THE CHALLENGE TO FRIENDSHIP
IN MODERNITY

Books of Related Interest

FOUCAULT
Editor: Robert Nola, University of Auckland

PLURALISM AND LIBERAL NEUTRALITY
Editors: Richard Bellamy, Reading University and Martin Hollis,
University of East Anglia

FEMINISM, IDENTITY AND DIFFERENCE
Editor: Susan Hekman, University of Texas at Arlington

TOLERATION
Preston King, Lancaster University

THINKING PAST A PROBLEM
Preston King, Lancaster University

The Challenge to Friendship in Modernity

Editors

PRESTON KING and
HEATHER DEVERE

FRANK CASS
LONDON • PORTLAND, OR

t published in 2000 in Great Britain by
FRANK CASS PUBLISHERS
Iewbury House, 900 Eastern Avenue,
Ilford, Essex IG2 7HH

nd in the United States of America by
FRANK CASS PUBLISHERS
c/o ISBS
5804 N.E. Hassalo Street
Portland, Oregon 97213-3644

Website: www.frankcass.com

British Library Cataloguing in Publication Data

The challenge to friendship in modernity
1. Friendship – Philosophy 2. Friendship – Political aspects
3. Trust 4. Friendship – Public opinion – History
I. King, Preston, 1936– II. Devere, Heather
177.6′2

ISBN 0 7146 5069 2 (cloth)
ISBN 0 7146 8118 0 (paper)

Library of Congress Cataloging in Publication Data

The challenge to friendship in modernity / editors, Preston King and Heather Devere
   p.   cm.
Includes bibliographical references and index.
ISBN 0-7146-5069-2 (hbk: alk. paper). – ISBN 0-7146-8118-0 (pbk.: alk. paper)
1. Friendship – History. I. King, Preston T., 1936– II. Devere, Heather.

BJ1533.F8 C42 20000   99-059740
177′.62 – dc21

This group of studies first appeared in a Special Issue on 'The Challenge to Friendship in
Modernity' of Critical Review of International Social and Political Philosophy 2/4
((Winter 1999) ISSN 1369-8320 published by Frank Cass.

Printed in Great Britain by Antony Rowe Ltd., Chippenham, Wilts.

Contents

1

Introduction

PRESTON KING

History

I begin from the assumption that one age is relevantly distinguished from another, not by the passage of time ('decade', 'century', 'millennium'), but by some determinate alteration in circumstance which, given recorded language, will commonly consist in, or be marked by, the rise or fall of some dominant philosophical paradigm or ideology. Passage from 'decade' to 'decade' or from 'century' to 'century' need not of itself bring substantive change, as in techniques (perhaps fishing or hunting) or ritual practice or ideological outlook. But it is at those points where we do abut upon altered practice or outlook, that we enter into relevant, substantive change of the sort that demarcates 'age' from 'age'. History in this sense is, indeed, to do with difference. Were there no significant and determinate change of circumstance, most especially in outlook and ideology and technology, then what we call 'history' would always amount to an account of the present – but a 'present' co-extensive with Eternity.

Where we must not be deluded is in supposing that history is *only* to do with change. For history works in two ways. First, it accounts for *change*, if always against the backdrop of duration. Second, it recounts *duration*, but here (inversely) against a backdrop of change. If one history may stress what has altered from that era to this, so may another history detail what has persisted from this period to that. Either sort of account – of variation, or of constancy – may entertain and may even matter. In the first case (mutation), nothing will have changed if something else has not stayed still. And in the second case (fixity), nothing will have stood still save by contrast with other things that have moved. Whether we are to do with identity or difference must be decided by the evidence. It will not necessarily and unarguably be true that 'liberty' in Ancient Athens was entirely different to, nor that it will be altogether at odds with, that which we now espouse.

If you suppose that every chronological unit is 'unique', then it must be difficult to envisage any continuity between fifth century Athens and twentieth century Washington. If you suppose the content of different chronological units to be identical, then it must be difficult to imagine discontinuity, otherness. Let us accept that history operates *in* the present. It will not follow that it attends only *to* the present (though we may and do have histories of the present). For history may (even more commonly) attend to the *past*, whether that particular past (it is always a *particular* past) is portrayed as different or enduring.

So we may say that to differentiate era from era is obviously and necessarily to attend to difference. Yet it is to attend to difference against a backdrop of duration. What differentiates era from era is not mere *chronological* succession, but *substantive* change of circumstance, and most importantly, for our present concern, changed patterns of thought. Formally, one may distinguish era from era merely chronologically, as where we speak of the second century by contrast to the third, or the sixth by contrast to the seventh, or the ninth by contrast to the tenth, etc. These time markers have a limited utility *qua* markers, just as any abstract number system will do. Otherwise, *in themselves*, they signal nothing substantive. We may well attribute some potent magicality to the year '2000' as distinct from '1999' or '2001'. But the fact that in the twenty-fourth hour we are located in 1999 and in the next hour transit to 2000 can be expected to have not the slightest impact on whether atrocities persist, tornadoes twist, roosters crow, elections loom, markets boom, or crash. (King 2000b: chs. 1/2.)

To distinguish *era from era* is not quite the same as differentiating past from present. We distinguish one era from another necessarily with a view to underscoring a difference. Without substantive difference, we should have *one* era, not substantively *distinct* eras. But we may distinguish *past from present* precisely in order to underscore a continuity; for the substantive rituals, techniques, behaviours, beliefs, paradigms of the chronological past may be identical with those of the chronological present – whether we find these substantive continuities banal or significant. We must get used to the idea of histories legitimately constituting accounts of a past whose substantive content may be either different or persistent. Whether some given stretch of the past, in some determinate respect, happens to be distinct, must remain a matter for investigation. Thus we shall not assume that the past is always or necessarily different. Equally, we shall not construe any and every assimilation of past to present as indiscriminately anachronistic.

By 'anachronism', we are casually disposed to mean 'reading history backwards'. It is a valid enough meaning, and yet not quite right. 'Not quite right' because there is no way in which we can avoid, strictly speaking, 'reading history backwards' – meaning 'back to front', which is to say from present to past. We cannot avoid constructing the past (a) within the present, nor (b) from present data, nor (c) from a (literally) present perspective. So let me put the point more finely, thus: The error of anachronism consists in *assuming* that some claim, p or q, that we do or think now, was or *must* also have been done or thought at some previous time, t_1 or t_2, when, as it happens, it *was not*.

It would appear to follow that to view history as a repository of *unique*, non-recurrent and non-persistent events is also to assume that any substantive identity which the historian forges between past and present is anachronistic. Those who are disposed to see the past as 'another country' – as necessarily distinct, unique, particular – cannot be well-placed to infer that, for example, Ancient Greece could possibly have accommodated anything like our present image or practice of 'liberty'. One may hypothesise that the Greek image of liberty, on the evidence, is *prima facie* significantly different from the image we entertain. One may account it an error to read back into Ancient Greece, especially the Greece of 2500 years ago – let alone Rome – the contemporary paradigm of liberty, putting quite to one side the various difficulties located in our present paradigm. Acton (1986: 68) put the point briskly enough: 'The ancient politicians aimed no higher than to diffuse power among a numerous class. Their liberty was bound up with slavery.' Indeed, the Ancients were more concerned with the fraternal management by citizens of a sovereign power from which a majority of residents were presumptively excluded; and they will sometimes have called this 'liberty' (*eleutheria* in Greek, *libertas* in Latin).

Today we are more concerned with governmental defence of every individual's private space to do just what he or she wills, consistent with a like respect for the 'liberty' of others. If I charge that the assimilation of Greek liberty to present liberty is anachronistic, then at least this cannot or should not be put down to the assumption that *any* substantive identity or continuity between past and present is impermissible – as must be the case with those who render anachronism overly encompassing and indiscriminate (to which historicists, particularists and methodological contextualists are unduly prone).

The Libertarian Paradigm

The dominant moral and political paradigm of our own age is constituted by a widespread aspiration to Liberty, grounded in Power. Liberty is the head, Power is the foot, of this aspiration. Our enthusiasm for such private liberty is open and sunlit; we fondle power by stealth and moonlight. The two are so joined that one cannot easily make out the hidden fibres that connect them. If citizens and subjects, following an analyst like Hobbes, contract to submit to government from fear of one another, then it is free choice, paradoxically, which generates power. Or, if one's freedom is absence of oppression, one way to secure this freedom, again paradoxically, is by oneself appropriating the instruments of oppression. Or, if negative liberty ('freedom from') is morally superior to positive liberty ('freedom to'), it remains, contrariwise, that the ultimate 'cash value' of removing a constraint consists precisely in being 'free to' do what the constraint would prohibit. There are many different ways in which we may express the same idea. But to fall back upon the simplest of illustrations: Proper defence of your free speech, at the one extreme, or of your 'consensual sex among adults', at the other, requires, at the limit, a police power to restrain those who would obstruct it. Hence we stand openly on the principle of liberty, while liberty stands on the plinth of power – this last shaded, and often shady.

The logical difficulty with the ideal of liberty is that it so readily converts into the ideal of power. What is power if not the dominance by A over B where B cannot resist? And what is liberty if not the repudiation of such dominance? Where we celebrate liberty, we (ostensibly) wish to deplore the power that stifles it. Yet we conceive few or no effective means to defend liberty, save by deploying power. We commonly think, like Lord Acton (1988: 519), that 'power tends to corrupt' and that 'Great men are almost always bad men'. We think power evil, a threat, an obstacle to liberty. But, like Morgenthau and Madison and indeed Montesquieu, we also think that power must be fought with power. We think to balance force against force, body against body, coalition against coalition, on the assumption that these will annul one another or give rise to something other than either. This may be taken to mean, 'anarchistically', that power can and ought to be destroyed. It may be taken to mean, more 'realistically', that the separation and balancing of powers plausibly sum to liberty. The liberty paradigm (reading this off as the avoidance of oppression) is rocked on its plinth by the reflections (a) that liberty is not secure without power and (b) that power always extinguishes someone's liberty.

One may suppose there to be some way round and beyond the 'paradox' of liberty. I assume that there is, and, if so, that it probably begins with recognising that the call for non-oppression is an appeal to a species of justice which is larger than non-restraint and thus larger than, and sometimes contradictory to, 'liberty' itself. Hence the repeated and possibly accelerating interest in insinuating some 'clear blue water' between the concern with 'liberty', on the one hand, and the larger, often countervailing, concern with 'justice', on the other. (Rawls 1971; Jackson 1986; Barry 1989; King 2000a: ch.7.) Liberty may well appear somewhat too primitive a moral paradigm to be allowed to stand alone – in so far as it stands at all. Obviously, a very great deal of important work has and continues to accumulate around it, whether recently formulated as 'liberty' (Berlin 1969; Hayek 1960), 'freedom' (e.g. Benn 1988; Cranston 1953; Raz 1986), 'autonomy' (Young 1986; Lindlay 1986), 'liberalism' (Rawls 1993; Kymlicka 1989), or otherwise. Equally, the libertarian paradigm stumbles over anomalies, paradoxes, inadequacies... relating to power, choice, voting, democracy, trust and so forth. It has a powerful intuitive appeal for us all, or at least for most of us, and the problem has become that of relocating it so that extremist absurdity does not trump sensibilities more cosmopolitan and just.

How disappointing therefore that my immediate concern here, *en passant* and uncontroversially, is to do no more than insist that liberty, fractured as it may be, is the dominant paradigm under which we labour. How long we have done so is another matter. Certainly, the emergence of modern liberty is often broadly associated with social contract theory – somewhat too comprehensively, since we may have a 'contract' of submission, as in Thomas Hobbes. Putting further argument to one side, I am tempted to trace this notion back to about the dawn of the eighteenth century – focusing in particular upon figures like Milton, Locke, Montesquieu, Rousseau, Voltaire especially, and the *philosophes* more generally. It is tempting to think to rush beyond this beachhead with a view to probing more important, analytical, liberty-related strong-points. If that is the sort of direction in which we should move, this, clearly, is not the occasion for such movement.

Classical Liberty as Anachronism

Many are commonly disposed to assume, in embracing the libertarian ideal, that the ancient Greeks and Romans, with whom we readily identify, were equally wedded to a negative ideal of non-oppression and statal neutrality. Even where we deny this claim to classical Rome (Finlay 1973; Dunn 1992), we risk falling over ourselves in retrojecting upon Athens, and the reforms associated with Cleisthenes in 508 BC, a libertarian aura. Popper (1962: I, 102), perhaps the most famous and acute of these gladiators, locates 'the basis of our western civilisation' in an individualism and altruism whose germ he espies in Ancient Athens, which is to say in the account by Thucydides (*Peloponnesean War*: II, 37-41) of Pericles' Funeral Oration.

Popper in effect supplies a construct of uncritical, closed 'tribes' being replaced by rational, civilised states, Athens exemplifying the latter. Hence, following Popper (I, 183), 'the open society [meaning a 'free society'] was already in existence' in fifth-century Athens. Surrounding and earlier peoples are conceived as 'closed', 'tribal', collectivist, totalitarian. He views the conquering state, built upon commerce and debate, as making a breakthrough into this species of enclosure, opening a window onto a freer, more cosmopolitan world. Indeed, for Popper (I, 184), 'the universalistic imperialism of the Athenian democracy and the instruments and symbols of its power' were all in the service of 'a new faith in reason, freedom and the brotherhood of all men'. Popper (I, 181) supposes there to be a clear distinction between 'tribal life' and 'civilisation', and concludes that the way to break down the former and introduce the latter is by force: 'tribalist exclusiveness and self-sufficiency could be superseded only by some form of imperialism'. Accordingly, Athens at least, not only for Popper (see Patterson 1991), is reckoned to entertain an ideal of freedom despite both slavery and imperialism, not to speak of the 'illiberal' urges of many of her most prominent intellectuals – Plato not least among them.

I signal Popper's views only because they illustrate a much larger tendency – to see smaller, 'tribal' peoples as somehow morally inferior, little capable of restraint, or rational debate, given only to despotism or licentiousness. In as far as it is especially hunter-gatherers with whom we are to do, the conclusion (for Popper) must be that what they require is a touch of the mailed fist, however much restrained that fist may be by reflective rationality. The *locus classicus* of this sort of view is really Hobbes (1651), who quite repudiates any such notion as that of a 'golden age'. Hobbes insists upon statelessness as a condition of chaos, and upon sovereignty – a form of rationally contracted subjection – as the only point of access to what we celebrate as civilisation. Popper *in esse* is saying little more than Hobbes, in this regard, except that he entertains a more elaborate construct of the nature of 'nature'. The characteristic that Popper (I, 172-173) claims to be "found in most, if not all, of these tribal societies [is an] irrational attitude towards the customs of social life, and the corresponding rigidity of these customs." Popper (I, 101) also takes it that 'the breakdown of tribalism' is a precondition for 'the rise of democracy'. Indeed, Popper's entire contrast between 'the open' and 'the closed' society is one between "the magical or tribal or collectivist society… and the society in which individuals are confronted with personal decisions". This rather distorted view of earlier, smaller, more self-sufficient societies as 'undemocratic', static, closed, rigid, unequal and anti-individualistic is, of course, rejected by many who know them, such as Richard Lee (1979) on the !Kung and Colin Turnbull (1961) on the Mbuti.

We have immense difficulties with conceiving even fifth-century Athens – putting Rome and certainly Sparta altogether to one side – as a 'free society'. Of course there are continuities: we encounter a certain rationality in public discourse; a belief that public policy is best tested by bringing many minds to bear upon it; that argument can bring both delight and benefit; that sovereignty should be vested in a public assembly; that there should be popular juries; that membership of public bodies should rotate, in part by election. None the less, we are not to do – not even in the case of Athens – with a society that supposes careers should be open to talent, that social mobility is somehow desirable, that humans are somehow equal, that all persons *qua* persons have rights, that presumptive social exclusion is wrong. The dominant element in all major Greek and Roman cities consisted only of citizens, only of males, and was numerically small. The subordinate element was fragmented, and we variably call them helots (Sparta), freedmen, dependent labour, peasants, tenants, debt-bondsmen, clients (*coloni*), poor (*penes*), plebs, metics, periokoi, slaves (*douloi, demosioi, servi*) of divers kinds and qualities, not to speak of women. Any society which excludes the bulk of its de facto membership from respect, regard, recognition, not to speak of office, cannot be called 'free' in the sense that we today intend. No society – valuing its existence, regarding this as legitimately grounded in slavery – can meaningfully view itself as aspiring to freedom in any standard contemporary sense of the term.

One was a citizen of Athens if one's father was a citizen, and later, under Pericles, if both parents were citizens. The firm principle, marked by rare exceptions, was citizenship through birth. The Athenian constitution designated a minority (of those residing) as sovereign. Wealth went largely, if not exclusively, with birth. Aristotle (*Athenian Constitution*, 2, ii) wrote of the poor, and of their wives and children, as being enslaved to the rich, the children being subject to seizure where parental rents went unpaid. No social system is entirely coherent, but it seemed to be assumed that citizens would have slaves, and that citizens would not themselves be slaves. Of course some did become slaves, as through indebtedness, even if the practice was to remove or sell such natives abroad. Slaves could be owned publicly or privately, they could be skilled and gifted or unskilled and dim. But their presence was pervasive, as was the acceptance of this presence.

Resident aliens were numerous and welcome as traders, taxpayers, even soldiers – but not as citizens. Citizens, in such an age, commonly worked. But they were not expected to work for others. It was demeaning, even if Socrates (following Xenophon) was disposed to argue against such inept *hauteur*. If Athenian slavery, and the general structure of exclusion, was complex, it seems reasonable to infer that slaves and other persons of subordinate and excluded status were abundant. Thucydides (VII, 27, v) refers to 20,000 skilled slaves deserting the Athenians in the war with Sparta. Even where we can secure no reliable grip on numbers, it is clear from Aristotle's account (*Politics* 1253b) that every 'complete household' would contain slaves, just as it would wives and children. It will be recalled that Aristotle assumes the slave to be such 'by nature' – an animate instrument that is subject to the will of a master. Here then we have an image of an intimate entity (*polis*) governed by a restricted class of citizens, who collectively (the 'statesman' is not for Aristotle a 'tyrant') fashion policy, but who easily exclude from mutual recognition and rights of participation the overwhelming mass of the population.

On the whole, in the Ancient world, including fifth century Athens, the bulk of the people were a subject, dependent, excluded population. The claims attributed by Thucydides (II, 37, 1) to Pericles, regarding access by the poor to power, would, if true, be markedly exceptional, more expressive of uncommon aspiration than of daily reality. To borrow one account: 'Not many Greek states of the classical period, and none at all in the ancient world at any other period, allowed poor men of obscure condition to play a positive constructive role in political life, and even in Athens it is almost impossible to find a man of modest means, let alone a really poor man, in a position of leadership.' (Finlay 1985: 37) To borrow another account: 'The figures show – and not just in the oligarchies, but also in the economically advanced democracies, that the sovereignty of the citizens was that of a minority – a minority moreover tending to shrink further....' (Ehrenburg 1982: 76) Power and standing belonged only to citizens, and these were few. If we accept for, example, for Rome (8 BC.) an Augustan census enumerating 4.2m. citizens out of 50m. residents, then we can allow the citizenry to constitute at best approximately 8.4 per cent of the total population (Finlay 1985: 47).

The body of Athenian citizens might be described as a democracy, in the sense of 'rule by majority', or even as 'mob rule', except that they are clearly not quite to do with either. How does the use of such an expression as 'democracy' (demos-ocracy) arise in the context of the Athenian constitution? Some part of its currency must surely be put down to the oppositional irony of Athens' detractors. What the Athenian system really instantiates is minority rule, even if that rule was more 'direct' than 'representative'. The Athenian citizenry were a decidedly engaged, 'hands-on' minority, but they were a distinct minority all the same. They were much given to argument and counter-argument as a part of the process of rule, but there was no assumption that just anyone might enjoy a prima facie right to participate. They had little if any concept of 'individual rights'. They had little respect for the liberty of *laisser faire*, or *laisser aller*, or of just doing what one likes. They were disposed to view citizens who absented themselves from civic duty – in the Ecclesia, or Council of Five Hundred, or popular juries – as more contemptible than splendidly eccentric. And even Socrates, following Plato (*Apology*), despite considered objections to these institutions, preferred to die than seek escape from their judgements.

As Garlan (1988: 20) observes, *douleia* in Plato significantly denotes 'not only slavery in the strict sense, ...but equally political subjection' – expanding into moral servitude and subjection generally. But this inclusive use of slavery to encompass subjection generally may mislead. Athens was of course a slaveholding society. But this is not to say that the condition of all non-citizens within it must be viewed as abjectly dolorous. Let us then accept, on the one hand, that the slave (*doulos*, *servus*) conventionally stands in opposition to the free (*eleutheros*). Let us accept, on the other hand, that this opposition may be unduly sharp in view of the many possible gradations of servile status – or (more neutrally) of 'dependency'. A free man in Athens or

Rome, for example, was not necessarily either powerful or independent. A man might be free, but only in the sense of having been freed; free, but not a citizen (*polites*); free, *qua* citizen, but poor; free, but without weight, or power. Like freedom, slavery too came in wildly different degrees. So we are right to be careful about any blanket opposition of *doulos* or *servus* to *eleutheros*. This does not mean that the opposition is simply unwarranted. It only means that the opposition between citizen and non-citizen, which has its own limitations, remains far more revealing.

Our concern becomes not, 'To whom do we oppose the slave?', but rather, 'To whom do we oppose the citizen?' This brings us much closer to locating domination in Athens, since it is not only over the slave. In Athens or Rome, the citizen excluded the non-citizen. The chattel slave may have been the most oppressed of the excluded. But many more besides were caught in the non-citizen net. The contrast between citizen and non-citizen is that between those with and those without direct access to power. To celebrate citizenship, membership, duty, belonging, 'freedom', participation, responsibility was also to celebrate this narrowly filtered access to power. If 'freedom' is an autonomous ideal in the ancient world, it is not the 'freedom from' of Berlin (1969). If it is ever aptly freedom at all, then it is – in the technically 'positive' sense – a 'freedom to'. It is capacity, a power.

The Athenian praise of participation, of engagement, is appealing. But it has another side: exclusion. Did Athens praise liberty? Yes, in so far as being free means not being subject. Did Athens condemn subjection? If we follow Aristotle's account, then not in the least. Slavery was everywhere, but few ancients worried about it even to the point of discussing it. So what was Athenian liberty? It was rational public discourse among a pre-selected and presumptively designated few: that is, of free-born, male citizens. This, however, is more the celebration of a particular expression of power, than a generalised, Kantian promotion of liberty. In Athens, liberty and power were joined at the hip. The liberty was discursive, located in wide-ranging debate, such as we do not find under a conventional despotism. But the power of decision, mediated through debate, was restricted to a limited class circumscribed by birth. And we must suppose exclusion (for those affected) to have been as emphatic as under any conventional despotism. In the end, the distinct minority of power-holders in Athens, however wide-ranging their debate, directly represented, and were answerable to none but, themselves.

The working Greek or Roman ideal was less our contemporary independence or freedom or rights. It was more to do with enjoying capacity, exercising power, being sovereign. An array of adjectives is plausible in relation to Classical Athens: small, autonomous, intimate, informal, lively, intelligent and so on. We can detect through these a link with the 'free society' or indeed the 'open society', in Popper's title. Yet we must distinguish. A dominant estate or class may itself enjoy liberty (non-oppression) without ever viewing such de facto liberty as an abstract ideal that either can or should be extended further or indeed universalised. A small band of citizens may participate discursively and dominate corporately without ever aspiring to incorporate all or most (of those who are subject to them) into either discourse or domination. Hence the paradox, more apparent than real, that any expansion of the Athenian or Roman citizen-body would equally require an expansion of dependent labour, not least slave labour, within it. As Finlay (1968: 72) once put it: "one aspect of Greek history... is the advance, hand in hand, of liberty *and* slavery." It would be extremely difficult to locate any generalised appeal to liberty, as moderns conceive it, in this.

If, with Finlay (1985: 45-48), we view the Athenian citizenry as a dominant 'order' or 'estate', one marked by various juridically defined privileges and obligations, where membership is hereditary, by fact or by law, where non-citizens are excluded from ownership of land and from political rights, however long their residence, whatever their numbers or contribution or wealth, and if we add to all of this the automatic subjection of women as such to male authority, then we are clearly to do with a narrowly circumscribed form of minority rule. The relevant liberty that might be celebrated here is that of insertion, that which facilitates a 'power to', even a 'power over'. What is in play here is the principle of attachment, of belonging. This principle commends proximity to the palace, membership of the assembly or court. And this belonging may be assorted with the fraternity peculiar to those who exercise discursive domination.

In the end, it seems implausible to suppose that the Greeks or Romans entertained an ideal which really resembles the modern notion of liberty. The differences are far starker than the continuities. For Aristotle (*Rhetoric* 1367a 32), the free man is merely one who is not dominated or constrained by another. But who thereby qualifies as 'free'? Not the slave, helot, wife, or child; not the labourer who works for another; not the craftsman who seeks a commission; not the retailer who depends upon the goodwill of customers; not the butcher, baker or candlestick maker; in short, not the vast majority of people. A 'free man' on this account is essentially one who has power – a 'power to' do things, and a 'power over' others to secure that things are done. This is not to say that the ancient writers directly praise power. (Plato's Socratic refutation of Thrasymachus in *The Republic* is a repudiation of 'might makes right'. Aristotle in *The Rhetoric* comments at length on nobility, which is partly to do with the proper use, not mere possession, of power.) But it is to say that their support of participation as a duty owed by a restrictive class is implicitly an endorsement of domination by the class of citizens. In the end, to impose upon Athens the ideal of liberty is overwhelmingly anachronistic.

The Salience of Friendship and its Decline

The first question with which we are left is whether there is a political or social ideal in the ancient canon which approximates to universality. Certainly neither liberty nor power serves as a generalisable ideal, cutting across all classes and periods in the ancient world. I cannot here argue the question out, but I hypothesise that that notion which most nearly fits the bill is friendship. Plato attributed to Socrates the statement, 'I have a passion for friends'. Aristotle claimed to value friendship more highly than justice, on the assumption that, with the first, there is no need for the second.

Friendship was central to the ethics of Socrates. His students, Xenophon and Plato, supply firsthand accounts of it. Aristotle, Lucretius, Cicero, Seneca, Plutarch and innumerable others wrote of and for friendship. Those who wrote in Latin were atypical. Virtually all philosophical writing, even of the Roman period, is in Greek –as in the case of the reflections of Epictetus (via Arrian) and of the meditations of the Emperor Marcus Aurelius. And most of the thinkers of this Greco-Roman period, whether they wrote in Greek or (more rarely) in Latin, were committed to this ideal . It is a defensible thesis that no major book on friendship has appeared since Cicero, 2000 years ago, and certainly not since Plutarch's Dialogue on Love (the *Amatorius*).

If we inspect the modern period, the disposition we most commonly encounter with regard to friendship, is one of indifference to hostility. I do not say that the prejudices and conclusions of major thinkers is necessarily embodied in the social practices of ordinary people. But I do say, if we concentrate upon major thinkers, that we immediately detect in the modern figures a sharp divergence from their ancient predecessors, at least in the attention they devote or deny to friendship. Virtually no modern figure – Bacon, Montaigne and Nietzsche (bizarrely) apart – has anything to say about or in praise of the subject. Not Machiavelli, Descartes, Hobbes, Locke, Spinoza, Leibnitz, Berkeley, Hume, Voltaire – not even Rousseau; not Bentham or the Mills; neither Hegel nor Marx. The earlier notion of the person always as some species of 'communion' (Schmalenbach 1939) with another or others, as achieving moral value only through valuing some other as one's own highest end, somehow dissolves into a later notion of the person as a self-subsistent individual in pursuit of self-interested ends, maximising personal utilities, often enough standing beyond and above communal values. Apart from indifference, friendship often meets with simple hostility – as in the work of Immanuel Kant, Sigmund Freud, Mary Douglas, Ayn Rand, and others.

Friendship is in fact a lead that has almost gone cold. The ancient analyses alone betray immense sophistication. Yet they are not much attended to. This volume seeks to contribute modestly to the task of re-inspection of friendship as a major philosophical category. The essayists mostly inspect work on friendship in the eighteenth, nineteenth and twentieth centuries. But the first essay, by Mulgan, explores the clarity and applicability of Aristotle's commitment to friendship as a political virtue. The second, by Hill and McCarthy, explores the contrasting views of David Hume, Adam Smith and Adam Ferguson on the capacity of modern commercial society to engender or to destroy friendship. The third, by Abbey, inspects Nietzsche's puzzling appreciation of friendship, which he approved in his youth and then seemed to cast aside in his later thinking. The fourth essay, by Rustin, retrieves the work of Martin Buber as one of the most significant of modern attempts to develop a philosophy of relatedness in which some form of friendship features in a major way. The fifth essay, by Dallmayr, critically reviews recent work by Jacques Derrida on friendship, noting that this writer's method of reviving the concept may secure an unhappy, contrary effect. The sixth essay, by Hutter, argues for the practice of friendship as a universal phenomenon, but one cut to the cloth of wildly varying historical conditions. Devere supplies an authoritative bibliographical essay on friendship, with particular reference to work on Greece and Rome.

REFERENCES

Acton 1986. [J.E.E. Dahlberg-Acton] *Essays in the History of Liberty: Selected Writings of Lord Acton*, vol. 1. Edited by J.R. Fears. Indianapolis: Liberty Classics.

Barry, B. 1989. *Theories of Justice*. London: Harvester-Wheatsheaf.

Benn, S.I. 1988. *A Theory of Freedom*, Cambridge: CUP.

Berlin, I. 1969. *Four Essays on Liberty*, Oxford: OUP.

Cranston, M. 1953. *Freedom: A New Analysis*, London: Longmans.

Dunn, J. 1992. *Democracy: The Unfinished Journey, 508BC to AD1993*,

Ehrenberg, V. 1982. *L'Etat grec*. Paris: Francois Maspero.

Finlay, M. I. 1968. *Slavery in Classical Antiquity*.

—. 1973. *Democracy Ancient and Modern*.

—. 1985. *The Ancient Economy*, Berkeley: Univ. of California. Press.

Garlan, Y. 1988. *Slavery in Ancient Greece*. London: Cornell Univ. Press.

Hayek, F. A. 1960. *The Constitution of Liberty*, London: Routledge.

Jackson, M. 1986. *Matters of Justice*. London: Croom Helm.

King, P. 2000a. *Fear of Power*. London: Frank Cass.

— 2000b. *Thinking Past A Problem*, London: Frank Cass.

Kymlicka, W. 1989. *Liberalism, Community and Culture*. Oxford: Clarendon.

Lee, R. 1979. *The! Kung San*. Cambridge: C.U.P.

Lindlay, R. 1986. *Autonomy*, London: Macmillan.

Miller, D. 1976. *Social Justice*. Oxford: Clarendon.

Patterson, O. 1991. *Freedom in the Making of Western Culture*. London: I.B. Tauris.

Popper, K. R. 1962. *The Open Society and Its Enemies*, Vol.1(Plato). London: Routledge.

Rawls, J. 1971. *A Theory of Justice*. Oxford: OUP.

Raz, J. 1986. *The Morality of Freedom*, Oxford: Clarendon.

Schmalenbach, H. 1939. *Geist und Sein*. Basel.

Turnbull, C. 1961, *The Forest People*. London: Chatto & Windus.

Walzer, M. 1983. *Spheres of Justice*, Oxford: Blackwell.

Young, R. 1986. *Personal Autonomy*: London: Croom Helm.

2

The Role of Friendship in Aristotle's Political Theory

RICHARD MULGAN

Debates Over Friendship

To what extent can Aristotle's ideas about friendship be pressed into useful service by modern political theorists? In particular, can they throw any light on the theoretical foundations of political communities and about the relationships of individuals within such communities? 'Communitarian' theorists have co-opted Aristotle to their cause as an advocate of intimate, friendly relations between fellow citizens and, by implication, as a critic of individualist premises for justifying political institutions (eg MacIntyre 1981, Barber 1984).

Other commentators, however, have sought to deny any particularly communal or fraternal interpretation of Aristotelian citizenship, emphasising the comparatively lukewarm nature of political friendship and its basis in mutual self-interest, thus aligning Aristotle more with modern liberal individualism (eg Yack 1993, Miller 1995, Bickford 1996). This debate cannot be settled with complete confidence because Aristotle's theory of friendship, particularly his view of political friendship – the friendship between fellow citizens – is itself among the more difficult parts of his ethical and political theory to interpret and is highly contested.

The main treatment of friendship as such occurs in the *Ethics* (both *Eudemian* and *Nicomachean*) rather than in the *Politics*. Given that the prime, defining instance is the relationship of a few virtuous individuals, friendship naturally finds its place among topics relating to the good life for individuals, the subject matter of the ethical treatises. Aristotle's view of the wider role of friendship in the political community draws on his account of the derivative types of friendship, the friendships based on pleasure and advantage or utility, which is obscure and controversial. In particular, it is unclear whether Aristotle intends to invest these friendships with any of the goodwill or altruistic concern for others which animates genuine friendship.

Moreover, while the concept of political friendship in the *Ethics* is textually obscure, in the *Politics* it is largely absent. The importance of friendship for politics is foreshadowed in the *Ethics* by the prefatory remark that friendship appears to hold states together and that lawgivers appear to care for friendship more even than for justice (*EN* 1154b 22; cf *EE* 1234b 23). This might suggest a prominent role for the concept when Aristotle embarks in the *Politics* on an explanation of the theoretical knowledge necessary for statesmanship. However, the notion of specifically 'political friendship' is not unambiguously referred to in the *Politics* – though *Pol* 1295b 23 may possibly be such a reference (Cooper 1990: 234n; Annas 1990: 246). Friendship is not mentioned at all in the opening chapters of Book I, where Aristotle lays the basis for his theory of the *polis*, nor in the opening to Book VII, which introduces the ideal *polis*. Nor is there any lengthy discussion of any theoretical puzzles surrounding political friendship, such as how large numbers of citizens can be friends with each other or how friendship might vary, like justice, between different constitutions. On the other hand, the theory of friendship outlined in the *Ethics*, though not further developed in the *Politics*, is certainly not forgotten. Aristotle draws on friendship to underline important arguments, such as the implausibility of Plato's collectivisation of the family (*Pol* 1262b 7-23), the origin of the state in collective activities within a given territory (*Pol* 1280b 38), the inconsistency of kings in treating people as friends while denying them a share of power (*Pol* 1287b 30-35), and the value of economic equality among the citizen body *(Pol* 1295b 21-33).

These references to the concept of friendship at key points show that the ideas implicit in the concept remain of central importance in Aristotle's political theory, even though the burden of explicit argument may be largely carried by other concepts with which friendship is logically connected. Thus, inevitably, a consideration of the role played by political friendship leads the interpreter into wider areas of Aristotle's political theory.

Degrees of Friendship

The importance of friendship in Aristotle's theory of politics is indicated by its presence in every *koinonia. Koinonia,* ie 'joint

enterprise' or (literally) 'community', is Aristotle's general term for a
social group and central to the theory of the *polis*. The *polis* is said to
be the *koinonia* which embraces all others *(Pol* 1252a 5-6) and is
formed out of the lesser *koinoniai* of the household and the village *(Pol*
1252b 27-30). Because the household and the village exist by nature,
so too does the *polis (Pol* 1252a 24 – b30–31). There are other types
of *koinonia* besides the household, village and *polis*, including more
limited associations such as commercial partnerships *(EN* 1163a 31)
and even sharing a sea voyage *(EN* 1161b 13). In spite of their variety,
all *koinoniai* share certain features. They all involve a common object
or purpose shared by all members *(Pol* 1328a 25-27). The members of
a *koinonia* must also be equals (either absolute or proportionally, in
Aristotle's terminology), thus laying a basis for relationships of justice
in their mutual dealings *(EN* 1159b 34–1160a 8). Most important for
present purposes, every *koinonia* includes not only justice but also
friendship *(EN* 1159b 27–8; *EN* 1161b 11). Friendship is thus, for
Aristotle, an integral part of any social group with a common purpose.

However, the presence of friendship in every *koinonia* does not
entail that all social groups involve the same extent of friendly
affection and concern. Different types of *koinonia* exhibit different
types and degrees of friendship. Indeed, the most important
characteristic of the concept of friendship as understood by Aristotle is
not so much its pervasiveness as its variety. In the *Ethics*, Aristotle
identifies three main types of friendship *(EN* VIII.2-3; *EE* VII.2),
depending on whether they are based on virtue, pleasure or advantage
(sometimes translated as 'utility'). The friendship based on virtue, in
which good people love each other for their virtuous characters, is
'complete both in respect of duration and in all other respects' *(EN*
1156b33) and is the first and defining sense of friendship *(EN* 1157a
30-31; *EE* 1236b 20–26, 1238a 30). Such friendship is found most
fully among truly virtuous people who love the virtue in each other's
character. It can also occur, however, whenever people love each other
for the sake of each other's character. Thus, though it is initially
described as 'friendship on account of virtue', it is also referred to as
'friendship on account of character' (eg *EN* 1164a 12), a phrase which
perhaps more accurately captures its meaning in the context of
Aristotle's general social theory (Cooper 1977, 629).

In contrast with friendships based on virtue and character,
friendships based on pleasure and advantage are called such 'by
comparison' or 'derivatively' *(EN* 1157a 31-35; *EE* 1236b 21). The
precise logical relationship between the main sense of friendship and

the other senses varies between the two *Ethics* and is itself a matter of scholarly dispute (Price 1989, 131–48). For the present, however, it is sufficient to note that virtue-friendship is the truest form of friendship and that the other varieties of friendship are so called because they approximate virtue-friendship to a certain extent. Examples of friendships based on pleasure are purely sexual relationships (*EN* 1156b 2-5), while the most common advantage-friendships are business relationships, though, significantly, the friendship of fellow citizens is also said to be a type of advantage-friendship (*EE* 1242a 6-7).

The main characteristic of true friendship based on virtue is that friends show mutual (and mutually recognised) goodwill to each other, wishing each other well for the other person's sake rather than·their own (*EN* VIII 2-3; 1166al-4). Such friendship is also a particularly stable type of friendship, because a person's character is itself stable, particularly in the case of the virtuous; it is also the most pleasurable, because it involves the highest degree of similarity (*EN* 1156b 6-24, cf *EE* 1236b 27–1237a 9).

Friendship also implies equality, being the mutual affection of people of similar qualities and interests, and the truest friends are said to be the most alike in virtue and character (*EN* 1156b 6). However, friendship based on virtue and character is also found between family members where the main family relationships, those of husbands and wives and of parents and children, are all unequal relationships between superiors and inferiors – though the degree of inequality differs significantly between each type. Aristotle is ambivalent about whether friendship can also exist between master and slave (*EN* 1161a 32-b 8; *Pol* 1255b 12–15). In unequal relationships, the contribution made by each party is proportional to their inequality, thus equalising the relationship as is proper among friends (*EN* 1158b 12–28). In Aristotelian terms, there is proportional or geometric equality rather than arithmetic equality between the family members. In other respects, however, the friendships of family members share the same degree of intimacy and mutual affection and concern found among friends. Indeed, the relationship of mothers towards their children is mentioned several times as a leading instance of friendship, in particular for its degree of unselfish concern and delight in the other person (*EN* 1159a 27–28; 1166a 6–9; *EE* 1241b 5–6; Schwarzenbach 1996: 101–2; Annas 1990: 244).

Finally, friendship also involves spending time together ('living together'), enjoying the same activities (*EN* 1156b 5, 20; 1157b 6–9; 1166a 5–6). Thus, because true friendship involves intimate relations and frequent contact between people, it is necessarily confined to a small circle of people, to one or a few like-minded companions, as well as to close family members (*EN* 1157a 11–13; 1170b 29–1171a 20).

By contrast, the derivative types of friendship are deficient and therefore less truly types of friendship. In the first place, they are less unselfish than true friendship, being valued for the benefits which each person receives from the relationship, whether their own pleasure or advantage, rather than for the benefits which each person is able to confer on the friend (*EN* 1156a 10–18). Consequently, they are said to be less stable than character-friendship because the partners are primarily concerned for their own individual pleasure and advantage, rather than the other's character, and the friendships lapse once their pleasure and advantage ceases (*EN* 1156a 18–20; 1157a 3–16).

Moreover, the exchanging of mutual benefits, as in advantage-friendship, does not require the degree of familiarity required among true friends. Derivative friendships may be less intense. People may therefore be advantage-friends, such as business associates and fellow citizens, with a much larger number of people than they can ever have as genuinely true friends (*EN* 1171a 10–21). Because the respective obligations of such distant friends are more limited than those of close friends, the injustice in breaking them is less. 'It is more terrible to defraud a comrade than a fellow citizen, more terrible not to help a brother than a stranger, and more terrible to wound a father than anyone else.' (*EN* 1160a 4–6).

The social picture that emerges from Aristotle's account of friendship is thus of a range of *koinoniai* or social groups of varying intimacy and intensity. At the centre of people's lives are the friendships of close companions and family, the friendships which are the most important of the 'external goods' without which happiness is impossible (*EN* 1169b 8–21; cf 1099b 5–6; 110a 7–8) and an indispensable part of the good life (Mulgan 1990: 200–1). Also intimate, but more transitory, are friendships of pleasure, such as relationships entered into for purely sexual gratification. Beyond this immediate circle of intimate relationships, there is a somewhat wider range of friendly relationships based on the extended family and personal acquaintances, institutions such as the 'brotherhoods' and religious cults which Aristotle mentions in the *Politics* as arising out of friendship and the desire to 'live together' (*Pol* 1280b 36–8). More distant still, in terms of intimacy and affection, is the network of business relationships generated by the city's economic activities. The friendship of fellow citizens, too, is more remote in character, lacking the intensity of intimate friendship.

It is this view of society that leads Aristotle to criticise Plato's attempt in the *Republic* to extend the feelings of parental love and affection beyond the immediate family to the whole guardian class. Where wives and children are held in common, the love of fathers for their children will be diluted and 'watery' (*Pol* 1262b 7–23). It is contrary to human nature and human experience for people to show towards thousands of fellow citizens the same intense concern and love they feel for family and friends. Such a conclusion is sensible and consistent, given that the mutual dealings which most fellow citizens of the Greek *polis* had with one another as individuals, beyond the circle of family and personal friends, were largely commercial and legal in character. It also fits with the picture of the good life which can be gleaned from the *Ethics* where the ethical virtues are exercised primarily in close personal relationships or in business dealings and where political participation is an optional extra (eg *EN* 1179a 5–7; Mulgan 1990). The *koinonia* of the *polis*, providing all the necessities of living and good living (*Pol* 1252b 28–30), was a complex and diverse society in which one could know only a few people really well and, for the rest, one would need to rely on more distant market relationships underpinned by the reciprocity of justice (*EN* 1132b 32; *Pol* 1261a 30).

Thus Aristotle's theory of friendship provides an argument for the greater intensity and superior value of close personal relationships compared with those which can exist between large numbers of fellow citizens. He rejects any political theory, such as Plato's, which attempts to build its foundations on sentiments of supposed 'fraternity' or 'camaraderie' extending throughout a whole political community. Such theories are likely to founder on the unwillingness and inability of human beings to extend intense sympathy and affection beyond their nearest and dearest. Fraternity and camaraderie are necessarily sentiments of intimacy which are not available for the world of politics. Conversely, and more positively, political theory should recognise and cater for the fact that people belong to a variety of social groups for a variety of reasons, ranging from the intimate and comparatively selfless relationships of family and friends to the more distant and instrumental relationships with neighbours and fellow citizens. People may not be able to care for all their fellow citizens with the same intensity of concern that they show towards their immediate circle. By the same token, however, they should not be expected to treat family, friends and neighbours with the same degree of detachment that they exhibit towards the mass of fellow citizens.

Friendship, Self-interest and Goodwill

Such an account of Aristotle's theory of friendship still leaves a number of questions unanswered. One concerns the extent to which the derivative types of friendship, particularly advantage-friendship, involve concern for the other partner as well as for oneself. By describing business partnerships, for instance, as 'friendships', is Aristotle meaning to imply that economic relationships, though based on mutual self-interest and the exchange of utility, none the less require at least a degree of unselfish attention to the other's interests? If so, his argument would constitute an important challenge to social theories which base their explanations of social interaction on individualist premises of rational self-interest. If the institution of individual rational self-interest *par excellence,* namely market exchange, cannot be explained on wholly self-interested grounds, then theories of rational self-interest are stopped in their tracks.

However, whether Aristotle is indeed making such a point is a matter of scholarly controversy. Against the view that the derivative types of friendship involve any altruistic concern for the other partner is Aristotle's clear statement that these friendships are based on the person's own self-interest and that such friends only wish pleasure and advantage to each other as means to their own personal pleasure and advantage (*EN* 1156a 10–21). In his separate analyses of 'goodwill' or 'well-wishing' (*eunoia*), Aristotle says explicitly that it is confined to virtue-friendships and absent from the friendships of pleasure and advantage (*EE* 1241a 4–7; *EN* 1167a 12–13). There are, indeed, major philosophical problems in identifying goodwill as common to all types of friendship. Though goodwill is obviously part of the friendship of the virtuous where a friend loves the other's virtue for its own sake, locating the same degree of disinterested concern for the other in the derivative types of friendship is problematic when the *raison d'être* for these types is the personal return to the individual friend. Friends for the sake of pleasure or advantage appear to enter into the relationship, and continue in it, purely for the sake of their own pleasure or advantage. Any concern for the interests of the friend would appear to be instrumental, as a means to securing one's own pleasure or advantage, and therefore not genuine goodwill.

Furthermore, Aristotle appears to confirm this hard-line denial of altruism in economic relationships by his distinction between two types of such relationship, depending on whether the terms of the agreement are spelled out clearly in advance, the 'legal' type, or whether the partners rely more on discretion and trust, the 'moral' type *(EN* 1162b 21–35; *EE* 1242b 31–1243b 14). In the *Nicomachean Ethics,* a further distinction is made within the former, 'legal' relationships between a 'purely commercial' variety where immediate payment is required and, a 'more liberal' variety which allows time for repayment and thus 'in the postponement provides an element of friendship' *(EN* 1162b 29). The latter, more liberal version of the 'legal' relationship thus comes closer to the 'moral' type, where the initial contribution is made without specification, 'a gift, or whatever, as if to a friend' with no stipulation about repayment *(EN* 1162b 32).

Aristotle recognises that the 'moral' type of business relationship, where everything is left to the partners' discretion, is particularly liable to lead to misunderstanding and recrimination because people may think they have received a gift for which no repayment is necessary *(EN* 1162b 31 – 1163a 9). Indeed, in the *Eudemian Ethics,* Aristotle claims that it is an 'unnatural' attempt to combine the friendships of utility and virtue *(EE* 1242b 38–39). Such partners associate for reasons of mutual advantage but 'represent their friendship as moral, like that of good men; pretending to trust one another they make out their friendship to be not merely legal' *(EE* 1243a 1–2). The only reliable and genuine form of advantage-friendship is therefore the 'legal' type, where terms are clearly specified in advance and no attempt is made to hide the fact that the basis of transactions is mutual advantage rather than mutual concern. Aristotle therefore appears to be making a clear distinction between friendly dealings, where people consider each other's welfare, and business dealings, where people consider only their own self-interest. Attempts to impose sentiments of friendly concern onto business relationships involve a dangerous confusion of categories because they deny the inherent selfishness of economic transactions.

On the other hand, the view that Aristotle means to deny any genuine goodwill to the derivative friendships faces its own difficulties. It seems to undercut the rationale for identifying them as types of friendship, if only derivatively. After all, concern for the other person rather than oneself is such a clear token of friendship, as Aristotle himself recognises. In the *Rhetoric,* for example, when introducing a comparatively non-technical discussion of friendship and enmity, he claims that friendship involves 'wishing for someone what one thinks are good things, for that person's sake not one's own' *(Rh* 1380b 36–37). In this case, to count as friendship, even in a minimal sense, some element of selflessness needs to be included. In the *Nicomachean*

Ethics, Aristotle claims, at one point, that some form of goodwill is present in all types of friendship *(EN* 1155 b31–1156a 5). Thus John M. Cooper has argued, in an influential analysis (Cooper 1977: 629–43), that even in relationships whose overall rationale is the self-interest of the respective parties, the individuals concerned may do each other incidental acts of kindness. Such acts are not justified on strict self-interest even though they take place within the overall framework of a profitable relationship and would cease once that overall profitability ceased. On this view, for instance, the 'moral' type of business relationship where terms are left unspecified, which is condemned as unnatural hypocrisy in the *Eudemian Ethics,* is defended in the more nuanced *Nicomachean Ethics* as the more genuine form of advantage-friendship (Cooper 1977: 639n). However, Cooper's attempt to explain away the denial of genuine goodwill to the friendships of pleasure and utility has been far from universally accepted (Irwin 1988: 613n; Price 1989: ch 5; Miller 1995: 209).

That the debate over goodwill in the derivative friendships has resisted resolution, in spite of lengthy and determined scholarly attention, suggests indecision on Aristotle's part. He appears unable to make up his mind whether all social activities, including those entered into on strictly utilitarian grounds, must involve an element of genuine altruism or collective concern beyond the pursuit of individual self-interest. On the one hand, he seems to consider that all action for a common purpose involves not just rules of justice agreed between the partners but also shared sentiments of concern. On the other hand, he holds that some social relationships are grounded in self-interest and do not share the genuine altruism of true friendship. This uncertainty is also reflected in his vacillation about the precise logical relationship between the central defining case of true friendship and the derivative cases.

In this case, the most prudent conclusion is to leave the question open, re-emphasising, however, the central theme of Aristotle's account of friendship, namely the moral superiority of the friendship of the virtuous few for each other. Even if Aristotle intends to attribute an element of altruism to all shared social behaviour, the extent of such altruism within the derivative types, including certain business relationships (and the relationship of fellow citizens), should not be over-emphasised nor the difference between the derivative types and true friendship minimised. Even where elements of altruism and goodwill are found in derivative friendships, they take place within an instrumental justification of the relationship as a whole. Partners enter into these relationships for their own selfish purposes and abandon them once their selfish interests cease to be met. Thus, though Aristotle could be taken to mean that any *koinonia,* that is any social group with a common purpose, must involve some genuinely co-operative, non-selfish behaviour between members; he is not claiming, and is indeed denying, that the rationale for all such social groups, the reason why they exist in the first place, is similarly unselfish. The main thrust of Aristotle's theory of friendship, that the relationships between fellow citizens are less intense and less valuable than those between close friends and family, remains intact.

Political Friendship and Political Consensus

The political role of friendship between fellow citizens is another issue of contention. Aristotle's classification of friendship between fellow citizens as a distant, derivative type of friendship may be a satisfactory account of how fellow citizens normally relate to each other in most of their individual dealings, person to person. But what of the collective activities of citizenship, such as political deliberation and military service? Did they not require a more intense personal commitment than that of individuals' business dealings? Does not the maintenance of civic order itself, the recognition of political and legal institutions and the acceptance of their decisions, depend on stronger sentiments of social solidarity than are associated with market exchange? How can a watery type of political friendship be sufficient to meet its assigned task of holding the city together?

Aristotle's most explicit account of political friendship is given in the *Ethics* where, as we have seen, it is classified as an advantage form of friendship which, unlike true friendship, can exist between large numbers of people. It is also closely connected with 'unanimity' or agreement *(homonoia).* Unanimity is defined as existing between people who have a shared interest and who agree about what action they should take and about other important matters of joint concern *(EN* 1167a 21–30; *EE* 1241a 16–18). It is a feature of the true friendship of virtuous individuals, who are of 'one mind' in their common activities and, conversely, absent from the relationships between bad people who tend to disagree with one another *(EN* 1167b 5–15; *EE* 1241a 24–30). Unanimity is also found between political friends and, indeed, may be identified with political friendship *(EN* 1167b 2; *EE* 1241a 33). Unanimity occurs among fellow citizens when they agree on important matters of common concern, such as how public officials should be selected, which individuals should be selected as rulers, or which other cities the state should be allied with *(EN* 1167a 31–33). The lack of such agreement amounts to 'faction' or disorder *(stasis)*. Thus it is unanimity which provides the collective aspect of the friendship between fellow citizens, the shared commitment to political institutions.

When political friendship is understood to be equated with this type of unanimity we can appreciate why it is that friendship appears to 'hold states together' and why lawmakers may care for it more than justice *(EN* 1155a 22–26). Citizens will not deal justly with one another unless they agree on how disputes are to be resolved. Public agreement or consensus on constitutional fundamentals and on the legitimacy of legal and political institutions is indeed the essential basis for political stability. In this respect, political friendship, though unnamed as such, is a central topic of the *Politics.* The avoidance of faction and revolution *(stasis),* that is the achievement of unanimity, is the most important political objective for everyday politics and provides the main theme of Books IV–VI. As the main source of *stasis* is disagreement about which concept of justice should determine the constitution of the *polis (Pol* 1301a 35–8), it follows that agreement on such matters is a prerequisite for political stability. Many of the steps which Aristotle recommends for statesmen and constitution-makers are designed to create agreement among the citizens about basic institutional questions, such as who should belong to the supreme deliberative body or how officials are to be selected, that is the types of issue associated with unanimity in the *Ethics.* Indeed, Aristotle adopts what may be called a 'maxim of unanimity' as one of the guiding principles of constitution building (Miller 1996, 269–74): if a constitution is to survive, all parts ought to wish that it continue *(Pol* 1270b 21–22; 1294b 34–40).

That Aristotle values political agreement among the citizen body is undisputed and uncontroversial. But what is added to this position by his identification of political agreement with political friendship? Does he mean to imply that collective political agreement arises out of the multiplicity of friendly relations which fellow citizens have with one another? Or is he simply describing such agreement as friendship without implying that it rests on any other sentiments of friendship between citizens? A number of commentators have attempted to interpret the friendship of fellow citizens as involving feelings of mutual concern sufficient to sustain political consent and joint political action, even though such friendship is more distant and more selfish than the true friendship between close friends and family members. Thus Cooper argues that each individual citizen in a political community will recognise the benefits that he draws from the law and legal institutions and, though not knowing most other citizens personally, will see that they too share a similar appreciation of the benefits of their joint institutions. Each will therefore be willing to act in a spirit of co-operation and forbearance to one another, thus providing consent and active support for these institutions (Cooper 1977: 646–8; 1990: 235). Cooper notes that Aristotle uses the human desire for friendship as a refutation of the self-interested alliance as a model for the state (*Pol* 1280b 30–1281a 2). This demonstrates, he claims, that the friendship which fellow members of the state have for each other goes beyond mutual self-interest and involves genuine concern for each other's welfare which, in turn, leads them to support their shared institutions (Cooper 1990: esp 232–5). Terence Irwin, though disagreeing with Cooper's comparatively altruistic reading of advantage-friendship, none the less argues that, at least in the best state, virtuous citizens recognise each other's virtue and are thus willing to offer them the type of concern that they would offer to their own close friends, thus underpinning the constitution with their collective friendship (Irwin 1988: 399–402; 1990).

The difficulty with interpreting Aristotle's theory of political friendship as an argument that political consent arises out of sentiments of mutual care and concern between fellow citizens is the lack of supporting explicit textual evidence (Annas 1990: 243; Miller 1995: 208–9). The passages in the *Ethics* simply identify political friendship with political agreement. They do not say that such friendship *leads to* agreement or, conversely, that such agreement *springs from* friendship. The conceptual link between political agreement and friendship in general is established through the fact that agreement is also a characteristic of virtue friendships. That is, political friendship shares with true friendship the fact that all parties are in agreement over matters of common interest. However, that is the limit of the stated similarity. There is no explicit suggestion that friendship among citizens also shares with true friendship sentiments of mutual concern and goodwill which, in turn, generate unanimity. Nor need there be. Fellow citizens may agree on the justice of shared political and legal arrangements and to that extent may be prepared to yield to each other's interests and to support particular institutions and decisions which favour others rather than themselves. But it does not follow that their political consent is based on a prior concern to help each other.

Nor is there any explicit suggestion in the *Politics* that sentiments of friendship between citizens lead to political agreement between them. The only reference to friendship in Books IV–VI comes in Book IV. 11 where Aristotle is discussing the merits of middle class rule. Class warfare in cities polarised into rich and poor is said to be 'the furthest removed from friendship and political community *(koinonia)*, for community *(koinonia)* is friendly' *(Pol* 1295b 23. See further Cooper 1990: 233 n 16; Annas 1990: 246). In this brief comment, friendship need mean no more than political agreement, the absence of conflict, rather than any further feeling between citizens. In Book 111.9, in the passage emphasised by Cooper *(Pol* 1280b 30–1281a 2), Aristotle certainly connects friendship with the human desire for living together for its own sake, a desire which is used to refute the contractarian view of the state as an alliance of self-interested individuals. But the institutions explicitly linked to friendship are not the city itself but the smaller associations, such as brotherhoods and cults, where people may enjoy personal relations with one another in a way which is not possible, on Aristotle's own admission, within the larger community of the city (Annas 1990: 242–3). As indicated by Aristotle's account of the good life in the *Ethics*, the communal living together which people particularly value for its own sake is that involved in their more immediate relationships of family and friends while the more distant relationships are looked on more instrumentally. The *polis* is certainly valued because the good life is impossible without its social diversity and legally enforced order. But this does not mean that all relationships within the *polis*, including that of fellow citizens, are equally important or equally valued for their own sake.

Thus, Aristotle certainly recognises the importance of civic consent and solidarity and equates it with political friendship. But he does not unambiguously base it in any sentiments of mutual goodwill arising out of the relationships of fellow citizens, sentiments which he recognises to be weak, especially when compared with the intensity of true friendship. Still less, though civic consent is described as 'friendship', is it the expression of any mutual goodwill or concern beyond that entailed by the consent itself. Rather, consent appears to be an independent attribute of shared citizenship, necessary for the maintenance of political order, and requiring its own independent means of inculcation and reinforcement. As such, it does not arise out of the friendship of fellow citizens, so much as complement the deficiencies of such friendship (Yack 1993: 114).

Such an account of political friendship may seem to downplay the importance not only of friendship between fellow citizens but also of political life itself. If the relationships which people value most are those of immediate friends and family while those between fellow citizens are largely instrumental, how does this square with Aristotle's doctrines that the *polis* is natural and his supposed endorsement of the centrality of citizenship to the good life? Aristotle's theory of friendship leads to a consideration of other major parts of his social theory which are beyond the scope of this paper. We may note, however, that the role of political participation in Aristotle's political theory is a similarly contested question. Many commentators have read Aristotle as an advocate of active citizenship who includes participation in politics as an essential component of the virtuous and happy life (eg Arendt 1958, Barber 1984). Such an interpretation may encourage a more positive and richer view of the friendship between fellow citizens. For instance, Cooper and Irwin, who see political friendship as involving feelings of mutual care and concern between fellow citizens, also assume that political participation is a necessary part of a communal good life. It is because people value their shared civic life as citizens that they develop friendly feelings towards one another (Cooper 1990: 238–41; Irwin 1990).

However, the assumption that specifically political activity is necessary for happiness is not sustained by a careful reading of 'the *Ethics* and is inconsistent with Aristotle's unwillingness to reject kingship and absolute rule on principle (Mulgan 1990; Miller 1996: 237–9; Duvall and Dotson 1998). Virtuous men will share in ruling when required, but exclusion from ruling does not deprive them of virtue or happiness in the same way as does loss of friends or family. Such a view is more compatible with a weaker interpretation of political friendship. If people do not consider the duties of citizenship to be essential to their happiness they are less likely to place value on their relationships with fellow citizens or to be concerned about the welfare of their fellow citizens.

Some commentators, admittedly, combine a minimalist interpretation of political friendship with a central role for political participation. Thus Bernard Yack, in his sustained attempt to rescue Aristotle from the communitarian embrace, claims that the essence of human beings' political nature is their capacity for reason (*logos*) which he understands as a capacity for argument and deliberation, in particular political argument and deliberation about the fundamental principles of justice. What characterises the body of citizens is not so much their shared values and friendship as their conflicting interests and differences over justice which they seek to reconcile through political debate (see also Bickford 1996: ch 2). Aristotle thus becomes aligned with those modern political theorists who see deliberative democracy as the escape route from the impasse caused by the inevitably conflicting interests of fellow citizens. However, while the points against excessive unity and camaraderie among Aristotle's citizens are well made, Aristotle cannot be convincingly co-opted into the ranks of ethical pluralists or deliberative democrats (Mulgan 1999). A stable political regime, for Aristotle, depends on some shared values from which collective deliberation can proceed in just the same way as a virtuous person requires an ethical disposition before he or she can reason virtuously. A capacity for deliberation and argument does not in itself provide a starting point for moral justification, either for individuals or communities. In each case, debate presupposes prior indoctrination and habituation, through parents and education in the case of individuals, through statesmen and laws in the case of cities.

Political consent thus depends on the inculcation of political values through the legal system and the political culture of the political community. Consent does not develop spontaneously either from the fellow feelings of individual citizens or from their capacity for reasoned speech and political participation. The naturalness of the city provides a rationale for such inculcation on the grounds that people need the city in order to live the good life but cannot be trusted to live justly without coercion from the city's system of justice (*Pol* I.2, esp 1253a 29–34). Ensuring that all citizens, or as many as possible, accept the justice of the regime is one of the most pressing tasks of statesmanship, for the very reason that citizens cannot be relied on to do so for themselves. No laws are needed to make parents love their children or close friends look after each other. But fellow citizens, whose personal dealings are distant and largely instrumental, will neglect their common interests and resort to faction and violence without the coercive power of the state.

Modern Lessons?

Where, then, does Aristotle's theory of friendship stand in relation to debates between liberal individualists and communitarians over the basis of political society? (The use of these terms may be justified as a convenient shorthand, though it overlooks the considerable variations within each camp [Mulhall and Swift 1996]). Not untypically, Aristotle occupies a middle position. On the one hand, he clearly rejects the extreme liberal–individualist assumption that all social institutions must be justified in terms of individual self-interest. His emphasis on the independent ethical value of genuine friendships, both in the family and between close companions, is a convincing refutation of hard-line individualists who would base even the most intimate relationships on self-interest. People engage in many social relationships for their own sake and genuinely care for the welfare of at least some others as indistinguishable from their own.

At the same time, however, his theory has less purchase against more moderate liberals who would draw a distinction between family and friends whose welfare is inextricably bound up with one's own, and the wider society of economic and political relationships where motives of self-interest are appropriate. True, Aristotle is careful not to draw hard and fast lines between genuine and derivative types of friendship. His picture of society is more one of a series of widening circles of friendship and acquaintance, with decreasing degrees of intimacy and commitment, rather than of a clear division between friends and others. In this respect, as so often, his social analysis is subtle and perceptive and reveals important characteristics not only of his own society but also of others, including our own. His weight can thus be lent to those who stress the social value of intermediate or mediating institutions existing between individuals and their families and the political community as a whole.

If Aristotle softens the crudities of a sharp 'us and them' bifurcation, he does not unequivocally reject the liberal assumption that relationships with fellow members of a political community are based primarily on considerations of self-interest. He follows common sense in supporting the superior moral weight of our duties to nearest and dearest. The 'friendship' that he attributes to fellow citizens is weak and instrumental and does not indicate a base of mutual concern on which could be built a justification for submerging individual self-interest into a community-wide public interest. In this respect, Aristotle does not provide the modern communitarian with a justification of political institutions in terms of sentiments of friendship or solidarity.

But the problem of justification still remains, for Aristotle as well as us. In Aristotle's scheme of values, the institutions of the state are justified in terms of justice, whether the complete justice of the ideal state or the partial justice of everyday states. In any stable political community, it is a particular conception of justice that determines who should rule, who should decide the laws and how the laws should be applied and administered. But what reasons do individuals have for accepting this conception of justice when it may, on occasion, require them to act against their own interests in the common interest? This is the critical question which lies at the heart of the modern debate between liberals and communitarians. It was also a central question in Greek political theory, raised by the sophists and articulated most tellingly by Plato though the mouth of Glaucon in *Republic* II.

Aristotle's theory of friendship does not provide an answer to the problem of justification unless the extent of genuine friendship between fellow citizens is expanded well beyond the texts. The theory, however, may be said to presuppose an answer because political friendship is identified with the agreement of citizens to accept common institutions and a common interest. Where does this agreement come from? Aristotle's rationale for political consent can be seen to involve an appeal to general consequences backed by brute force. Just institutions are needed to provide the society necessary for living the good life because, without political stability, the prerequisites for people's happiness, namely their lives, property, family and friends, cannot be guaranteed. However, individuals cannot be trusted to pursue the common interest unprompted. Law and coercion are necessary to inculcate public values and constrain free riders. Ultimately, agreement rests on enforced beliefs not rational acquiescence. It is a tough-minded, realistic conclusion, likely to satisfy neither the collective idealism of the communitarian nor the liberal individualist's faith in rational self-interest.

REFERENCES

Annas, J. 1990. 'Comments on J. Cooper' in G. Patzig (ed), *Aristoteles' 'Politik'*, Göttingen: Vandenhoeck and Ruprecht, pp.243–49
Arendt, H. 1958. *The Human Condition*, Chicago: University of Chicago Press.
Barber, B. 1984. *Strong Democracy*, Berkeley: University of California Press.
Bickford, S. 1996. *The Dissonance of Democracy*, Ithaca: Cornell University Press.
Cooper, J. M. 1977. 'Aristotle on the Forms of Friendship' *Review of Metaphysics* 30, pp.617–48, reprinted in abridged form as part of 'Aristotle on Friendship' in A. O. Rorty (ed), 1980. *Essays on Aristotle's Ethics*, Berkeley: University of California Press, pp.301–40.
Cooper, J. M. 1990. 'Political Animals and Civic Friendship' in G.Patzig (ed), *Aristoteles' 'Politik'* (Gottingen: Vandenhoeck and Ruprecht, pp.221–42.
Duvall, T. and Dotson, P. 1998. 'Political Participation and *Eudaimonia* in Aristotle's *Politics*', *History of Political Thought*, pp.19, 21–34.
Irwin, T. 1988. *Aristotle's First Principles*, Oxford: Clarendon Press.
Irwin, T. 1990. 'The Good of Political Activity' in G. Patzig (ed), *Aristoteles' 'Politik'* Göttingen: Vandenhoeck and Ruprecht, pp.73–100.

MacIntyre, A. 1981. *After Virtue,* Notre Dame: University of Notre Dame Press.
Miller, F. R. 1995. *Nature, Justice, and Rights in Aristotle's* Politics, Oxford: Clarendon Press.
Mulgan, R. 1990. 'Aristotle and the Value of Political Participation', *Political Theory,* 18, 195–215.
Mulgan, R. 1999. 'Aristotle, Ethical Diversity and Political Argument', *Journal of Political Philosophy,* pp.7, 191–207.
Mulhall, S. and Swift, S. 1996. *Liberals and Communitarians,* Oxford: Blackwell.
Price, A. W. 1989. *Love and Friendship in Plato and Aristotle,* Oxford: Clarendon Press.
Schwarzenbach, S. A. 1996. 'On Civic Friendship', *Ethics* 107, 97–128.
Yack, B. 1993. *The Problems of a Political Animal: Community, Justice, and Conflict in Aristotelian Political Thought,* Berkeley: University of California Press.

3

Hume, Smith and Ferguson:
Friendship in Commercial Society

LISA HILL and PETER McCARTHY

During the period in which Adam Smith, David Hume and Adam Ferguson lived and wrote, Scotland experienced enormous social and political upheavals. Although it would be inaccurate to describe 'capitalism' as the dominant mode of economic organisation in eighteenth-century Scotland (Camic 1983: 95), they were witness to the advent of commercialism and its profound effects both in Britain and abroad. The most dramatic revolutions occurred in the agricultural economy of the highlands and this exerted a marked effect on village life (Strasser 1976: 53). Other significant industrial changes were: the mechanisation and specialisation of labour, enormous increases in productive output, the geographical concentration of manufacture, the division of the manufacturing population into either owners and employers of wage labour and workers, and the urbanisation of Britain.[1] Because Britain was the first industrial and commercial state there was much debate at the time about the likely social and moral effects of commercialism. One such topic was the likely effect of industrial life on patterns of association.

It has been suggested by Allan Silver (1997) that Hume, Smith and Ferguson all saw commerce as exerting a positive effect on the capacity for people to form and maintain friendships. Rather than contaminating and blurring the distinction between genuine and utilitarian friendships, now genuine friendship begins to be more easily separated from the instrumental and involuntary ties of clan and kin because of the clarifying effect of contracts. Others have also suggested that Smith, Hume and Ferguson all regard 'modern' friendship as improved because more voluntary and, therefore, somehow more authentic under commercial conditions. Alan Wolfe (1989: 29), for example, suggests that friendship in the Smithian world is superior because governed by a natural sympathy that 'enrich[es] and deepen[s]' our 'moral obligations to one another'. Severyn Bruyn (1998: 1–2) likewise claims that the new civility of market society enhances mutual sentiments and generates 'trust and respect between agents' (see also Chaplin, 1990). In these readings, friendship is not seen to rely on instrumentalism, but on the presumably more benign mechanism of 'sympathy'. Sympathy breaks down the mandatory and particularistic constraints of class and clan thereby increasing the general quantity of goodwill (Silver 1990: 1480–81). The new congeniality is an antidote to the allegedly hostile, particularistic and suspicious tenor of bonds defined by 'custom' and 'station' (Silver 1997: 59), reflecting and adding lustre to the optimistic, universalistic atmosphere of the Enlightenment (Silver 1990: 1481; 1997: 50).

But, as is frequently the case in general discussions of the Scottish Enlightenment, insufficient care has been taken to distinguish between the views of its various luminaries. While it is certainly the case that Smith and Hume are optimistic about the new age, this does not necessarily mean that they are *all* celebrating the liberation of a new and more ubiquitous form of voluntary friendship or for the same reasons. Ferguson is the notable exception. To begin with, he does not really have a theory of sympathy; in fact, he often complained about Smith's use of the term. Second, Ferguson did not agree that commerce brought with it a 'superior' form of sociability; rather, he disagreed bitterly. Nevertheless, these analyses (particularly Silver's) illuminate nicely the optimism of Hume and Smith about the new strangership of modern life.

Smith and Hume

When Adam Smith described the new moral economy of the commercial age, he enthusiastically heralded the passing of feudal and pastoral friendships based on 'beneficence' and the emergence of those animated by the cooler and more constant virtues of 'prudence' and 'justice'. Smith provided what was probably the most subtle account to date of the impracticality of benevolence as the basis for social life. With that shift came a new understanding of friendship.

Fundamental to Smith's account of the evolution of friendship is the breakdown of the extended family. In feudal or 'pastoral' orders, extended families remain united for the purpose of 'common defence'. However, in commercial states, 'where the authority of law is always perfectly sufficient to protect the meanest man in the state', family members 'naturally separate and disperse, as interest or inclination may direct'. After a while, relations lose contact and 'in a few generations, not only lose all care about one another, but all remembrance of their common origin'. The more established the 'state of civilization', the more 'remote relations become' (Smith 1976: VI.ii.1.12–3, 222–3). Biological affiliation is displaced by proximity, but such a revolution is by no means catastrophic for the survival of community. Smith recognised that the disintegration of tight-knit communities did not reduce interdependence; rather, it transformed the quality and means of our interdependence.

Smith celebrated the breakdown of feudalism and the diffusion of freedom and individual power brought on by commercialisation. He witnessed first hand the transition from social organisations based on mechanistic solidarity to those characterised by organic solidarity. That transition saw the passing of clan and village life, the breakdown of extended families, the growth of cities, the increasing development of task specialisation and the extension of markets. It also saw the decline of arbitrary and diffuse forms of rule and the concomitant rise of the modern state. Smith's greatest objection to the feudal age relates to the necessary and compulsory dependence associated with the system of great landholders and retainers. Dependency is bad because it breeds servility (Smith 1979: III.iv.4–7, 412–5). 'Nobody but a beggar', says Smith, 'chuses to depend chiefly upon the benevolence of his fellow-citizens' (1979: I.ii.2, 27). The new order brings with it a new moral energy and a new affective tone. The feudal order, in which the distribution of goods occurred according to dependency relations or blood ties, is displaced by a more impersonal rationality. 'Natural affection' is superseded by a kind of friendship which Smith refers to as 'necessitudo'. The 'necessity of the situation', by which Smith means the constraints of market society, gives rise to this new type of association because amity between people in the workplace is desirable and conducive to business:

> Among well-disposed people, the necessity or conveniency of mutual accommodation, very frequently produces a friendship not unlike that which takes place among those who are born to live in the same family. Colleagues in office, partners in trade, call one another brothers; and frequently feel towards one another as if they really were so. Their good agreement is an advantage to all; and, if they are tolerably reasonable people, they are naturally disposed to agree. We expect that they should do so; and their

disagreement is a sort of a small scandal. The Romans expressed this sort of attachment by the word *necessitudo*, which, from the etymology, seems to denote that it was imposed by the necessity of the situation.[2]

The new voluntaristic friendship is welcomed as an adjunct to the growth of the market, which is both natural and good because it results from the natural 'propensity to truck, barter, and exchange' (Smith, 1979: I.ii.1, 25). In addition, it represents and embodies two important Enlightenment ideals: first, progress, which is inevitable and always positive; and second, cosmopolitanism, because commerce progressively enlarges markets (Hume 1987e: *passim*) and therefore expands circles of cool friendship.

Smith and Hume both reject the simple social forms admired by Ferguson in favour of large-scale, non-particularistic communities based on 'calculation and self-interest' and regulated by impartial justice (Smith 1978: 326–8, 538–9; Hume 1987i: 272–8; Berry 1992: 80–2). Only in such conditions, in a world regulated by the predictable and temperate rhythms of 'sympathy', are justice, virtue, happiness and prosperity to be discovered.

For Hume, a felicitous side-effect of 'industry and refinements in the mechanical arts' is that such advances are inevitably accompanied by refinements in the 'liberal' arts. As a consequence 'Profound ignorance is totally banished, and men enjoy the privilege of rational creatures, to think as well as to act, to cultivate the pleasures of the mind as well as those of the body.' Where the liberal arts flourish, where science is forever advancing and where there is, therefore, always something to talk about, people naturally become more 'sociable'. In stark contrast to Ferguson's fond portrait of his intimate pre-commercial 'knot of friends' united by beneficence and common interest (1995: V.III, 208), Hume regards barbarity as a state of 'solitude' in which each was compelled to 'live with their fellow citizens' in a 'distant manner'. The barren affective climate of pre-commercial life is contrasted with the vivacity and sociability of commercial society; here, people 'flock into cities; love to receive and communicate knowledge; to show their wit or their breeding; their taste in conversation or living, in clothes or furniture' (Hume 1987i: 270–71). Commercial life generates a new type of civil society characterised by candour, openness, friendliness, and a proliferation of 'clubs and societies' which reflect the breakdown of exclusivistic social categories. Indeed, Hume regards himself as a 'Kind of ... Ambassador from the Dominions of Learning to those of Conversation' (1987c: 535). Now even the two 'sexes meet in an easy and sociable manner', while the tempers and manners of everyone are observed to improve and 'refine apace' (1987i: 271).

Hume is particularly delighted at the introduction of women into polite society. Compared to 'barbarous nations' where polygamy is practised and women are sequestered and reduced to 'abject slavery', 'among a polite people' women are treated with 'civility', 'respect' and (an albeit patronising) 'complaisance'. The company of women is both a sign and preservative of civility: 'What better school for manners, than the company of virtuous women; where the mutual endeavour to please must insensibly polish the mind ... where the delicacy of that sex puts every one on his guard, lest he give offence by any breach of decency' (Hume 1987j: 133–4; 1987g: 184–5). The admittance of women to Hume's cool circles of fellowship is a most valuable addition, for 'the Fair Sex' are to him, not merely the true 'Sovereigns of the Empire of Conversation', but cherished allies in the 'League ... against the Enemies of Reason and Beauty, People of dull Heads and cold Hearts' (1987b: 535–6).

The polished age instates women in their rightful (that is, natural) place in relation to men, no longer tyrannised chattels but more properly 'lovers' and 'friends'. Habitual interaction with women also improves relations between men because it demystifies and desexualises women, erasing the distorting jealousies and anxieties attendant on the practice of polygamy (or in Britain's case, effective seclusion); this jealousy is 'as destructive to friendship as to love. Jealousy excludes men from all intimacies and familiarities with each other. No one dares bring his friend to his house or table, lest he bring a lover' to his wife or wives. A relaxation of controls on women in barbarous nations would undoubtedly bring about a revolution in human happiness because it would safeguard the only thing of value: 'Destroy love and friendship; what remains in the world worth accepting?' (Hume 1987g: 184–5; 1978: I.IV.VII, 269–70.)

This perpetual amicable commerce, in which people are regularly sharing and entering into each other's sentiments, gives rise to a more humane atmosphere with the effect that each is constantly 'contributing to each other's pleasure and entertainment' and thereby increasing the common fund of happiness. Smith likewise welcomes the new friendliness which is generated outside intensely emotional and exclusivistic social units such as the family, noting that the habits of congeniality are now acquired more diffusely and impersonally through interaction with the world at large: self-command, 'equality of temper' and other norms of interaction peculiar to 'men of the world' are products of 'conversation' and the 'bustle and business of the world' (1976: I.i.4, 23; III.3.25, 146).

Hume diverges slightly here; he does not seem to share in Smith's view that the new sociability exists for the sake of commerce (about which he is perfectly complacent) but for the sake of civility itself; civility, and the new type of temperate friendship to which it gives rise, seems to be an end in itself. Modernity and the 'vulgar commercial arts' create that condition which 'soften[s] and humanize[s] the temper, and cherish[es] those fine emotions, in which true virtue and honour consists'. Persons 'of taste and learning' are usually averse to those 'passions of interest and ambition' which Smith celebrates. Love of money, which Smith peddles euphemistically as a morally indifferent imperative to self-preservation, is a 'vice' which appears to bewilder and bemuse Hume. Though he agrees with Smith that avidity is often socially productive, and most definitely 'insatiable' and ineradicable (Hume 1978: III.II.II, 492), he nevertheless regards it as a 'frosty, spiritless' passion attaching only to those 'without regard to reputation, to friendship, or to pleasure' (Hume 1987a: 571). What Hume and Smith do share in common (though for different reasons) is an embrace of the new 'strangership' which renders life more tranquil, predictable, just, orderly and, above all, more sociable (see, for example, Hume 1987i: 272).

Sympathy and Strangers

Commercial society is a society of strangers. There is no total state or absolute moral code to coerce and control, aside from the limited strictures of positive law (justice). Sympathy becomes the primary method of social control. We all want to attract the sympathy of those around us, whether or not they are known personally to us. Accordingly, we constantly moderate or mould our behaviour according to the judgements of a hypothetical observer who is impartial. The impartial spectator reduces conflict and brings order, 'tranquillity' and 'concord' (Smith 1976: I.i.4.8–10, 22–3). Like Hume (1978: II.I.XI, 320–22), Smith stresses that we possess a 'natural disposition to accommodate and to assimilate, as much as we can, our own sentiments, principles, and feelings, to those which we see … in the persons whom we are obliged to live and converse a great deal with' (1976: VI.ii.1.17, 224).[3] The goodwill and civility required to 'lubricate' social life is just as necessitous as that requisite to the maintenance of ascribed and kinship relationships, however, now its manufacture is a less particularistic enterprise. Under commercial conditions, there is a greater general fund of goodwill from which everyone may benefit in an impersonal way. No one need suffer, Smith writes, if one's 'beneficence' toward another does not elicit commensurate 'kindness' or 'gratitude'.

> No benevolent man ever lost altogether the fruits of his benevolence. If he does not always gather them from the persons from whom he ought to have gathered them, he seldom fails to gather them, and with a tenfold increase, from other people. (Smith 1976: VI.ii.1.19, 225.)

The fact that amicable strangership, rather than the alternatives of intense enmity or intense friendship, is now the norm means that people must habitually moderate their behaviour and attitudes (Smith 1976: III.3.25, 146–7). The faceless mass of strangers becomes internalised in the moral personality as the 'impartial spectator' who constantly monitors and corrects the 'strongest impulses of self-love' (Smith 1976: III.3.38, 153–4; III.3.4, 137; VI.3.18, 244–5; Hume 1978: II.II.I, 331–2). As Mizuta puts it:

> The stranger is not a friend from whom we can expect any special favour and sympathy. But at the same time he is not an enemy from whom we cannot expect any sympathy at all. Everyone in society is as independent of every other as a stranger, and is equal with every other as they can exchange [their] situations. The famous impartial spectator is no one else but the spectator who is indifferent to, and does not take the part of either side (1975: 122, n4).

Sympathy and the new strangership generate a pervasive atmosphere of goodwill and politeness. We stand in need of much greater numbers of people than ever before and this gives rise to a softening of manners and a diminution of conflict. However, rather than being symptomatic of a proliferation of warm friendships, the character of sympathy is more properly understood as a new form of instrumentalism. The fact that it is universalisable and voluntary does not mean that it is any more benign than the necessitous alliances of pre-commercial times. Since all strangers are now potential contractees and not potential enemies, the exchange culture has a surface appearance of calm friendliness which belies its competitive and passionless character.

Smith differs from Hume in the sense that he has a far narrower view of how much community is required to sustain human life. Whereas Hume celebrates the new conviviality for the preservation of impartial justice and general sociableness, Smith wants a world with less socialising and more exchanging. Friendship is one of life's lower order priorities; Smith's ideal agent never sacrifices the duties of business and work to the pleasures of sociability and friendship (1976: VI.i.13, 215–6). The prudent agent is honest, 'always sincere', but 'not always frank and open'. He is 'capable of friendship', but avoids 'ardent and passionate' attachments and 'is not always much disposed to general sociality'. Attendance on 'convivial societies' is restricted because it might 'interfere with the regularity of his temperance, might interrupt the steadiness of his industry, or break in upon the strictness of his frugality' (Smith 1976: VI.i.8–9, 214).

The commercial agent is not particularly interested in friendship, nor should he be according to Smith, because there is far too much specialising and exchanging to be done (after all, our desire for wealth is insatiable and relentless) (Smith 1979: II.iii.28, 341). The archetypal calm friendship permits of no one-sided dependency nor any imperfect reciprocity; there may be no breaches of privacy, nor may any of the parties take liberties with the rules or seek to corrupt the natural independence of the other by offering too much. The prudent agent refrains from meddling or any of the other things that 'true' friends are inclined to do. To use the modern terminology, he has extremely firm personal 'boundaries'. Sometimes Smith is apt to shock us with his insistence on the 'firmness' of these boundaries. Note what happens to friendship when one of the parties fails to exhibit the commercial virtue of prudence, the ability to take care of oneself. People who decline to pursue the 'extraordinary and important objects of self-interest' appear 'mean-spirited'. It is entirely natural for us to despise such a person, who may find himself quite justifiably 'abandoned by his friends, as altogether unworthy of their attachment' (Smith 1976: III.6.7, 173; see also Hill 1999).

The New Interdependence

Civilised society permits greater interdependence, paradoxically, because each 'stands at all times in need of the co-operation and assistance of great multitudes despite the fact that his whole life is scarce sufficient to gain the friendship of a few persons' (Smith 1979: I.ii.2, 26). The almost complete self-sufficiency of 'savages' and 'barbarians' did not benefit them; rather, it gave them a world of meagre and somewhat one-dimensional moral relations. The knot of intimate conspecifics is affectively barren compared to the rich new 'strangership' of the commercial age. In pre-commercial society, as Silver puts it so well:

> the space between friend and enemy was not occupied, as in commercial society, with mere acquaintances, or neutral strangers, but charged with uncertain and menacing possibilities. ... [Whereas] strangers in commercial society are not either potential enemies or allies, but authentically indifferent co-citizens — the sort of indifference that enables all to make contracts with all. (1990: 1482–3.)

Forbearance and mutual non-interference are Smith's favourite virtues. The 'impartial spectator' monitors our 'passions and appetites', constantly judging 'how far' each of them was 'either to be indulged or restrained' (Smith 1976: III.5.5, 165). The impartial spectator does not seek to reduce selfishness, but merely to regulate the self-regarding passions and ensure that contracts are honoured. Virtuous commercial agents ask little of each other, beyond a demand for fair play, respect for the other's autonomy and the extension of reciprocal non-interference (Smith 1976: II.ii.2.1, 83; III.6.10, 175).

For Smith, it is not the 'soft spark' of beneficence (the philosophical equivalent of Christian love) that makes social life possible in the modern age; large-scale societies are too unwieldy to be held together by spontaneous affection. What holds an industrialising society together are the bonds of contract (the primary mechanism of association) and the irresistible attractions of mutual enablement. Specialisation generates unprecedented levels of interdependence and association becomes a matter of purely instrumental, mutual 'good offices':

> man has constant occasion for the help of his brethren, and it is in vain for him to expect it from their benevolence only. He will be more likely to prevail if he can interest their self-love in his favour, and shew them that it is for their own advantage to do for him what he requires of them. ... Give me that which I want, and you shall have this which you want, is the meaning of every such offer; and it is in this manner that we obtain from one another the far greater part of those good offices which we stand in need of. (Smith 1979: I.ii.2, 26.)

Exchange is now the primary mode of association; the urge to 'truck, barter, and exchange one thing for another' is innate and therefore natural. By this means, the equally natural institution of society is held together. (Smith 1979: I.ii.1–3, 25–7.)

Strangers and the Golden Emotional Mean

According to Smith, the exigencies of the commercial age require that the fierce passions attendant on feudal alliances are relinquished in favour of something tamer. The golden mean is emotional equilibrium, not benevolent passion. Smith admonishes excessive displays of 'humanity, kindness, natural affection, friendship [and] esteem' (1976: VI.iii.15, 243) and regards passionate expressions of 'friendship and humanity' as a form of 'weakness'. Such intemperate sensibilities can never be 'disagreeable', however they are most certainly 'unfit for the world' of commerce and contract (1976: I.ii.4.3, 40; V.ii.10, 207; V.i.3.15, 243). Hume follows suit: cultivating 'the polite arts' improves our taste for the circumspect 'tender and agreeable passions' while rendering 'the mind incapable of the rougher and more boisterous emotions' (1987c: 6). Though people become milder and less furious in their emotions with 'politeness and refinement', their 'sense of honour', which is after all a 'stronger, more constant, and more governable principle, acquires fresh vigour by that elevation of genius which arises from knowledge and a good education' (Hume 1987i: 274). Impartial justice displaces passionate personalism and the world becomes a place that is easier to live in and more congenial to our basic desire for love of 'company', a love often mistaken for the grander and more lofty passion of universal benevolence (Hume 1978: III.II.I, 482).

Ferguson

Ferguson is particularly troubled by Smith's reasoning. Though he admits that the desire for 'attention and personal consideration … frequently inclines us to be connected with our fellow-creatures', nevertheless this desire can just as easily cause us to use others instrumentally as 'tools of our vanity' (Ferguson 1995: I.VIII, 55–6). Ferguson seems to agree that there is now greater organic solidarity in society and greater interdependence brought on by specialisation and the ever-increasing need to exchange. But whether market life brings more or better patterns of association is questionable to Ferguson's mind because modern life is becoming increasingly purged of such emotionally sustaining primary virtues as beneficence, charity, philanthropy and chivalry.

Ferguson's opposition to the Smithian-Humean perspective is thus extremely strong. Rather than being the 'sociable' society, market society is the (potentially) weak and anomic society. It nurtures the self-regarding passions and provides poor encouragement for the development of the other-regarding passions. Advanced or 'polished' nations afford few opportunities for the development of the more important civic virtues since 'the habits of a vigorous mind are formed in contending with difficulties, not in enjoying the repose of a pacific station' (Ferguson 1995: VI.IV, 242). On the one hand, commerce provides opportunities for the expression of 'a busy, inventive and versatile spirit' (Ferguson 1995: III.I, 107); on the other, it is the cause of moral and social breakdown.

For Ferguson, the new contract society can be alienating, isolating and affectively sterile; he believed that modes of association had become so debased that 'the duties of friendship are exacted by rule' and we 'consider kindness itself as a task' (1995: II.II, 87). Ferguson described *The Theory of Moral Sentiments* as 'a Heap of absolute Nonsense' and referred to Smith's use of the term 'sympathy' as an abuse of language (1960: 228–31). He is also impatient with Smith's moral relativism and his reliance on the need to 'accommodate and to assimilate' moral principles (Smith 1976: VI.ii.1.17, 224). But Smith's greatest sin consists in his substitution of sympathy for genuine moral sentiments and the lower virtues of the market for the higher, social virtues. It should be noted that Ferguson also endorsed the cool virtues, however, his complaint is with the ranking Smith accords them. The primary virtue of beneficence is displaced in Smith by cool, negative virtues such as propriety and prudence, which is nothing more than the 'capacity to take care of one's-self' (Smith 1976: VI.i.16, 216). Ferguson's derision is unbridled: 'who ever heard of Sympathizing with a person who pays his Debts?' (1960: 229.) Hume's claims that society is bound by a purely instrumental justice and that the value of the 'sociable', 'friendly' and 'beneficent' virtues consists partly in their utility (1975: II.I–II, 176, 181–2) are equally irritating to Ferguson, who attacks him by attributing to him the belief that 'Virtue is founded on Utility and that Virtue is only a Cow that gives milk of a particular Sort.' (1960: 226.) He also rejects Smith's axiom that people are more concerned to be admired than loved (Smith 1976: I.iii.2.1, 50). To 'prefer interest, fame and power, to acknowledged happiness' (that is, the exercise of beneficent friendship) is an error of the 'vulgar, as well as the learned'. The claim of both Smith and Hume that mutual utility is what holds society together is unconvincing because it ignores the comparative anthropological evidence which suggests that the 'bands' of society are actually *stronger* in communities where material conditions are extremely difficult and hostile (Ferguson 1995: I.III, 21–4). Hume and Smith have little or no faith in the power of beneficence to regulate society, insisting that 'each person loves himself better than any other single person' (Hume 1978: III.II.II, 487; Smith, 1976: III.3.10, 140) even going so far as to deny the existence of the universal variety (Hume 1978: III.II.I, 481).

According to Ferguson, the new commercial ethic obliterates communal sentiments and leads to the gradual disintegration of society. 'The members of a community may … be made to lose the sense of every connection … and have no common affairs to transact but those of trade … in which the national spirit … cannot be exerted.' (Ferguson 1995: V.III, 208.) Specialisation 'loosen[s] the bands of political union' (Ferguson 1995: V.III, 206–9), while 'commercial spirit' comes to displace vital civic spirit. Martial valour inevitably dissipates as armies specialise and professionalise; soon, 'an admiration, and desire of riches' brings with it 'an aversion to danger' (Ferguson 1995: VI.I, 231). Simple or 'barbarous' nations do not suffer these afflictions because in them 'the public is a knot of friends', bound together by the relentless threat of external attack (Ferguson 1995: V.III, 208).

Whereas Hume is progressivist, optimistic and unsentimental about what may be lost in the advance of market society, Ferguson is extremely worried about the emergence of the individuated society, reflecting nostalgically on the putative golden age of the small tribal community where the 'friendly intercourses of men … is affectionate and happy' (1995: II.III, 104). Ferguson recalls the intimacy of the Athens of Pericles which Thucydides referred to in Pericles' Funeral Oration and to the ancient Germany of Tacitus' reports where citizens enjoyed friendships based on spontaneous affection rather than expectation of reward (1995: V.III, 207; II.II, 86–7). Market society is dominated by a spirit of individualism, competition and legalism where relationships are defined and constrained by contracts and the profit motive. Ferguson seeks to correct Smith's individualism and Hume's blithe optimism by drawing attention to the alienating, soul-destroying and isolating effects of life in the market economy. Here 'man is sometimes found a detached and a solitary being: he has found an object which sets him in competition with his fellow-creatures, and he deals with them as he does with his cattle and his soil, for the sake of the profits they bring' (Ferguson 1995: I.III, 24; 1975: II.V.IV, 376–7).

In direct contradiction to Hume, Ferguson idealises village life and is apprehensive about the development toward large-scale social organisations (1995: V.III, 208–9; V.IV, 216). Ferguson lists 'People' before 'Wealth and Revenue' as the premier 'National resource'. But he provides the important qualification that mere size of the population does not reflect its value. Rather, the value of the key national resource is proportionate to a peoples' sense of 'union and character' (Ferguson 1978: VII.I–II, 242–5).

Ferguson disagrees with Smith and Hume on the desirability of order, tranquillity and the pleasant cadences of 'polite society'. According to Smith, modernity is better because it has better ways of delivering material accommodations (1979: I.i.11, 23–4), while for Hume, life in 'ancient nations' is in most important respects 'inferior' to that in the modern, which is happier because more calm, predictable and pacific (1987f: 420–21). On the one hand, Ferguson welcomes the more civilised expressions of conflict witnessed in modern times; however, he is worried that too much politeness will lead to inertia and political corruption. Ferguson seems to have had a more robust idea of what social activity consisted in; war, for example, provides the perfect occasion for the exercise of the social virtues. Here, 'Sentiments of affection and friendship mix with animosity; the active and strenuous become the guardians of their society; and violence itself is, in their case, an exertion of generosity as well as of courage.' (Ferguson 1995: I.IV, 29.)

Thus, even violence is a benefit when exercised by the 'patriot and warrior' for it results in the most illustrious career of human virtue (Ferguson 1995: I.IV, 29). There is a direct correlation between the strength of our social passions and the lengths we are prepared to go in order to defend them and this is nowhere better exemplified than in the actions of the true warrior whose aggression and belligerence are perfectly legitimate expressions of sociability (Ferguson 1995: II.III, 104–5). War preserves civil society, inspiring extraordinary acts of altruism, corporate sentiments, and communities which are 'faithful, disinterested and generous' (Ferguson 1995: II.III, 99). The universal, restrained amity of the Smithian-Humean vision is rejected in favour of the warm passions ignited in the particularistic tight-knit communities of the pre-commercial age. Ferguson probably has in mind the familiar highland clans when he speaks nostalgically of those 'small and simple tribes, who in their domestic society have the firmest union, are in their state of opposition as separate nations, frequently animated with the most implacable hatred' (1995: I.IV, 25; see also Waszek 1986: 162–3). True friendship is demonstrated by the capacity to love and hate with intensity, not by a willingness to honour contracts, assimilate the opinions of those around us, or engage in polite conversation.

Another important contrast between Hume and Ferguson is that Ferguson regards political faction fighting as a desirable and legitimate form of social activity (Ferguson 1995: III.II, 124–5). His discussion of party faction and the perils of political quiescence can be read as a critical commentary on Hume (Forbes 1966: xxxvi), who had written that factions undermine the rule of law and 'subvert government' (1987h: 55). Hume's 'ideal commonwealth' is one in which 'inveterate' party strife is minimised (1987d: 514; 1987i: 274), whereas Ferguson welcomed the inevitable ructions of class society.

Closing Remarks

It would be inaccurate, therefore, to characterise Ferguson in the same light as Smith and Hume. Ferguson did not see the instrumentalism of commercial society as purifying personal interactions. Rather, he saw it as a contaminant of such friendships.

Hume does not particularly value commercialism for its capacity to clarify friendship either; rather, he values commerce because it is accompanied by greater civility and politeness, thereby expanding the delightful circles of friendship congregating in coffee-houses and salons. For his part, Adam Smith welcomes the new sociability, not for the sake of 'authentic' friendship, but because it brings on the congenial strangership so necessary for the functioning of expanding market societies.

There are two fundamental differences between Ferguson and his adversaries which go a long way toward explaining their divergent attitudes to friendship in the commercial age. First, Ferguson's value system is less 'proto-liberal' in nature. He still adheres to a belief in an absolute moral code (Ferguson 1995: I.VI, 36–7) and is far more attracted to classical values (such as his celebration of warrior culture and the primary virtues). Hume regards his attitude as naive and somewhat primitivistic. 'To declaim against present times, and magnify the virtue of remote ancestors' is natural but nevertheless silly (Hume 1987i: 278). Contrary to Ferguson's prejudices, modern agents are no more venal than their ancient counterparts; in fact, the best way of 'restrain[ing] … the love of money' is not by appealing to antiquated virtues, but by bringing on the age of 'knowledge and refinement' (Hume 1987i: 276).

Second, the three thinkers entertain starkly competing conceptions of the point and chief happiness of life, conceptions which roughly correlate with their views on how friendship is affected by progress. Hume sees the purpose of all human effort as 'the attainment of happiness'; happiness consists of 'three ingredients; action, pleasure, and indolence' (1987i: 269; 1987k: 148). Since life's greatest pleasure is friendship, and since commerce expands the possibilities for the type of calm, decent and just friendship that Hume values, commerce is seen as positive. For Smith, the *telos* of human existence is also happiness, defined more narrowly as prosperity and material abundance (1976: VI.ii.3.5–6, 236–7; III.5.7, 166; 1979: I.viii.36, 96). Witness the 'serenity' and 'happiness' of the wealthy compared to the 'misery and distress' of the poor (Smith 1976: I.iii.2.1, 51); contrast the forlorn poverty of the 'savage' age with the 'general security and happiness which prevail in ages of civility and politeness' (Smith 1976: V.2.8–9, 205). It is self-interest, not beneficence, which is the cause of all this happiness (Smith 1979: II.iii.31, 343); hence his valorisation of the new strangership in which 'mutual good offices' are maximised by ever-enlarging circles of cool friendship. But Ferguson is far less worldly; the point of all human effort is union with the mind of God (1975: I.III.XIII, 313; II.II.III, 129; II.II.IV, 136) and, here on earth, this consists in the exercise of warm friendship and the sublime virtue of beneficence (1975: II.I.IV, 36). Happiness is synonymous with the practice of beneficence (Ferguson 1995: I.VIII, 55–6; 1975: I.III.XIII, 313; II.V.IV, 364; see also Hill, 1997), a virtue made increasingly redundant in the commercial age. Smith and Hume are perceived as contributing actively to its exile, hence his incensed opposition to them. Thus, the Scots present us with different, and in many ways troubling pictures of the potential for friendship in the modern world.

NOTES

1. These changes were fully realised in the nineteenth century (Mahon 1982: 43–5).
2. *The Oxford Latin Dictionary* defines '*necessitudo*' as 'a bond or tie between persons, obligation, connection, affinity ... a bond or affinity between things'. Lewis and Short's *Latin Dictionary* defines it as 'a close connection ... relationship, friendship, intimacy, bond'.
3. It should be stressed, however, that there are important differences in the way in which each thinker develops the idea of sympathy. See, for example, Campbell 1971: 95–6, 104–5; Raphael 1975: 86–7.

REFERENCES

Berry, C. J. 1992. Adam Smith and the virtues of commerce. *Nomos*, XXXIV, pp.69–88. New York, New York University Press.
Bruyn, S. T. 1998. The moral economy. *Ethics Colloquium*, 19 February 1998. Boston, Boston Theological Institute. http://www.bu.edu/sth/BTI/colloquium/ethbruyn.htm.
Camic, C. 1983. *Experience and Enlightenment: Socialization for Cultural Change in Eighteenth Century Scotland*. Edinburgh, Edinburgh University Press.
Campbell, T. D. 1971. *Adam Smith's Science of Morals*. London, George Allen & Unwin.
Chaplin, J. E. 1990. Slavery and the principle of humanity: a modern idea in the early lower South. *Journal of Social History*, Vol.24, No.2 , pp.299–315.
Ferguson, A. 1960. Of the principle of moral estimation: a discourse between David Hume, Robert Clerk, and Adam Smith: an unpublished ms by Adam Ferguson. Ed. Mossner, E. C. *Journal of the History of Ideas*, XXI, April–June 1960, pp.222–32.
    1975 [1792]. *Principles of Moral and Political Science*, Vols.I and II. Hildesheim, Georg Olms.
    1978 [1773]. *Institutes of Moral Philosophy*. New York, Garland.
    1995 [1767]. *An Essay on the History of Civil Society*. Ed. Oz-Salzberger, F. Cambridge, Cambridge University Press.
Forbes, D. 1966. Introduction. In *An Essay on the History of Civil Society 1767, by Adam Ferguson*, pp.xiii–xli. Edinburgh, Edinburgh University Press.
Hill, L. 1996. Ferguson and Smith on 'human nature', 'interest' and the role of beneficence in market society. *History of Economic Ideas, Adam Smith Special Edition*, Vol.IV, Nos.1–2, pp.353–99.
    1997. Adam Ferguson and the paradox of progress and decline. *History of Political Thought*, Vol.XVIII, No.4, winter, pp.677–706.
    1999. *Homo economicus*, 'difference voices', and the liberal psyche. *International Journal of Applied Philosophy*, Vol.13, No.1, spring, pp.21–46.
Hume, D. 1975 [1777]. *An Enquiry Concerning the Principles of Morals*. Eds. Selby-Bigge, L. A. and Nidditch, P. H., third edn. Oxford, Clarendon Press.
    1978 [1739–40]. *A Treatise of Human Nature*. Eds. Selby-Bigge, L. A. and Nidditch, P. H., second edn. Oxford, Clarendon Press.
    1987a [1777]. Of avarice. In *Essays Moral, Political and Literary*, ed. Miller, E. F., rev. edn. Indianapolis, Liberty Classics.
    1987b [1777]. Of essay writing. In *Essays Moral, Political and Literary*, ed. Miller, E. F., rev. edn. Indianapolis, Liberty Classics.
    1987c [1777]. Of the delicacy of taste and passion. In *Essays Moral, Political and Literary*, ed. Miller, E. F., rev. edn. Indianapolis, Liberty Classics.
    1987d [1777]. Idea of a perfect commonwealth. In *Essays Moral, Political and Literary*, ed. Miller, E. F., rev. edn. Indianapolis, Liberty Classics.
    1987e [1777]. Of the jealousy of trade. In *Essays Moral, Political and Literary*, ed. Miller, E. F., rev. edn. Indianapolis, Liberty Classics.
    1987f [1777]. Of the populousness of ancient nations. In *Essays Moral, Political and Literary*, ed. Miller, E. F., rev. edn. Indianapolis, Liberty Classics.
    1987g [1777]. Of polygamy and divorces. In *Essays Moral, Political and Literary*, ed. Miller, E. F., rev. edn. Indianapolis, Liberty Classics.
    1987h [1777]. Of parties in general. In *Essays Moral, Political and Literary*, ed. Miller, E. F., rev. edn. Indianapolis, Liberty Classics.
    1987i [1777]. Of refinement in the arts. In *Essays Moral, Political and Literary*, ed. Miller, E. F., rev. edn. Indianapolis, Liberty Classics.
    1987j [1777]. Of the rise and progress of the arts and the sciences. In *Essays Moral,*

Political and Literary, ed. Miller, E. F., rev. edn. Indianapolis, Liberty Classics.
1987k [1777]. The Stoic. In *Essays Moral, Political and Literary*, ed. Miller, E. F., rev. edn. Indianapolis, Liberty Classics.
Mahon, J. 1982. Engels and the question about cities. *History of European Ideas*, Vol.3, No.1, pp.43–77.
Mizuta, H. 1975. Moral philosophy and civil society. In *Essays on Adam Smith*, eds. Skinner A. S. and Wilson, T., pp.114–31. Oxford, Clarendon Press.
Raphael, D. D. 1975. The impartial spectator. In *Essays on Adam Smith*, eds. Skinner, A. S. and Wilson, T., pp.83–99. Oxford, Clarendon Press.
Silver, A. 1989. Friendship and trust as moral ideals: an historical approach. *European Journal of Sociology*, XXX, pp.274–97.
1990. Friendship in commercial society: eighteenth-century social theory and modern sociology. *American Journal of Sociology*, Vol.95, No.6, May 1990, pp.1474–504.
1997. 'Two different sorts of commerce' — friendship and strangership in civil society. In *Public and Private in Thought and Practice: Perspectives on a Grand Dichotomy*, eds. Weintraub, J. and Kumar, K., pp.43–74. Chicago, University of Chicago Press.
Smith, A. 1976 [1790]. *The Theory of Moral Sentiments*. Eds. Raphael, D. D. and Macfie, A. L., *Glasgow Edition of the Works and Correspondence of Adam Smith*. Oxford, Clarendon Press.
1978. *Lectures on Jurisprudence*. Eds. Meek, R. L., Raphael, D. D. and Stein, P. G., *Glasgow Edition of the Works and Correspondence of Adam Smith*. Oxford, Clarendon Press.
1979 [1784]. *An Inquiry into the Nature and Causes of the Wealth of Nations*. Eds. Campbell, R. H. and Skinner, A. S., two vols. Oxford, Clarendon Press.
Strasser, H. 1976. *The Normative Structure of Sociology: Conservative and Emancipatory Themes in Social Thought*. London, Routledge & Kegan Paul.
Waszek, N. 1986. *Man's Social Nature: A Topic of the Scottish Enlightenment in its Historical Setting*. Frankfurt, Peter Lang.
Wolfe, A. 1989. *Whose Keeper? Social Science and Moral Obligation*. Berkeley, University of California Press.

4

Circles, Ladders and Stars: Nietzsche on Friendship

RUTH ABBEY

Although the name of Friedrich Nietzsche is often invoked in discussions of subjectivity, it rarely appears in accounts of how relations with others shape and influence identity. The idea that Nietzsche could contribute to an understanding of friendship seems odd, if not misguided. This blend of Nietzsche and friendship appears even stranger in light of the fact that he is typically seen to purvey an ultra-individualistic ethos which disavows dependence on others and valorises autonomy, self-responsibility and solitude.[1] For example, in *Beyond Good and Evil* (henceforth referred to as BGE), he advises free spirits 'Not to cleave to another person, though he be the one you love most – every person is a prison, also a nook and corner'.[2]

One of the major purposes of this article is to show that friendship was one of Nietzsche's central concerns and that he shared Aristotle's belief that it takes higher and lower forms. Yet Nietzsche's interest in friendship is overlooked in much of the secondary literature.[3] An important reason for this is that this interest is most evident in the works of his middle period, and these tend to be neglected in commentaries on Nietzsche. This period comprises *Human, All Too Human* (1878) (henceforth, Volume One is referred to as HH), 'Assorted Opinions and Maxims' (1879) (henceforth, this part of HH Volume Two is referred to as AOM), 'The Wanderer and His Shadow' (1880) (henceforth, this part of HH Volume Two is referred to as WS), *Daybreak* (1881) (henceforth referred to as D) and the first four books of *The Gay Science* (1882) (henceforth referred to as GS).[4] The middle period is demarcated at one end by Nietzsche's early writings with their enthusiasm for Wagner and Schopenhauer and at the other by *Thus Spoke Zarathustra* (1883) (henceforth referred to as Z) and the subsequent works.[5]

In the works of the middle period, Nietzsche suggests that there is a close connection between friendship and selfhood, contending that an individual's friendships reflect something about his or her identity. Following Aristotle, he believes that friendship can make a significant contribution to self-knowledge and self-improvement,[6] which are both closely associated with his notion of self-overcoming. Nietzsche encourages individuals to adopt an aesthetic approach to the self: they should refashion themselves by consolidating their strengths, minimising their weaknesses and developing themselves in new directions. The works of the middle period suggest, however, that not only can friendship foster self-overcoming, but that the talent for friendship is one of the marks of a higher human being. Recognising this requires some reconsideration of Nietzsche's putative individualism and the belief that he holds great individuals to be utterly independent and indifferent to the judgements of others. It also requires a revision of the common interpretation that he is unremittingly sceptical about pity and other forms of fellow-feeling. Yet while Nietzsche generalises about friendship in the works of the middle period and contrasts its superior and inferior forms, he remains sensitive to its particularity. He never adopts a wholly formulaic approach to this relationship, but recognises that difference and responsiveness to particularity are among its central characteristics. Comparing Nietzsche's views on friendship in his middle period with those in his later works suggests that as his work 'progresses', the importance attributed to friendship recedes.

Friendship in Context

According to Jacques Derrida, 'the great canonical meditations on friendship ... belong to the experience of mourning, to the moment of loss – that of the friend or of friendship'.[7] This goes some way toward explaining Nietzsche's concern with friendship in the middle period. The years 1878–79 saw his break with his old friend Carl von Gersdorff and the death of Albert Brenner.[8] His friendship with Wagner deteriorated and collapsed over this phase. However, he was also sustained by many important friendships during this time. The powerful role friendship played in Nietzsche's life is evident from his correspondence before and during the middle period.[9] Both the existence and the content of his letters testify to friendship's importance: he often writes to his friends about friendship. He invites his friend Erwin Rohde to 'Think what life would be like without a friend. Could one, would one have borne it? *Dubito.*[10] Writing to Franz Overbeck, he describes being separated from his friends as 'the darkest melancholy'.[11] The importance of friendship is illustrated again in a letter to Paul Rée: 'in my entire life I have not had as much pleasure as through our friendship during this year, not to speak of what I have learned from you. When I hear of your studies, my mouth waters with anticipation of your company; we have been created for an understanding of one another...'.[12] The vitality of these relationships must be considered alongside loss and mourning as forces that inspire Nietzsche's reflections on friendship at this stage of his life.[13]

Yet Nietzsche's interest in friendship was not simply a consequence of his personal experiences. It was also connected to his theoretical interest in history, culture and what he later called the revaluation of values, as seen, for example, in *Ecce Homo* (henceforth referred to as EH).[14] In each of the middle-period works, he notes how important friendship was to the Greeks.[15] The particularity and elitism of friendship in the ancient world[16] was, however, transvalued by Christianity into a more diffuse and egalitarian injunction to love one's neighbour.[17] Just as Nietzsche attacks the value of neighbour-love by exposing the base drives that often fuel it and the damage it does to individual well-being, so he wants to resurrect some of the qualities of classical friendship, seeing it as a nobler model for engagement with others. His claim that the Greeks have been 'so far the last, to whom the friend has appeared as a problem worth solving' (HH, s.354) implies that in taking up the baton of friendship, he is carrying on where they left off. Yet this depiction of the philosophical history of friendship is, even in Nietzsche's terms, too sparse. As he later concedes, antiquity 'almost buried friendship in its own grave' (D, s.503) – almost but not quite, for some of his favourite writers in the middle period, such as Montaigne, La Rochefoucauld and Chamfort, also belong to this tradition of delineating and celebrating friendship.[18]

Nietzsche follows Aristotle and the French moralists by distinguishing higher from lower friendships. He says, for example, that most people cannot keep their friends' confidences (HH, s.327) and warns that idle people are not good friends, having too much time to talk about and interfere in their friends' business (AOM, s.260). Most so-called friends cannot be relied upon in times of real danger – the support and protection they seem to offer is only apparent (HH, s.600). He also claims that deliberate attempts to establish intimacy are not the mark of true friendship (HH, s.304). Such characterisations of inferior friendships serve two, and possibly three, purposes. The first is to demonstrate that only higher types have the talent for true friendship. The second is to provide a foil for this sort of superior friendship, for a clearer sense of what it is emerges when its counterfeit forms are exposed (D, s.471). The third possible purpose is to warn readers against these inferior friendships.

Friendship and Selfhood

The importance Nietzsche attributes to friendship is evident in more and less subtle ways throughout the works of the middle period. It manifests itself subtly when, among examples of 'proud indifference to great losses', he lists indifference to 'one's own existence and that of one's friends' (HH, s.477). Painting a picture of grief, he evokes the feelings of a hero 'on the evening after a battle that has decided nothing but brought him wounds and the loss of his friend' (GS, s.337). Friendship appears in a subtle, but important, way in the aphorism 'Collective spirit', which claims that 'A good writer possesses not only his own spirit but also the spirit of his friends.' (HH, s.180.)

Friendship's importance is more obvious in the longer passage entitled 'The talent for friendship' (HH, s.368). Here Nietzsche's general point is that friends reflect one's personality. Individuals who 'possess a particular gift for friendship' can be divided into one of two types: they are either like a ladder or like a circle. When like a ladder, 'in a state of continual ascent' (HH, s.368), individuals find new friends for each phase of their development. As a consequence, those who have been the individual's friends differ considerably from, and are unlikely to engage with, one another. The second sort of individual, the circle, takes different types of people as friends at the same time. The variety of this person's relationships is not diachronic but synchronic; it is a function of the breadth of personality rather than its serial metamorphoses. Those who are friends with this type of person can associate together even though they are quite different from one another. This is because sharing the nodal friend and being drawn to such a multifaceted individual provides some basis for attraction to and involvement with one another. As Nietzsche says, 'One can call such a man a *circle*, for in him this solidarity between such different natures and dispositions must in some way be prefigured.' (HH, s.368.) The idea that friends reflect the self is echoed in his observation that 'If we greatly transform ourselves, the friends of ours who have not been transformed become like ghosts of our past': these ghosts haunt us with the sound of how we once were, 'younger, more severe, less mature'

(AOM, s.242). The close link between friendship and selfhood is suggested in a negative way in the depiction of 'The friend we no longer desire'. When a friend has expectations we cannot meet, estrangement is preferable to living with the constant reminder of our failure (D, s.313). As Nietzsche later says, always being 'taken for something higher than one is' is 'the most painful feeling there is' (AOM, s.344).

Friendship and Knowledge

Nietzsche acknowledges that the survival of a friendship can require silence, discretion or ignorance about some of the partner's characteristics. The passage 'One is judged falsely' implies that friendship is incompatible with full knowledge of the other and that to remain such, friends must misjudge one another to some extent: 'would they be our friends if they knew us well?' (HH, s.352.) The passage 'Two friends' returns to this question of how much truth a friendship can bear when Nietzsche notes that some relationships founder when one of the friends feels too well known by the other (D, s.287). This suggests that perspicuity is not one of friendship's essential features.[19] However, this passage also acknowledges that friendship can falter when one friend feels insufficiently understood by the other, so while delineating some of the defining features of friendship, Nietzsche remains alive to the variety of forms it takes and emotions it accommodates.

The value of feeling understood by friends emerges again in the discussion of 'Presumptuousness'. Tallying the costs of the desire 'to signify more than he is *or counts for*', Nietzsche warns that one should only display a proud demeanour when 'one can be quite sure one will not be misunderstood and regarded as presumptuous, for example in the presence of friends and wives' (HH, s.373).[20] The need to feel known and understood by one's friends recurs when he points to the value of an environment in which one is free either to remain silent or to communicate things of the utmost importance (D, s.364).[21] Without this freedom, a dissatisfaction with one's self and the world develops that is anathema to individual well-being. Nietzsche further claims that one can only learn to say strong things in a simple way when surrounded by those who believe in one's strength; such an environment 'educates one to attain simplicity of style' (GS, s.226). However, when the company is inadequate, one 'will usually be a good letter-writer' (HH, s.319), illustrating again the importance Nietzsche attributes to communicating with, and being understood by, select others.

The possibility that the survival of a friendship might require a measure of ignorance about the other is echoed in another of Nietzsche's long reflections on friendship:

> such human relationships almost always depend upon the fact that two or three things are never said or even so much as touched upon: if these little boulders do start to roll, however, friendship follows after them and shatters. Are there not people who would be mortally wounded if they discovered what their dearest friends actually know about them? (HH, s.376.)

He points out that myriad differences separate even the closest of friends (HH, s.376; compare HH, s.32), that friendship is a fragile achievement and that each individual is ultimately alone. However, what begins as an apparent attack on the illusions of solidarity and intimacy becomes an injunction to celebrate the reality of human relationships rather than lament their imperfections. A variation on Nietzsche's critique of free will, the passage argues that when one sees that one's friends must be as they are, any regret that they are not otherwise evaporates. Echoing Aristotle's suggestion that we relate to ourselves as we relate to our friends,[22] Nietzsche recommends that we view ourselves as we view others: 'It is true we have good reason to think little of each of our acquaintances, even the greatest of them; but equally good reason to direct this feeling back on to ourself.' (HH, s.376.) Acceptance of others and their apparent limitations should, therefore, be the corollary of self-knowledge, for if we learn to see ourselves clearly and thus 'despise ourself a little' (HH, s.376), tolerance of others grows. To acquire more realistic expectations about friendship in this way, to see the self and the friend more clearly, frees us eventually to celebrate it, despite its imperfections.

This question of how closely each partner in a friendship can and should know herself and her friend is taken up again in the passage 'Self-observation'. Rather than self-knowledge being a precondition of realistic friendship, honest friends become a prerequisite of self-knowledge. Because the pursuit of self-knowledge is hindered by the many barriers and defences individuals erect against themselves, it is only through the observations of others that a more accurate view of the self can be attained. Friends (and enemies) can pierce this ignorance about the self (HH, s.491). In contrast to some of his previous claims, here Nietzsche concedes that friendship can be open and honest and thereby provide an invaluable service to the individual in quest of self-knowledge.

In fact, the desire for self-knowledge could be the variable resolving the apparent contradiction in Nietzsche's musings about how much knowledge of the other a friendship can endure. Individuals who really want to know themselves will value direct and open exchanges with others who point out their foibles, failures and shortcomings. Among such individuals, perspicacity and honesty are not threats but fillips to friendship. In enumerating 'The good four' virtues, Nietzsche again draws this connection between honesty, friendship and self-knowledge, advocating that we be '*Honest* towards ourselves and whoever *else* is a friend to us' (D, s.556). This suggests that in being honest with oneself, one is being a friend to oneself. So while Nietzsche follows Aristotle in seeing the friend as 'another self', there are also some grounds for thinking that he sees the self as another friend.[23] In both cases, friendship can challenge the self-other separation.

Yet Nietzsche does not demand total frankness of all friendships; this would be too formulaic an approach to an area in which he is highly sensitive to difference and particularity. As the passage 'Attitude towards praise' indicates, other considerations can outweigh honesty: deception is acceptable if it protects friends' feelings (HH, s.360). That individuals should be responded to differently appears in Nietzsche's claim that 'in our relations with people who are bashful about their feelings, we must be capable of dissimulation' (GS, s.16). As the passage goes on to relate, without such sensitivity to individuality, friendships can be destroyed. Although the need to conceal oneself in order to spare others' feelings or prevent harm to them is repeatedly acknowledged throughout the middle period,[24] this rationale for wearing masks receives little attention in the literature on Nietzsche.

Friendship and Higher Individuals

The aphorism 'Friend' defines friendship as 'fellow rejoicing' (HH, s.499) and Nietzsche later depicts the ability to 'imagine the joy of others and to rejoice at it' as a rare human quality (AOM, s.62). That the capacity for 'rejoicing with' is the preserve of the noble personality is evident in his claim that in most social interaction, 'if we let others see how happy and secure in ourselves we are in spite of suffering and deprivation, how malicious and envious we would make them!' (AOM, s.334). It is impossible for those with 'petty natures' to be true friends because 'in order to maintain in themselves a sense of self-respect ...

[they] are obliged to disparage and diminish in their minds all the other people they know' (HH, s.63; compare AOM, s.263). The association of generosity and friendship with higher types appears again when Nietzsche contrasts 'the unpleasant character who is full of mistrust [and] consumed with envy' with one 'who readily rejoices with his fellow men, wins friends everywhere, welcomes everything new and developing, takes pleasure in the honours and successes of others'. Such a person is 'an anticipatory man striving towards a higher human culture'.[25]

As this equation of friendship with 'joying-with' and his admiration for such generosity indicate, in the works of the middle period, Nietzsche takes the talent for true friendship to be the mark of a higher human being. A strong statement of how noble and unusual this is comes in the conclusion of the passage entitled 'The things people call love'. After arguing that love and avarice are not antitheses, but, rather, different phases of the desire to have, he evokes a different, unusual type of love. Its participants do not crave exclusive possession of one another, but share 'a higher thirst for an ideal above them' (GS, s.14). This uncommon love is friendship. Yet, the attitude of higher individuals toward friendship differs from most: they choose friendship from a position of self-possession and sufficient self-love and do not need approval from others as imprimaturs to their choices and decisions (HH, s.360). When the noble personality seeks recognition, this is a choice rather than a need and is based on acknowledgement of the power of another's judgement. As Nietzsche says, 'He who really possesses himself … henceforth regards it as his own privilege to punish himself, to pardon himself, to take pity on himself: he does not need to concede this to anyone else, but he can freely relinquish it to another, to a friend for example' (D, s.437).

Nietzsche sometimes goes beyond claiming that friendship's higher form is the preserve of noble personalities to suggest that friendship can sustain and spur them on to even greater heights. The value of kindred spirits for superior types emerges clearly in the discussion of 'Seeking one's company':

> Are we then seeking too much if we seek the company of men who have grown gentle, well-tasting and nutritious like chestnuts which have been put on to the fire and taken from it again at the proper time? Who expect little from life, and would rather take this as a gift than as something they have earned. (D, s.482.)

The value of friendship to higher individuals is further explored in the passage 'The tyrants of the spirit', which predicts that future cultural authority will emanate from 'the *oligarchs of the spirit*'. This new oligarchy will be a group of like-minded higher humans who, despite their 'spatial and political division', will constitute a 'close-knit society whose members *know* and *recognize* one another' (HH, s.261). These superior spirits need and nurture one another:

> how could the individual keep himself aloft and, against every current, swim along his own course through life if he did not see here and there others of his own kind living under the same conditions and take them by the hand ... The oligarchs have need of one another, they have joy in one another, they understand the signs of one another – but each of them is nonetheless free, he fights and conquers in his *own* place, and would rather perish than submit. (HH, s.261.)

Their relationship evinces many of friendship's characteristics. It is a relationship among superior types who see one another as equals, who take joy in one another, who respect distance among themselves and provide support and intimacy without quashing individuality.[26] Nietzsche's awareness that friends can be spurs to greatness also appears in the vignette of a relationship uniting one person who had great works with another who had great faith in his works. The individual with the great works 'depended wholly' on his companion (WS, s.234). The description of this pair as 'inseparable' provides another indication that Nietzsche sees blurring the boundaries of individuation as possible and sometimes desirable.

Yet despite the importance attributed to friendship in the middle-period works, few of Nietzsche's readers recognise its importance for his superior types. Even those who discuss his interest in agonal striving accord friendship little or no role in this, believing instead that Nietzsche internalises the agonistic struggle, so that various parts of the self battle with each other.[27] However, the works of the middle period offer no reason why working on the self must be conceived of as a solitary effort: they betray no necessary antagonism between agonism within and without. Rather, these can be complementary forces in self-making, so that friends can assist in the self's struggle with itself. It is true that the passage 'In praise of Shakespeare' initially appears to deny the possibility that friendship can be a spur to greatness.[28] It declares:

> Independence of the soul! ... No sacrifice can be too great for that; one must be capable of sacrificing one's dearest friend for it, even if he should also be the most glorious human being, an

ornament of the world, a genius without peer – if one loves freedom as the freedom of great souls and he threatens this kind of freedom. (GS, s.98.)[29]

But as the hypothetical final clause makes clear,[30] friendship and independence are only sometime rivals and the middle period's many passages in praise of friendship testify to Nietzsche's belief that not all friendships jeopardise nor constrict the growth of individuality.

Friendship and Difference

Nietzsche often suggests that acknowledging, tolerating and even relishing difference is a vital characteristic of robust friendship, which prevents his idea of higher friendship from degenerating into advanced narcissism.[31] In the passage entitled 'A different kind of neighbour love', he describes the sort of relationship preferred by those capable of grand passion:

> it is a kind different from that of the sociable and anxious to please: it is a gentle, reflective, relaxed friendliness; it is as though they were gazing out of the windows of their castle, which is their fortress and for that reason also their prison – to gaze into what is strange and free, into *what is different*, does them so much good! (D, s.471.)

When one partner chooses a different path from her friend's, this can nourish, rather than undermine, their relationship. Nietzsche calls such divergence 'a high sign of humanity in closer association with others' (AOM, s.231). The passage 'Of friends' (HH, s.376) shows the value of accepting then growing to celebrate friends' differences, and Nietzsche seems to privilege the 'circle' model of friendship over the 'ladder' in discussing the talent for friendship (HH, s.368).[32]

   This admiration for friendships that accommodate diversity suggests that while Nietzsche acknowledges that friendship can transcend the boundaries of individuation, total assimilation into, or identification with, the other is not encouraged. The section on 'A good friendship' (AOM, s.241) cautions against becoming too close and 'confounding the I and Thou'. The need to maintain a balance between connection and individuation is also apparent in the warning 'Too close':

> If we live together with another person too closely, what happens is similar to when we repeatedly handle a good engraving with our bare hands: one day all we have left is a piece of dirty paper.

The soul of a human being too can finally become tattered by being handled continually ... One always loses by too familiar association with friends and women.... (HH, s.428.)

The importance of balancing connection and individuation is expressed in a more positive and elegant way in the aphorism 'In parting', where Nietzsche says that 'It is not in how one soul approaches another but in how it distances itself from it that I recognize their affinity and relatedness.' (AOM, s.251.)

Just as higher friendships are nourished by difference, base ones are destroyed by it (D, ss.484, 489). Yet as the section entitled 'Star friendship' acknowledges, radical divergence can destroy even higher friendships. But Nietzsche hopes that when a once strong relationship has been rent by differences, its erstwhile partners will not be bitter. A more elevated view is available: 'That we have to become estranged is the law *above* us; by the same token we should also become more venerable for each other – and the memory of our former friendship more sacred.' (GS, s.279.) In this context, he again applies his analysis of the necessity of actions to friendship, and concludes that when action is seen as necessary rather than freely chosen, it becomes inappropriate to impute blame when the relationship falls apart.

Friendship and Suffering

Nietzsche is typically cast as an implacable critic of forces such as pity, empathy, sympathy and benevolence.[33] However, appreciating the importance he attributes to friendship in the works of the middle period requires a reappraisal of this commonplace. Rather than rejecting all forms of pity as disguised egoism, the middle period's works suggest that friendship is a forum in which pity's positive characteristics can manifest themselves.[34] In one passage, for example, Nietzsche claims that our most personal suffering is incomprehensible to 'almost everyone' among our neighbours and would-be benefactors. The exceptions to this incomprehension are our friends, for he counsels helping 'only those whose distress you *understand* entirely because they share with you one suffering and one hope – your friends' (GS, s.338).[35]

How one friend responds to the suffering of another is also explored in the passage 'Growing tenderer' (D, s.138). The first reaction is shock, for it had been assumed that the happiness radiated by the friend signalled his well-being. The next is greater tenderness so that 'the gulf between us and him seems to be bridged, an approximation of identity seems to occur' (D, s.138). The aim then becomes to comfort the friend, not, as pity would, by presuming to know his palliative, but by trying to discern what would best soothe his particular pain. This discrete, sensitive, respectful and particularised pity contrasts markedly with the garrulous sympathy that 'bears the sick man's bed into the public market-place' (AOM, s.282). Yet so many of Nietzsche's readers are oblivious to the fact that while he castigates most shows of pity, he not only allows for, but values highly, this sort of intimate, individualised response to suffering.[36] They mistake Nietzsche's critique of the morality of pity for a rejection of all forms of pity.[37]

In the middle-period works, Nietzsche also adumbrates an alternative response to the suffering of a friend, one which seeks to transcend the misery of suffering rather than add to it, as even genuine pity must. Instead of pitying the friend, an attempt can be made to both soothe and inspire him beyond his misery, interrupting the cycle of suffering. This alternative is intimated in the claim that 'in dark states of distress, sickness or debt we are glad when we perceive others still shining and they perceive in us the bright disk of the moon' (AOM, s.61). It is more evident when he observes that:

> the question itself remains unanswered whether one is of *more use* to another by immediately leaping to his side and *helping* him – which help can in any case be only superficial where it does not become a tyrannical seizing and transforming – or by *creating* something out of oneself that the other can behold with pleasure: a beautiful, restful, self-enclosed garden perhaps, with high walls against storms and the dust of the roadway but also a hospitable gate. (D, s.174.)

So when it comes to the suffering of a friend, Nietzsche moots a more emancipatory alternative than pity, one which retrieves the ancient practice of relieving suffering by offering it something creative and joyful. 'In regard to an existence of suffering the ancients sought forgetfulness or some way or other of converting their feelings into pleasurable ones: so that in this matter they sought palliatives' (AOM, s.187). As this indicates, neither ignorance of, nor indifference to, the suffering of others is a corollary of his excoriation of the morality of pity. Rather, he gestures toward an alternative response to the suffering of oneself or one's friends, one that breaks the cycle of suffering and averts the increase in overall misery promoted by simply sympathising with suffering.

Friendship and Solitude

Nietzsche bemoans the fact that 'no one learns, no one strives after, no one teaches – *the endurance of solitude*' (D, s.443). However, appreciating his attitude to friendship in the works of the middle period prompts a reappraisal of the meaning of solitude. Just as he prizes the sort of intimacy that maintains its strength and delicacy by leaving some space between its partners, so he implies that solitude need not exclude friendship. At one point he discusses the boredom that 'a solitude without friends, books, duties or passions' (cws, s.200)[38] can bring. While the idea of solitude encompassing the last three items is unremarkable, to suggest that it can embrace the friend is certainly unconventional. When being alone can include a friend, the normal boundaries of self and other have clearly been transgressed. The possibility that solitude can include friendship is also countenanced when, lamenting the contemporary obsession with work, Nietzsche predicts that 'soon we may well reach the point where people can no longer give in to the desire for a *vita contemplativa* (that is taking a walk with ideas and friends)' (GS, s.329). Given the traditional equation of contemplation with solitude,[39] he is once again upsetting conventional boundaries between self and other. Yet if a friend can sometimes know me better than I know myself, the idea that being with oneself can include the company of friends becomes less paradoxical. Similarly, as this sort of intimacy keeps a respectful distance and does not totally subsume individuality, it is unlikely to be the sort of intrusion from which solitude is usually sought.

Nietzsche's other discussions of solitude do not adopt this inclusive stance but betray a more conventional understanding. 'Society as enjoyment', for example, points out that time spent alone heightens enjoyment of 'the society of men', because company becomes 'a rare delicacy' (AOM, s.333). Taking a bleaker view of social interaction, 'From the land of the cannibals' poses a stark choice for the solitary person: either she consumes herself or she is consumed by the crowd (AOM, s.348). The imagery of comestibles recurs in the aphorism on 'The socialiser', which diagnoses the person who loves company as unable to love themselves: 'Society's stomach is stronger than mine, it can digest me' (WS, s.235).[40] Yet while all these aphorisms associate solitude with isolation, none repudiates the unconventional, inclusive variety sketched above because they repose upon the individual-society dichotomy and ignore the intermediate category of friendship. In fact, this holds for much of the middle period's praise of solitude: it celebrates refuge from the wider world rather than from friendship.[41]

Yet irrespective of whether it encompasses friends, Nietzsche does not always praise solitude. He suggests, for example, that the conceit of 'the Winter of life' only has meaning if it refers to 'those cold recurring seasons of solitude, hopelessness and unfruitfulness, our *periods of illness*' (WS, s.269). In the passage 'Gardener and garden', both solitude and being in the company of those who are not our friends are inimical to well-being: 'Out of damp and gloomy days, out of solitude, out of loveless words directed at us, conclusions grow up in us like fungus ... and they gaze upon us morose and grey.' (D, s.382.) Nietzsche points again to the dangers of solitude when he claims that 'being alone implants presumptuousness' (HH, s.316). The sort of modesty he admires in the middle period is, conversely, fostered in good company: 'One unlearns arrogance when one knows one is always among deserving people' (HH, s.316). Yet ever attuned to the complexities of the psyche, Nietzsche allows that sometimes solitude can have the reverse effect, making some individuals undervalue themselves. Such people need others to restore their sense of self: 'they have to be compelled to acquire again a good and just opinion of themselves from others' (HH, s.624). This need not come from witnessing the inferiority of others; instead, Nietzsche allows that self-esteem can be fostered by others in a much more positive way.[42]

Overview

In the works of Nietzsche's middle period, friendship is not portrayed as antagonistic to self-development, but as something that can enhance this process through its perspicacity and honesty. Friends can assist one another in the quest for self-knowledge because a friend can know one better than one knows oneself, a possibility that challenges the image, so typically associated with Nietzschean thought, of the sovereign self clearly delimited from others. Yet while Nietzsche endorses compromising the boundaries of individuation in this way, he also insists that they not be eliminated: friendship's closeness should be contained. Friendship only threatens individuality when it compensates for self-development by allowing the friends to meld into, instead of take strength from, each other.[43] Nietzsche values a respectful distance between individuals whereby intimacy does not preclude separation or boundaries, but is nourished by a delicate balance of closeness and distance. He therefore adduces an ideal of intimacy that is simultaneously lovingly close and respectfully distant.[44] Because friends can behold in one another something that draws them out of and beyond the self, Nietzsche acknowledges that there can be an intersubjective aspect to greatness. Friendship can be a spur to self-overcoming. The works of the middle period also suggest that this higher form of friendship can unite individuals in a way that retains some of pity's positive features while overcoming its degenerate ones. Friendship can be governed by genuine knowledge of, and sympathy for, another, blurred individuation and the overcoming of egoism.

Although Nietzsche looks to antiquity as an era when friendship was more fully appreciated, he maintains that true friendship is still possible. At one point, he associates the demise of higher friendship with the increasing pace of modern life. He criticises the lack of delicacy, the 'gross obviousness' that characterises so much of people's dealings with their friends and other familiars when they wish to be honest with them (GS, s.329). This suggests that the infrequency of higher friendships is not just a function of the failures, foibles and weaknesses of the individuals contracting friendships, but that there are also wider social and cultural forces militating against individuals achieving higher friendships. However, another important reason for the rarity of higher friendship is that, for Nietzsche as for Aristotle, such friendship is only possible among equally superior types; it requires equality among firsts. Being such a friend not only requires exceptional qualities, but one's friends must also be exceptional types.[45]

The infrequency of associations between equally superior individuals is illustrated in the aphorism 'Lack of friends', in which Nietzsche points out that envy can kill friendships, but concludes wryly that 'Many owe their friends only to the fortunate circumstance that they have no occasion for envy.'[46] (HH, s.559.) Friendship's rarity need not, however, detract from its reality and importance.

Zarathustra and Beyond

Although the middle-period writings end with the conclusion of Book IV of *The Gay Science*, some belief in the possibility and importance of friendship among higher types is still evident in Nietzsche's next work, *Thus Spoke Zarathustra*. The eponymous protagonist of this work seeks 'fellow-creators, those who inscribe new values on new tables'.[47] Some of the features from the middle period recur in this book's picture of friendship. The intimacy and blurring of boundaries is suggested in Zarathustra's claim that 'Your friend's face is … your own face, in a rough and imperfect mirror.'[48] The idea that friendship is essentially 'joying with' and that friends can foster one another's greatness is implicit in his wish, 'May the friend be to you a festival of the earth and a foretaste of the Superman ... I teach you the friend in whom the world stands complete, a vessel of the good – the creative friend who always has a complete world to bestow ... in your friend you should love the Superman as your principle.'[49]

The promise of friendship is hinted at in an aphorism from Nietzsche's subsequent work, *Beyond Good and Evil*, which declares that 'With hard men intimacy [*Innigkeit*] is a thing of shame – and something precious.' (s.167.) The claim that 'all company is bad company except the company of one's equals' (BGE, s.26) is hardly lavish praise for friendship, but it does allow that other humans can provide good company, in contrast to the later Nietzsche's more usual insistence on solitude for higher types. Similarly, one of the ingredients of master morality is 'a refined conception of friendship' (BGE, s.260). Concomitant with this is the need for enemies as the channels for the emotions that threaten friendship, emotions such as 'envy, quarrelsomeness [and] arrogance' (BGE, s.260). Here enemies serve not to spur one to greatness, but to facilitate one's being a good friend to someone else. The value of superior types interacting among themselves returns in Nietzsche's image of the noble soul moving 'among these its equals and equal-in-rights with the same sure modesty and tender reverence as it applies to itself ... it is in no doubt that the exchange of honours and rights, as the *essence* of social intercourse, is likewise part of the natural condition of things' (BGE, s.265).

However, none of this comes close to the powerful image of friendship offered in the middle period; after *Thus Spoke Zarathustra* there are no blurred boundaries of individuation nor any sense that these equals can do anything but recognise greatness in one another; they do not seem capable of enhancing or promoting it. Whereas Zarathustra recommended friends who could provide the services of enmity,[50] in the subsequent works, it is enemies, not friends, who spur higher individuals on.[51] However, Nietzsche's focus has become the development of a strong character rather than the quality of one's relations with other people; enemies are indispensable because they provide resistance to the developing personality. The struggle against such forces enables great individuals to expand and it provides a yardstick of their progress. 'The undertaking is to master, *not* any resistances that happen to present themselves, but those against which one has to bring all one's strength, suppleness and mastery of weapons – to master *equal* opponents...'[52]

The works after *Thus Spoke Zarathustra* betray little sense of higher human beings benefiting from anything other than this sort of adversarial engagement. In contrast with the middle period's images of great individuals spurring one another on, now the individual striving for greatness 'regards everybody he meets on the way either as a means or as a delay and hindrance – or as a temporary resting-place. The lofty *goodness* towards his fellow men which is proper to him becomes possible only when he has reached his height and he rules.' (BGE, s.273.) Whereas the middle-period works explored the value of feeling understood by one's friends, now one's 'good friends' are disposable: 'one can laugh at their expense – or get rid of them altogether these good friends – and still laugh!' (BGE, s.27.) Friends are to great individuals temporary means to their goals, impediments to their ultimate goal or useless. Indeed, friends can be dangerous to the development of free spirithood: even those who are well loved must be released for, as indicated above, 'every person is a prison, also a nook and a corner' (BGE, s.41). In the later works, then, friendship seems to be the prerogative of the herd; friendliness features as a slavish virtue, along with pity, patience and humility (BGE, s.260). The philosopher, by contrast, 'hates to be disturbed by either enmities or friendships; he easily forgets or despises'.[53]

In the later works, then, most of Nietzsche's praise for friendship occurs in the first few books; after *Beyond Good and Evil* it is rare to find friendship lauded in any way. Contrast its image of great types moving among their equals with 'modesty and tender reverence' (BGE, s.265) with the depiction in *The Genealogy of Morals* (henceforth referred to as GM) of great individuals who have the strength of will to keep promises without the fear of punishment. It is natural for this type of individual 'to honour his strong and reliable peers, all those who promise like sovereigns' (GM, II, ii), but modesty, tenderness and reverence are no longer associated with such interaction. Instead, these works bristle with praise of the solitude that does exclude all others.[54]

Conclusion

Throughout the later works there is a gradual enervation of Nietzsche's depiction of friendship and its importance for higher human beings; indeed, his lively concern with the realm of intersubjective relationships in general atrophies in those works. Perhaps the attrition of friendship's importance can be partly explained by its diminishing presence in Nietzsche's own life.[55] But whatever its cause, it is only by recognising the power and vitality he once attributed to friendship that we can even begin to trace this demise. Only by reading the works of the middle period can the image of the bounded, autarchic individual be seen as an evolution, rather than a fixture, within Nietzsche's thought. Only when we appreciate the significance he once accorded friendship can it emerge that the later works involve a deliberate rejection of what he once took to be its benefits and pleasures.

As this suggests, it is not possible to reconcile the importance attached to friendship in Nietzsche's middle works with the rabid individualism of his later image of the sovereign *übermensch*.[56] What was seen as a healthy merging of identities and mutual support in self-overcoming in the middle period becomes associated with weak, slavish other-dependence in the later works. One reaction to these rival evaluations of friendship might be to dismiss the middle-period works and to maintain that the later works necessarily embody the more mature, reflective, authoritative Nietzsche. However, a different way of responding to this rift is intimated by Nietzsche's own discussions of friendship. His analysis operates at two levels and can be extended to a third. First, by his own practice in the middle period, Nietzsche suggests that theorists of friendship should remain sensitive to its particularity and temper their generalisations in the light of this. Second, he reminds friends that responsiveness to difference and to the individuality of their friends are crucial to the health of their friendships. When these insights are applied at a third level, they allow us to become friendly readers of Nietzsche.[57] This means not seeing Nietzsche the thinker and writer as a single, stable identity, but as one who changes across his *oeuvre*. The temptation to generalise about his work should be tempered by openness to its differences and to the particularities of certain texts or periods.

ACKNOWLEDGEMENT

Thanks are due to Jeremy Moon, Douglas J. Den Uyl and Preston King for comments on an earlier draft, and to Jeanette Kennett.

NOTES

1. On the importance of solitude for Nietzsche, see Dannhauser, W. 1974. *Nietzsche's View of Socrates*, p.183. Ithaca, Cornell University Press; Donnellan, B. 1982. *Nietzsche and the French Moralists*, p.13. Bonn, Bouvier; Sadler, T. 1993. The postmodern politicization of Nietzsche. In *Nietzsche, Feminism and Political Theory*, ed. Patton, P., pp.226, 232. Australia, Allen & Unwin; Berkowitz, P. 1995. *Nietzsche:*

The Ethics of an Immoralist, pp.171–3, 303 note 21. Cambridge (MA), Harvard University Press.

2. Nietzsche, F. 1973. *Beyond Good and Evil*, No.41. Trans. Hollingdale, R. J. Harmondsworth, Penguin.

3. Judith Shklar identifies Nietzsche as a misanthropist (in Shklar, J. 1984. *Ordinary Vices*, pp.194–5, 222–3. Cambridge (MA), Harvard University Press) and defines misanthropy as 'the absence of friendship' (pp.198–9). Tanno Kunnas contends that Nietzsche is cynical about friendship and does not believe it can ever be sincere (in Kunnas, T. 1980. *Nietzsche ou l'esprit de contradiction*, p.203. Paris, Nouvelles Editions Latines). Alan Bloom reduces the many differences between Nietzsche and Socrates to 'that most ultimate form of human community, mutual understanding ... Socrates talks of his good friends, Nietzsche of his best enemies.' See Bloom, A. 1993. *Love and Friendship*, pp.542–3. New York, Simon & Schuster. Compare Honig, B. 1993. *Political Theory and the Displacement of Politics*, p.41. Ithaca, Cornell University Press.

4. The following editions of Nietzsche's works are cited: Nietzsche, F. 1996. *Human, All Too Human*, Vols.1 and 2. Trans. Hollingdale, R. J. Cambridge, Cambridge University Press; Nietzsche, F. 1997. *Daybreak*. Trans. Hollingdale, R. J. Cambridge, Cambridge University Press; Nietzsche, F. 1974. *The Gay Science*. Trans. Kaufmann W. New York, Random House. Section numbers are given for each quotation from these sources.

From my claim about the general neglect of the middle-period works, it should not be inferred that each of the three works has been equally neglected: GS has enjoyed considerable critical interest and HH has had more attention than D. According to Michael Tanner, the latter is the most neglected of Nietzsche's works. See Tanner, M. 1994. *Nietzsche*, p.26. Oxford, Oxford University Press. His view is echoed by Maudemarie Clark and Brian Leiter in their new introduction to Hollingdale's translation of D (p.vii). However, the fact that the Cambridge University Press has recently also republished Hollingdale's translation of HH with a new introduction by Richard Schacht suggests that there is a growing interest in these works.

5. In so far as attention has been paid to Nietzsche's views on friendship, it is usually by those familiar with the works of the middle period. This includes Kaufmann in his introduction to GS (p.6); Tanner, in his introduction to D (p.ix); and Derrida, J. 1993. Politics of friendship. *American Imago*, 50/3, p.353, compare pp.363–4. Graham Little uses Nietzsche as a source for his analysis of friendship, but draws mainly from Z. See Little, G. 1993. *Friendship. Being Ourselves With Others*, pp.24–6. Melbourne, Text Publishing. However, none of these commentators explores Nietzsche's views in the detail offered here.

6. See Aristotle. 1980. *The Nicomachean Ethics*, 1169b33–5, 1172a5. Trans. Ross, W. D. Oxford, Oxford University Press. For a fuller discussion of Aristotle's views on friendship, see Sherman, N. 1993. Aristotle and the shared life. In *Friendship: A Philosophical Reader*, ed. Badhwar, N. K., pp.91–107. Ithaca, Cornell University Press; Bowden, P. 1997. *Caring: Gender-Sensitive Ethics*, pp.60–100. London, Routledge.

7. Derrida, J. 1993. Politics of friendship. *American Imago*, 50/3, p.385. Derrida's own reflections on friendship and mourning seem to have been spurred by the death of his friend Paul de Man. He writes of 'the unique and incomparable friendship that ours was for me...'. Derrida, J. 1986. *Memoires for Paul de Man*, p.19. New York, Columbia University Press.

8. Parkes, G. 1994. *Composing the Soul*, p.286. Chicago, University of Chicago Press.

9. As Leslie Chamberlain notes, 'his friendships depended on correspondence'. Chamberlain, L. 1997. *Nietzsche in Turin*, p.14. London, Quartet Books. Fritz Stern attributes considerable importance to Nietzsche's letters: 'How magnificent, how

revelatory, that correspondence is ... To his friends Nietzsche confides so much.'
Stern, F. 1996. The trouble with publishers. *London Review of Books*, 19 September
1996, pp.8–9. Nietzsche's 'solicitous affection for his friends, and his compassion for
them' (p.9) strikes Stern powerfully and leads him to contrast the public, published
Nietzsche with the private correspondent. Characterising the former, he attends to the
'harshness and stridency, the verbal violence, the indifference to or indeed exaltation
of, suffering, the brutal outbursts and the contempt for "the botched and the
bungled"'. The letters, by contrast, deliver a Nietzsche who 'craves and extends love,
lives by gratitude and generosity' (ibid.). The Nietzsche that emerges from a study of
the works of the middle period is much closer to the personal Nietzsche that Stern
finds only in his letters.

10. From a letter dated 12 December 1870 in Levy, O. ed. 1921. *Selected Letters of
     Friedrich Nietzsche*, p.97. New York, Doubleday Page.
11. From a letter dated 28 February 1883 in Leidecker, K. F. trans. and ed. 1960.
     Nietzsche. Unpublished Letters, p.103. London, Peter Owen.
12. From a letter dated 19 November 1877 in Salomé, L. A. 1988. *Nietzsche*, p.61. Trans.
     and ed. Mandel, S. Connecticut, Black Swan Books.
13. Parkes identifies Rée as a 'major stimulus' to Nietzsche's interest in psychology and
     their relationship as 'crucial' to Nietzsche's development. Parkes, G. 1994. *Composing
     the Soul*, pp.3–4. Chicago, University of Chicago Press. Attention to the role of
     Nietzsche's friends in stimulating his thought provides a useful complement to Carl
     Pletsch's emphasis on mentor or father figures such as Schopenhauer, Wagner and
     Ritschl in Pletsch, C. 1991. *Young Nietzsche*. New York, Macmillan. With people such
     as Rée, Lou Salomé and Franz and Ida Overbeck, Nietzsche enjoyed relationships that
     fostered his intellectual formation, but were more equal and cooperative than most of
     the relationships Pletsch explores. Compare Del Caro, A. 1989. *Nietzsche Contra
     Nietzsche: Creativity and the Anti-Romantic*, p.170. Baton Rouge, Louisiana State
     University Press.
14. Nietzsche, F. 1979. Daybreak. In *Ecce Homo*, trans. Hollingdale, R. J., No.1.
     Harmondsworth, Penguin.
15. See HH, s.354; D, s.503; GS, s.61.
16. See Den Uyl, D. J. and Griswold, C. L. 1996. Adam Smith on friendship and love.
     Review of Metaphysics, 69, March 1996, pp.609–37.
17. Derrida, J. 1993. Politics of friendship. *American Imago*, 50/3, p.359.
18. See Montaigne, M. de, 1892. Of Friendship. In *Essays*, trans. and ed. Screech, M. A.
     London, George Bell; La Rochefoucauld. 1977. *Maximes et Réflexions Diverses*. Intro.
     Truchet, J. Paris, Garnier-Flammarion; Chamfort. 1968. *Maximes et pensées,
     caractères et anecdotes*. Pref. Dagen, J. Paris: Garnier-Flammarion. On Nietzsche's
     relationship with Montaigne see Donnellan, B. 1982. *Nietzsche and the French
     Moralists*, pp.18–37, 134–6. Bonn, Bouvier; Andler, C. 1920. *Nietzsche, Sa Vie et Sa
     Pensée*, Vols.1 and 2. Paris, Editions Brossard; Williams, W. D. 1952. *Nietzsche and
     the French*. Oxford, Basil Blackwell. For comparisons of his views on friendship with
     those of La Rochefoucauld and Chamfort, see Abbey, R. 1994. 'Descent and Dissent:
     Nietzsche's Reading of Two French Moralists'. Ph.D. Dissertation. McGill University.
19. Dannhauser picks up on this dimension of Nietzsche's view of friendship, but fails to
     acknowledge that it is only one such dimension. See Dannhauser, W. 1974. *Nietzsche's
     View of Socrates*, p.163. Ithaca, Cornell University Press.
20. For a discussion of the idea that Nietzsche even conceives of marriage as a form of
     friendship in the works of this period, see Abbey, R. 1997. Odd bedfellows: Nietzsche
     and Mill on marriage. *History of European Ideas*, 23/ 2–4, pp.81–104.
21. As Bowden says, 'In order to know and support our friends ... an environment is
     required that is hospitable to their integrity – an environment which they can inhabit

as persons on their own unique terms.' Bowden, P. 1997. *Caring: Gender-Sensitive Ethics*, p.83. London, Routledge. Nietzsche depicts Schopenhauer as one of those who wanted love and needed 'companions before whom they can venture to be as simple and open as they are before themselves and in whose presence they can cease to suffer the torment of silence and dissimulation'. See Nietzsche, F. 1983. Schopenhauer as educator, part three. In *Untimely Meditations*, trans. Hollingdale, R. J., p.140. Cambridge, Cambridge University Press. An excerpt from a letter to his sister Elisabeth from these years suggests that he is also of this type: 'It is precisely we solitary ones that require love and companions in whose presence we may be open and simple, and the eternal struggle of silence and dissimulation can cease. Yes, I am glad that I can be myself, openly and honestly with you, for you are such a good friend and companion...'. From a letter dated 22 January 1875 in Levy, O. ed. 1921. *Selected Letters of Friedrich Nietzsche*, pp.101–2. New York, Doubleday Page.

22. Aristotle. 1980. *The Nicomachean Ethics*, Book IX, Ch.4. Trans. Ross, W. D. Oxford, Oxford University Press.

23. In *A Passion for Friends*, Janice Raymond suggests that this inversion helps us understand women's friendships. This is discussed in Bowden, P. 1997. *Caring: Gender-Sensitive Ethics*, pp.92–100. London, Routledge.

24. HH, ss.253, 293, 360; AOM, ss.246, 393; WS, s.175; D, s.273.

25. HH, s.614, compare s.497; GS, s.55.

26. Compare Little, G. 1993. *Friendship. Being Ourselves With Others*, p.24. Melbourne, Text Publishing.

27. See Honig, B. 1993. *Political Theory and the Displacement of Politics*, pp.8–9. Ithaca, Cornell University Press. Compare Bergmann, P. 1987. *Nietzsche, "The Last Antipolitical German"*, p.108. Bloomington, Indiana University Press. In Thiele, L. P. 1990. The agony of politics: the Nietzschean roots of Foucault's thought. *American Political Science Review*, 84/3, September 1990, the author also insists upon the importance of agonism in Nietzsche's thought (pp.909–10) and portrays this as an inner struggle (p.913). He does note that Nietzsche wants his friends 'to be his fiercest opponents' (p.910), but the view that prizes friends as ersatz enemies is more characteristic of the later than the middle writings. Moreover, Thiele's account passes imperceptibly from friends as enemies to the enemy within.

28. Contrast my reading with Donnellan's claim that while Nietzsche valued friendship during the middle period, he ranked the claims of individuality ahead of it because friendship is a static relationship that must not be allowed to impede individual growth. Donnellan, B. 1982. *Nietzsche and the French Moralists*, pp.84–5. Bonn, Bouvier. As a young man, Nietzsche seems to have experienced friendship's spur himself. Writing to Paul Deussen in October 1868, he describes how he flourishes 'in the circle of ambitious friends and associates and only regret that I do not have around me the excellent Paul Deussen'. Leidecker, K. F. trans. and ed. 1960. *Nietzsche. Unpublished Letters*, p.49. London, Peter Owen.

29. That Nietzsche is thinking of his relationship with Wagner is suggested by a letter to Reinhart von Seydlitz: 'His and my endeavours are widely apart. This hurts me sufficiently, but in the service of truth one must be prepared to bring any sacrifice.' From a letter dated 11 June 1878 in Leidecker, K. F. trans. and ed. 1960. *Nietzsche. Unpublished Letters*, p.75. London, Peter Owen.

30. '...*wenn man nämlich die Freiheit als die Freiheit grosser Seelen liebt und durch ihn dieser Freiheit Gefahr droht*'.

31. The belief that difference can nourish friendship surfaces in Nietzsche's correspondence too. He described Ritschl and his wife as having 'quite an incredible love and esteem for me ... They really are extremely liberal people with a great deal of strength of their own. They permit whatever they differ with to exist cheerfully and

without bias, thus doing honour to themselves.' In Leidecker, K. F. trans. and ed. 1960. *Nietzsche. Unpublished Letters*, p.55. London, Peter Owen. Compare his remark to Overbeck in September 1882 about his relationship with Salomé: 'Our intelligence and our tastes are of one kind deep down. But apart from that the contrasts are so many that we constitute mutually the most instructive objects and subjects of instruction.' (Ibid., p.92.)

32. This preference seems to shift over the course of the middle period. In GS, s.295, for example, preferring short to enduring habits, Nietzsche numbers 'human beings' among the former and 'constant association with the same people' among the latter. This seems to promote the ladder model of friendship.

33. Dannhauser's Nietzsche 'deprecates pity' in Dannhauser, W. 1974. *Nietzsche's View of Socrates*, p.21. Ithaca, Cornell University Press; Berkowitz concludes that pity 'is definitely a catastrophe for higher types' in Berkowitz, P. 1995. *Nietzsche: The Ethics of an Immoralist*, p.105, compare p.214. Cambridge (MA), Harvard University Press; and Little sees Nietzsche as suspicious of pity in Little, G. 1993. *Friendship. Being Ourselves With Others*, p.43. Melbourne, Text Publishing. Ellen Kennedy holds that pity is one of the virtues Nietzsche transvalues because of its feminine and life-denying nature (see Kennedy, E. 1987. Nietzsche: women as *untermensch*. In *Women in Western Political Philosophy*, eds. Kennedy, E. and Mendus, S., p.183. Sussex, Wheatsheaf Books), while Charles Taylor claims that Nietzsche 'declared benevolence the ultimate obstacle to self-affirmation' (see Taylor, C. 1989. *Sources of the Self*, p.343, compare p.518. Cambridge (MA), Harvard University Press). As such, it must be repudiated by those aspiring to 'higher fulfilment' (ibid., p.423, compare pp.455, 499, 516).

34. As Thiele says, 'Nietzsche did not desire the extirpation of fellow-feeling but the vanquishing of its decadent form.' See Thiele, L. P. 1991. Love and judgement: Nietzsche's dilemma. *Nietzsche Studien*, Band 20, p.90.

35. This important qualification to Nietzsche's criticism of pity is ignored in Randall Havas's analysis of this emotion in Havas, R. 1995. *Nietzsche's Genealogy*. Ithaca, Cornell University Press. Citing this very passage, Havas concludes that Nietzsche's 'attack on the morality of pity turns on his rejection of the idea that compassion lifts the pitier out of himself and places him in a more intimate relationship to the sufferer than he normally enjoys ... it is precisely the idea that the emotion of pity allows the pitier as it were to *inhabit* the sufferer that, in Nietzsche's view, prevents the pitier from listening to him in the right way...' (ibid., p.220, compare p.221). While this is one aspect of Nietzsche's attack on the morality of pity, it ignores his concession that pity can be genuine when expressed in a particular way among friends. Indeed, Havas contends that what animates Nietzsche's various analyses of pity is the desire 'to emphasise the sufferer's *solitude* – his or her unavailability to the pitier' (ibid.).

36. Reading Nietzsche in this way brings out the parallels with the ethic of care outlined in Gilligan, C. 1982. *In a Different Voice*, pp.17, 58–9. Cambridge (MA), Harvard University Press.

37. According to Havas, for example, Nietzsche condemns pity because it is presumptuous; it presupposes knowledge of things that are actually mysterious, such as how another is suffering, how to relieve this and how to bridge the gap between sufferer and pitier. Hence, he claims that for Nietzsche the emotion of pity is 'insufficiently sceptical toward the sufferer'. See Havas, R. 1995. *Nietzsche's Genealogy*, p.221, compare pp.222, 224. Ithaca, Cornell University Press. Pity also strives to eliminate, rather than acknowledge, suffering (ibid.).

38. '...*eine Einsamkeit ohne Freunde, Büchern, Pflichten, Leidenschaften...*'.

39. Consider Aristotle's discussion of contemplation in Aristotle. 1980. *The Nicomachean Ethics*, Book X. Trans. Ross, W. D. Oxford, Oxford University Press. The accent is on

self-sufficiency, both in contemplation being an end-in-itself and in the suggestion that this highest source of human happiness is a solitary pursuit (ibid., 1178b ff).

40. D, s.482 and GS, s.167 also describe human relationships in terms of the imagery of comestibles. Nietzsche's use of this imagery is not unprecedented: Chamfort makes eating a metaphor for social relations in Chamfort, 1968. *Maximes et pensées, caractères et anecdotes*, No.1032. Pref. Dagen, J. Paris: Garnier-Flammarion. Bacon does this too, as noted by Little in Little, G. 1993. *Friendship. Being Ourselves With Others*, p.21. Melbourne, Text Publishing. One reason for this could be that so much social life has traditionally revolved around eating. Moreover, eating breaks down the boundaries of inside and outside, just as close human relationships can.

41. D, ss.323, 440, 473, 491, 499; GS, s.50. However, D, s.485 does distinguish friendship from solitude and reiterates the earlier point that friendship cannot survive too much proximity between its partners. Solitude also denotes removal from friends in other passages from this work (D, ss.479, 531).

42. That Nietzsche does not always celebrate solitude also emerges in his correspondence: to Salomé he wrote that 'not only health but still more *The Gay Science* drive me into solitude. I want to put an end to it.' (From a letter dated 10 June 1882 in Leidecker, K. F. trans. and ed. 1960. *Nietzsche. Unpublished Letters*, p.86. London, Peter Owen.) The following month he told her that 'from now on when *you* will be my guide, I shall be *well* advised and need not be afraid ... I do not want to be lonely any longer and desire to learn how to become human'. In mid-December, he wrote to her and Rée: 'I am touched in the head, half ready to be confined to the lunatic asylum, totally confused by my long loneliness.' (Ibid., p.96.)

43. The importance of friends taking strength from one another was a persistent theme of Nietzsche's correspondence before and during the middle-period years: to Rohde he writes, 'If I had not my friends, I wonder whether I should not myself begin to believe that I am demented. As it is, however, by my adherence to you I adhere to myself, and if we stand security for each other, something must ultimately result from our way of thinking – a possibility which until now the whole world had doubted.' (From a letter dated 31 December 1873 in Levy, O. ed. 1921. *Selected Letters of Friedrich Nietzsche*, pp.91–2. New York, Doubleday Page.) The following year he reflects on 'how very lucky I have been during the last seven years and how little I can gauge how rich I am in my friends. Truth to tell, I live through you, I advance by leaning on your shoulders, for my self-esteem is wretchedly weak and you have to assure me of my own value again and again...' (From a letter dated 7 October 1874, ibid., p.98.) He later writes that 'Friends like yourself must help to sustain me in my belief in myself and this you do when you confide in me about your highest aims and hopes.' (From a letter dated 24 March 1881, ibid., p.135.)

44. Consider Nietzsche's claim that intimacy is only denigrated by those incapable of 'warm and noble intimacy' (*die edel herzliche Vertraulichkeit*') (D, s.288).

45. This suggests that for Nietzsche, as for Aristotle, higher friendship must unite equals. Those who conclude with Berkowitz that Nietzsche 'denounced the belief in human equality as a calamitous conceit' fail to take account of the place of friendship in his thought. See Berkowitz, P. 1995. *Nietzsche: The Ethics of an Immoralist*, p.1. Cambridge (MA), Harvard University Press. Nietzsche's remark in a letter to his sister, Elisabeth, written after the middle period is interesting in this context: 'perfect friendship is only possible *inter pares*! *Inter pares* is an intoxicating word; it contains so much hope, savour and blessedness for him who is necessarily always alone; for him who is "different..."'. From a letter dated 8 July 1886 in Levy, O. ed. 1921. *Selected Letters of Friedrich Nietzsche*, p.182. New York, Doubleday Page.

46. But Nietzsche does not see envy as a thoroughly unredeeming characteristic. He concedes that some of those who envy others can also be 'striving for higher things'

(HH, s.351). In such cases, envy of 'the man of excellence' can mutate into love for him. This signals again just how sensitive he remains to particularity in the works of the middle period.

47. Nietzsche, F. 1972. Zarathustra's prologue. In *Thus Spoke Zarathustra*, trans. Hollingdale, R. J. Harmondsworth, Penguin.

48. Ibid., Part I, 'Of the Friend'.

49. Ibid., Part I, 'Of Love of One's Neighbour'.

50. Ibid., Part I, 'Of the Friend'.

51. Nietzsche, F. 1979. Why I am so wise. In *Ecce Homo*, trans. Hollingdale, R. J., No.7. Harmondsworth, Penguin.

52. Ibid.

53. Nietzsche, F. 1965. *The Genealogy of Morals*, Book III, Ch.viii. Trans. Golffing, F. New York, Doubleday.

54. Nietzsche, F. 1979. Why I am so wise. In *Ecce Homo*, trans. Hollingdale, R. J., No.8. Harmondsworth, Penguin. Compare Nietzsche, F. 1977. Maxims and arrows. In *Twilight of the Idols*, trans. Hollingdale, R. J., No.3. Harmondsworth, Penguin. Fredrick Appel (in Appel, F. 1999. *Nietzsche Contra Democracy*, pp.81–93. Ithaca, Cornell University Press) relies largely on evidence from Z and BGE to make his argument that friendship was an important good for the later Nietzsche.

55. In the later period, he bemoaned his lack of friends to Elisabeth: 'my pour soul is so sensitive to injury and so full of longing for good friends "who are my life". Get me a small circle of men who will listen to me and understand me – and then I shall be cured!' From a letter dated 8 July 1886 in Levy, O. ed. 1921. *Selected Letters of Friedrich Nietzsche*, p.183. New York, Doubleday Page.

56. Appel argues differently in Appel, F. 1999. *Nietzsche Contra Democracy*. Ithaca, Cornell University Press.

57. Nietzsche himself draws connections between friendship and readership in the epilogue to HH. In the poem 'Among Friends', he first depicts scenes of friendship and then addresses readers. Rather than any strong separation between the two categories, similarities between them are suggested. Section 1, for example, echoes the idea of friendship as 'joying-with', while Section 2 is addressed to readers 'who laugh and joy in living'.

5

Martin Buber and the Ontological Crisis of Modern Man

CHARLES RUSTIN

Through an ontological 'shift' away from the Cartesian *cogito*, Martin Buber offers an alternative interpretation and understanding of global society and the means to improve it. Buber asserts that self and society are constructed, often unconsciously, by people's relation to being. In Buberian terms, the amount of social conflict in a society depends upon whether subjective thought, as is currently the case, or unity and relation, are understood as the ground of being. Buber's work implies that seemingly irreconcilable differences in society result from a situation in which subjective (rational) thought and its social products are considered to exist prior to man's relation to his fellows and to the unity of being.[1]

Buber regards the crisis of (post)modern man as ontological and related to the prevailing understanding of Descartes' *Cogito Ergo Sum* as the foundation of modern thought. Descartes is commonly understood to have placed inordinate faith in subjective thought as the ground of being and knowledge. For Buber, by contrast, thought is a tool to be used as and when it is needed rather than the ground of existence itself.[2] In the social sphere, when thought is considered as a foundation rather than a tool, this results in excessive trust being placed in existing social structures seen as the product of these subjective thought processes. In this way, Buber's work may be seen as an attempt to emancipate humankind from the damaging products of subjective thought by drawing attention towards the primacy of human relations and their edifying potential. Buber does not deny self and society to be constructs of subjective thought, but rather suggests that unity of being and relation are prior.

Neither Buber nor this presentation of his ideas suggests that Cartesian thought is the root cause of certain undesirable by-products of subjective difference in global society. Difference, and the social problems which result from it, clearly existed long before Descartes formulated his notion that individual consciousness should be understood as the foundation of knowledge. The point is not that Descartes, but rather that a particularly prevalent misreading[3] of the Cartesian *cogito*, provides justification for a sociological process which results in the objectification and 'normalization' of the products of subjective thought.

Where Descartes' system may be understood as providing justification for the defence of the objective social by-products of subjective 'truth', Buber's thought represents an attempt to re-locate human relations as the foundation for knowledge, thereby rejecting subjective thought as a justification for social wrongs. Buber's desire to focus our attention upon the primacy of relation and the ultimate unity of being in place of the violent disunity which inevitably results when subjective thought is placed as the basis of knowledge is thus intended to illustrate how difference in global society need not result in prejudice and conflict. Rather, by acknowledging the initial similarities which unite humankind, Buber's work implies that social difference should be understood as a positive resource to be used in the edification of society rather than the justification for – often violent – conflict.

By drawing attention away from an attitude to being which can only lead to the assumption that divisions in international society, such as the sovereign state, and Hobbesian conflict are 'natural' phenomena, Buber seeks to turn our attention toward the fundamental unity of being and the priority of relation.[4] Ever conscious of the way in which the norms of human society may become accepted as 'natural', rather than imagined or social phenomena, and though accepting that there cannot be a humanity without division and difference, Buber's concern is to illustrate how these negative aspects of difference may be transcended. In this way, the central theme in Buber's work may be understood as a plea to humankind to reappraise its place in the world and its relation with the other and the ground of being in order that difference and plurality may be regarded as positive, rather than destructive, features of human society. In the words of one scholar, Buber's work is an attempt to illustrate how, '[i]n touching the human we [may] close the gap that separates peoples. In closing the gap we repair the tear in human relations. And in repairing the tear in the sphere of the human we repair the tear in the world'.[5]

This study of Buber's thought suggests that it is only having understood the significance of his ontological 'shift' that it makes sense to turn attention toward the more frequently considered notions of the I-It and the I-You relationships which constitute the focus of his magnum opus '*I and Thou*'.[6] With the benefit of a clear understanding of Buberian ontology it subsequently becomes possible to interpret the I-It and the I-You as Buber himself intended. That is to say, by emphasizing the personal responsibility required to acknowledge the primacy of relation and the unity of being, Buber illustrates how society can only be improved through individuals' movement away from the apathy and passivity which currently prevail. It is thus Buberian ontology which acts as a key to the comprehensive understanding of his diagnosis of, to paraphrase Lyotard,[7] humanity's post-modern condition.

A correct understanding of Buberian ontology and his insistence upon the personal responsibility that is required for social improvement helps to explain his interpretation of history which distances itself from Christianity's belief in fate and a Kantian understanding based upon the power of Providence and nature. For Buber, history is very much dependent upon whether, based upon an acknowledgement of the primacy of relation and the unity of being, humankind in general decides to take responsibility for its actions. The alternative is a continued allegiance to the primacy of subjective thought and consequently the negative aspects of difference and conflict which currently prevail.

The Secularisation of Cartesian Thought

Prior to examining Buber's ontological shift away from the Cartesian *cogito* it is worth noting that one of his shortcomings as a scholar is the frequent lack of reference in his work to the sources under consideration. The reason for this lack of attention to detail is unclear but in the case of his critique of Descartes might be attributable to the fact that his criticism, while explaining how the Cartesian *cogito* is an unacceptable basis for knowledge, is particularly focused upon the pervasive influence of one particular (mis)reading of the Cartesian subject in modern philosophy.[8] A clear distinction is thus made between the Cartesian corpus on the one hand and its practical influence upon modern thought on the other due to the fact that it is arguably a series of selective (mis)readings of Descartes' work which transmit his legacy to the modern audience.

Buber's decision to consider Descartes' influence rather than the corpus itself is thus based on the suggestion that it is the latter's practical influence rather than his actual writings which present a divisive problem in (post)modern society. Buber's approach may be considered as an example of astute scholarship in the sense that, if Descartes' influence is based upon a selective (mis)reading of his work, Buber's only option in terms of drawing attention away from the prevailing interpretation of the Cartesian cogito was to criticise the interpretation itself rather than the original writings upon which it is based. It is thus to these different readings of Descartes' corpus that we now turn prior to examining how Buber justified his movement away from the dominant interpretation of Descartes' cogito ergo sum.

The two readings of Descartes' corpus referred to above are those which hold sway respectively inside and outside France. While clearly a generalization, this example is intended to illustrate how the work of a particular philosopher may illustrate very different positions depending upon how the corpus in question is presented. Although it might at first appear to be a contradiction in terms, within France, Descartes' influence is seen as compatible with the attempt to locate the foundations of philosophy in religion and the grounding of reason in faith. This suggestion may appear all the more strange in the light of the Enlightenment's supposed emancipation of philosophy from religion and of reason from faith.[9]

Outside of France, Descartes' corpus is generally understood as a 'foundationalist' or rationalist attempt to locate reason as the ground of being, thereby emancipating reason from the stranglehold of faith. In this view, Descartes' objective was to illustrate how the 'cogito', or 'I think', is the only reasonable evidence upon which knowledge can be based. Accordingly, it is the certainty of individual consciousness which rejects belief in God as the grounds of knowledge on the basis that there is no 'objective' evidence for the existence of God that could provide such a foundation. This reading of Descartes creates an immediate conflict between religion and philosophy, reason and faith, which is not so readily apparent in France where attention is also paid, as it was by Buber,[10] to the role of God in the Cartesian corpus.

Where other interpretations of Cartesian foundationalism find incompatibility between reason and faith, the French reading locates continuity. In accordance with the French and Buberian readings of Descartes, Tom Rockmore suggests that, '[a]lthough Descartes is often understood as a resolutely secular thinker, the insistence that knowledge depends on the certainty of faith is a persistent doctrine running throughout his writings from the beginning to the end.'[11] While one may wish, on historical grounds, to suggest that Descartes' inclusion of God's role in his corpus was an attempt to outwit the religious censors of the time, it is worth acknowledging that his writings were, nevertheless, placed on the *Index* and that, as Rockmore observes, any reading of Descartes cannot ignore the extensive role which he attributes to God, not only in parts but rather throughout his entire work.[12]

Thus it is that Descartes writes in the fourth part of the 'Discourse on Method' that, '[f]or to begin with, that which I have just taken as a rule, that is to say, that all the things that we very clearly and very distinctly conceive of are true, is certain only because God exists, and that He is a Perfect Being, and that all that is in us issues from Him.'[13] Similarly, in the thirteenth of his *Principles*, Descartes suggests that the mind 'can have no certain knowledge until it is acquainted with its creator'.[14] These examples serve to illustrate that it is perhaps not the true Descartes who is represented when his work is read as an example of enlightened rationalism in which faith and religion are vanquished by the certainty of reason. Rather, Descartes' consideration of God the creator appears to sustain the suggestion that his corpus should be understood as an attempt to ground reason in faith, a position which would, contrary to what many believe, reinforce the links between philosophy and religion as opposed to weakening them.[15] Nevertheless, the problem remained, and it is this which has allowed the rational aspect of the Cartesian cogito to be emphasised at the expense of the religious, that '[h]owever orthodox men like Descartes, Locke and Leibniz might be, their Christian orthodoxy was tacked on to systems of thought which were as logically viable without it.'[16]

Just as the Christian churches were worried, not about the original intentions of the philosophers themselves but rather, about the potential implications of an influence that would eventually create a rift between philosophy and religion, reason and faith, this work is emphasizing the implications of Descartes' influence upon modern society rather than the original work itself. In this way, the current examination of Buber's critique of Descartes may be regarded as a repetition of history in terms of the Christian churches' initial misgivings, which turned out to be only too accurate, about the potentially divisive influence of the Cartesian cogito upon an 'enlightened' society, so called.

Descartes' Foundational 'Truth'

Having now illustrated the crucial distinction between Descartes' corpus on the one hand and its practical influence on the other it remains to elaborate the details of the Cartesian cogito prior to examining Buber's significant criticism of it and the influence that it has had upon the predicament of modern man. Descartes' understanding of how an individual's consciousness becomes the foundation of knowledge and the basis for 'truth', a position which has come to dominate philosophical discussion in the modern age,[17] is well-summarised by the following passage:

> whilst I thus wished to think all things false, it was absolutely essential that the "I" who thought this should be somewhat, and remarking that this truth "*I think, therefore I am*" [cogito ergo sum] was so certain and so assured that all the most extravagant suppositions brought forward by the sceptics were incapable of shaking it, I came to the conclusion that I could receive it without scruple as the first principle of the Philosophy for which I was seeking.[18]

Reading this excerpt, it is easy to comprehend how focus on a secular *cogito* at the expense of the religious aspect of Descartes' corpus should eventually result in what Buber termed the 'Eclipse of God' and Nietzsche before him referred to as the 'Death of God'. In both cases, what is being referred to is not the end of God per se, and in this sense Buber's message is perhaps more easily understood than Nietzsche's, but rather that rational thought has, perhaps only temporarily, hidden God from view. Buber's metaphor of God as the sun being eclipsed by rational thought in the form of the moon accurately illustrates how, in his view, rational thought founded upon a secular *cogito* has vanquished religion because the existence of God is not, at least to modern man, quite so certain as Descartes' conscious 'I'. However, where Nietzsche's 'Death of God' has a pessimistic air of finality about it, Buber's 'Eclipse of God' appears to be an optimistic attempt to illustrate how humankind has the capacity to reverse this situation should it so wish.

This note of optimism with regard to humankind's potential for improvement is an ever present element in Buber's thought.[19] The predominant 'meliorist'[20] message in Buber's ontology is an attempt to illustrate how prioritising the secular Cartesian *cogito* instead of relation can only lead to destructive divisions in global society in the sense that subjective thought creates many conflicting 'truths' and social structures. What Buber was so concerned to explain was his understanding that, if the unity of being and relation are understood as occurring prior to the Cartesian *cogito* then previously accepted subjective 'truths' and social structures, seen as the product of individuals' thought and personal opinion, might not be defended so dogmatically and violently in global society as they are at present.

Buber's position in no way rejects the value of difference but rather emphasizes its importance in the creative evolution of society. What it does reject, however, is the failure of humankind to acknowledge the importance of relation prior to this subjective difference. In the words of Peter Bertocci, Buber resisted an 'ultimate unity in which all cows are black' but rather wished to 'keep a unity in which plurality will be meaningful and individuality productive.'[21] In this sense, subjective difference, seen as a product of individuals' thought, is important for the healthy functioning of global society but not to the extent where it provides the foundation for positions which, in overlooking the original unity of being and the priority of relation, advocate violent conflict as a 'reasonable' or 'natural' form of behaviour.

Contrary to a Hobbesian understanding of humanity, Buber did not believe that man is born in a violent state of nature. Furthermore, humankind is able to reduce the occurrence of social conflict without assistance from outside, in the form of Divine intervention, for example.[22] Whether humanity succeeds in reducing societal woes depends, for Buber, very much upon how successfully the bonds of subjective thought are broken and replaced with an ontology which emphasizes the unity of being and the priority of relation in addition to the personal responsibility that is clearly involved in such an ontological shift.

Any theory which stresses the importance of what are, at root, subjective differences prior to the original unity of humankind and the primacy of relation can ultimately only lead to some form of 'Inside/Outside' distinction and from there to physical conflict in defence of these values. Walker suggests that exclusionary discourse represented by, for example, the sovereign state, possesses significant ethico-political implications and 'expresses a theory of ethics'.[23] If the defence of exclusionary social structures, such as the sovereign state, is understood as constituting a particular 'theory of ethics', or custom, the present examination of Buber's thought may be considered to be part of the search for an inclusive ethic for global society which values human life prior to exclusionary social structures such as sovereign states which are frequently defended with violent means.

Buber and the Frustration Occasioned by his 'Pointing'

At a time near the end of his life, Buber was asked in *Replies to My Critics* to respond to various critiques of his ideas. He readily acknowledged that his philosophy made no attempt to enunciate a fixed system of thought and he explained how the ultimate significance of his work lies in pointing towards the primacy of human relation which, prior to his own writings, 'had not or had too little been seen'. In this context, Buber's consideration of being goes only so far as to facilitate an understanding of the primacy of human relation.[24] The desire to *point the way*[25] towards the primacy of relation while offering no fixed or comprehensive system of thought to his readers follows the understanding that the path towards the position which he himself had reached is of a very personal nature and requires a conscious effort, in addition to the development of personal responsibility, in order to get there.

It is exactly this element of obscurity in Buber's writings, and his unwillingness to spoon-feed his readership, that can be seen as the root cause of much of the frustration which may result from prolonged contact with his work. This frustration, understood as flowing from Buber's great desire that his readers should think for themselves, is what in many ways makes a comprehensive appreciation of his ideas such a challenge. Prolonged contact with Buber's ideas may give one the impression that he actually wished his readers to experience at least some of the intellectual angst and struggle he himself must have felt in arriving at his conclusions. Moreover, what can only add to the sense of yearning engendered by contact with Buber's thought is the fact that the I-You relation which forms a central part of his work affords no 'objective' knowledge of itself.

This situation is clearly uncomfortable for a readership so used to asking almost automatically for 'objective' proof. It is in the knowledge that modern readers are profoundly influenced by a misreading of the Cartesian *cogito* (most of the time quite unconsciously) and by a resultant demand for the 'objective' grounding of a given idea, that Buber's critique of this situation is of such interest. The great irony, to which Buber's writings bear witness, is the search for objective foundations of ideas which, having no material form, can only be found in ideas themselves; i.e. in the conscious 'I' of subjective thought!

Buber's avoidance of fixed systems of thought makes him, in the language of Richard Rorty, an 'edifying philosopher' who attempts to locate the alienating and conflict-causing elements of society. This stands in contrast to the 'normal philosopher' intent on formulating a philosophical system which, he or she believes, will generate an accurate description of reality. Interestingly, Buber's thought bridges these two approaches in the sense that by locating the causes of social conflict he also describes humanity's existence in the world.

The edifying potential which Buber attributes to the primacy of relation and the unity of being places him alongside other edifying philosophers whose purpose is to 'help their readers break free from outworn vocabularies and attitudes, rather than provide "grounding" for the intuitions and customs of the present'.[26] In this way, edifying philosophers reject faith in objectivism and 'the more concrete absurdity of thinking that the vocabulary used by modern science, morality, or whatever has some privileged attachment to reality which makes it more than just a further set of descriptions'.[27] Rorty's description of the edifying philosopher is thus in full accordance with the above consideration of Buber's desire to illustrate how existing social structures and conflicting relationships are not quite as 'natural' as we are frequently led to believe.[28]

The Divisive Cogito and Buber's Ontological Shift

Having examined how Descartes positioned the individually conscious 'I' as the basis of truth and knowledge in society, we now consider Buber's critique. As previously mentioned, Buber's motive for criticising the Cartesian influence is that when the individually conscious 'I' is understood to be the foundation of knowledge, this results in societies in which subjective thought (i.e. differences of opinion) become objectified and concretised into the unquestioned 'natural' norms of society. Once this has occurred, human beings become prepared to defend, with their lives if necessary, these 'objective' differences which originated as an idea in somebody's mind.

The great irony to which Buber's thought bears witness is that human beings require an 'other' in order to develop their own identity. While representing an integral part in the constuction of individuals' identity, however, this 'other' subsequently becomes a focus and outlet for the expression of the various forms of anxiety which are an inherent aspect of human existence. The challenge for humanity, to which Buber continually pointed, is that individuals must assume responsibility through relation with their fellows for locating the peaceful means to balance existential instability and the temptation to use the 'other' as an outlet for conflict, both physical and emotional. In this sense, a peaceful balance must be located between feelings of otherness and the sameness that is represented by a common humanity.

Buber's critique of Descartes may be summarised as follows. While it is possible that the individual child may think (i.e. have thoughts) prior to relation, in order to become a conscious 'I' or Cartesian *cogito* that child must first enter into relation, perhaps pre-linguistic in form, with an 'Other'. It may be that relation and the arrival of the conscious 'I' occur at the same time, though Buber argues that this is not the case. What is clear is that Descartes ignored, the potentially unifying aspect of, relation in the coming into being of the individually conscious 'I'. In fact, Buber argues, Descartes attempted to create a concrete foundation for knowledge upon a philosophical abstraction; i.e. thought. This abstraction for Buber is unacceptable since relation, the concrete foundation towards which Buber continually turns our attention, is 'irrevocable'.[29] Moreover, in the words of Dan Avnon, 'as thought is not [objective] reality, it cannot be a proof of one's existence, unless one adheres to a philosophy that claims that nothing is real and hence one form of self-illusion is as good as another. This perspective is clearly unacceptable to a thinker such as Buber.'[30]

A distinction is thus made by Buber between thought, the result of thinking, and an individual's consciousness of being an 'I'. In effect, 'I' become conscious (i.e. aware) of being me only in relation to an other. While Descartes suggested that 'I think, therefore I am', Buber draws our attention to the fact that prior to this potentially divisive 'truth', which 'was so certain and so assured',[31] there is relation in which a thinking child enters into relation with an other and, as a result, becomes aware (conscious) of being an 'I'. Only after this initial relation can the child, now a conscious 'I', possibly arrive (unconsciously?) at Descartes' 'truth' that 'I think, therefore I am'. In this way, Buber replaces Descartes' foundational 'truth' with an observation which may be expressed thus, 'I' relate, therefore 'I' am.

The path to becoming a conscious 'I' is explained as follows. Firstly, and as confirmed by modern social psychology,[32] Buber suggests that there can be no conscious 'I' prior to relation with an 'Other' human being. In Buber's words, 'IN THE beginning is relation... THERE IS no I taken in itself, but only the I of the primary word *I-Thou* and the I of the primary word *I-It*... THROUGH THE *Thou* a man becomes I.'[33] In this way, Buber explains that, not only does relation come before the evolution of a conscious 'I' but, furthermore, this primary relation is of the I-You variety. It is only with the experience of an I-It relation that a person becomes fully conscious of being an 'I'.[34] The primal relation is therefore an I-You relation of 'natural combination', however, it is only with the experience of an I-It relation of 'natural separation' between subject and object that a person becomes an individually conscious 'I'.[35]

According to Buber, prior to all of this stands the unity of being or God. However, since Buber made it clear that his reference to the unity of being and God went only so far as to facilitate an understanding of the primacy of human relation, so this interpretation will adopt Buber's method and refer to the unifying element of being and God only as and when such reference is deemed necessary in clarifying Buber's thought upon the primacy of relation.[36]

Buber's explanation of the primacy of relation in 'I and Thou' focuses upon the child. He suggests that with the child 'it becomes crystal clear to us that the spiritual reality of the primary words [I-You and I-It] arises out of a natural reality, that of the primary word *I-Thou* out of natural combination, and that of the primary word *I-It* out of natural separation.'[37] For Buber, the child's first relation, which is 'one of purely natural combination, bodily interaction and flowing from the one to the other', is with its mother while still in the womb. At the same time, according to Buber,

> [the unborn child's] life's horizon, as it comes into being, seems in a unique way to be, and yet again not to be, traced in that of the life that bears it. For it does not rest only in the womb of the human mother... Every child that is coming into being rests, like all life that is coming into being, in the womb of the great mother, the undivided primal world that precedes form.[38]

In this passage, Buber draws our attention to the fact that, though babies are born unique in the sense that no two human beings are exactly alike, what ultimately unites them is the fact that all life derives from the 'undivided primal world' that is being or God. It is in this sense that Buber suggests that his reference to the unity of being and God goes only so far as to facilitate an understanding of the primacy of human relation. Seen in this light, the above passage is an attempt to illustrate how human beings, though themselves individually different and unique, are all related to the undivided primal world of being and God which creates all life. It is here that the spiritual aspect of Buber's thought becomes visible.[39] Returning to his consideration of the child as an illustration of the primacy of relation, Buber suggests that, once born,

> [t]he primal nature of the effort to establish relation is already to be seen in the earliest and most confined stage... It is simply not the case that the child first perceives an object, then, as it were, puts himself in relation with it. But the effort to establish relation comes first – the hand of the child arched out so that what is over against him may nestle under it; second is the actual relation, a saying of *Thou* without words, in the state preceding the word-form; the thing, like the I, is produced late, arising after the original experiences have been split asunder and the connected partners separated. In the beginning is relation – as category of being, readiness, grasping form, mould for the soul; it is the *a priori* of relation, *the inborn Thou*.[40]

In this passage Buber illustrates how relation comes prior to the Cartesian cogito. According to Buber, first comes the child's instinctive desire for relation. Second comes relation in its pre-linguistic form. Thirdly, only after this pre-linguistic relation can the child become a conscious 'I'. Fourthly, having entered into pre-linguistic relation, the child then wishes to communicate and it is here that we have the arrival of language. In this way, the origin of language is seen to rest in the pre-linguistic desire to communicate and share one's observations about the world.[41]

While it is obviously difficult to illustrate the temporal arrival of thought in connection to relation and which one comes prior to the other, in following the sequence of events described above it becomes clear that a human being must have entered into relation prior to becoming a conscious 'I'. The important distinction which Buber made in negating the Cartesian *cogito* is therefore that thinking, and being conscious of oneself as an 'I', are two entirely separate propositions. For Buber, both relation and thought are prior to the conscious 'I' which is itself an impossibility without the interaction of the two former variables.

Having now considered Buber's rejection of Descartes' foundation for knowledge, and the humanistic alternative which he proffers in its place, attention now turns to how the observation that relation and the unity of being come prior to the self-conscious Cartesian 'I' might have a practical edifying influence upon post-modern global society in which the divisive influence of the Cartesian *cogito* has become so firmly established as the norm. In pursuit of a satisfactory explanation as to how his ontological shift might have a positive practical effect upon global society, consideration of Buber's thought now turns to the

I-You and the I-It which constitute the two types of relation which individuals may have with the world in addition to social relations and the societies which they serve to create. Though experienced by individuals these two kinds of relation are both influenced by, and reflected in, human communities.

There may, for some readers, be an immediate temptation to draw similarities between Buber's understanding of man's twofold relation to the world and the 'instrumental' rationalisation of capitalist society that was so critically noted by members of the Frankfurt School, beginning with Lukacs' interpretation of Max Weber and continued, through the work of Adorno, Horkheimer, and Marcuse, to the present day critique of Jurgen Habermas.[42] However, where the 'Critical' theorists of the Frankfurt School were primarily concerned with the undesirable effects of the ever increasing instrumental rationalisation of capitalist society, Buber's corpus is chiefly concerned with the primacy of relation and with the edifying effect that acknowledgement of this might have for the re-humanisation of modern societies and in the resolution of social and political conflict. For Buber, it is not capitalist society in particular which attracts criticism but rather any society, be it local or global, which does not place man's common humanity prior to subjective and conflicting pluralities.

With the benefit of a clear conception of his unifying ontology which in turn provides the foundation for an understanding of humankind's relation to the world, we are now in a position to explain the way in which the improvement of society depends for Buber upon individual responsibility and the manner in which human beings decide to live their 'twofold' relation to the world. Such a philosophy rejects fatalism, apathy, and a lack of personal decision-making and responsibility in the attempt to emphasise humankind's mastery over its own social history. As will become clear, Buber's ontology is one which constructs society from the bottom up, beginning with the relationships which individual human beings have to the world, and only later considering the social structures which individuals and communities construct as a result of their relationships with each other.

I-You and I-It Relations

Following Buber, it is important to recognize that the two 'primary words', I-You and I-It, both constitute different forms of relation. Buber states that 'PRIMARY WORDS [I-You and I-It] do not signify things, but they intimate relations'.[43] With reference to questions concerning the desirability of the I-It relation, it must be made clear that what is at issue with regard to the I-It is its relative prevalence in society vis-à-vis the I-You. The I-It relation is unquestionably desirable for Buber since it is an essential component of humanity's everyday life. 'The *It* is the eternal chrysalis, the *Thou* the eternal butterfly'[44] and in this way the one presupposes the other. What is therefore undesirable is not the I-It per-se but rather situations in which it predominates over the I-You. It is in this context that Buber states at the end of the first part of I and Thou that, 'without *It* man cannot live. But he who lives with *It* alone is not a man'.[45] What concerned Buber, and is now of concern to the present study, is the observation that, 'THE HISTORY of the individual and that of the human race, in whatever they may continually part company, agree at least in this one respect, that they indicate a progressive augmentation of the world of *It*'.[46]

Buber directly attributes the condition of a given society to the balance that exists therein between the I-You and I-It relations. In this sense, the I-It does not, for Buber, constitute some sort of 'non-relation' and is desirable for humanity's day to day existence on the assumption that its fulfilment should not come at the expense of the *I-You*. It is as a result of the fact that in modern societies the I-It takes precedence over the I-You that this study has focused on humankind's ontological crisis and the way in which the objectification and reification of subjective thought impedes humanity's recognition of the primacy of relation and the unity of being.[47] At the domestic level this results in a lack of community spirit, the predominance of a materialistic way of life fuelled by the continual advance of commerce and industry, and ultimately alienation from one's fellow human beings and the primacy of relation. In the international sphere this predominant I-It attitude to being and reality establishes the normality of competing social structures, such as the sovereign state, of 'imagined communities'[48] in the form of contending nationalisms, in addition to the physical force and conflict which is used in the defence of such principles.

Primary Words and the Quality of Relation

Buber's formulation of the two primary words, I-You and I-It, is intended to illustrate the quality of relationship that is being experienced. They represent the state of an individual's inner attitude towards being and reality and serve to establish a mode of existence. The I-You and the I-It thus express an individual's mode of being in the

world. While the I-You 'can only be spoken with the whole being', the
I-It 'can never be spoken with the whole being.'[49] Buber explains that
there can be no 'I' except for that which is in relation with a 'You' or
an 'It'. Furthermore, the 'I' of the primary word I-You is a different 'I'
from that of the 'I' of the primary word I-It.[50]

For Buber, each individual is the sum of his or her relations with
other people and things. A person is as he or she relates to a particular
environment. Rather than being composed of certain fixed attributes
which more accurately define an individual's character, Buber
understood human beings to be dynamic in the sense that each person
is in a state of becoming. A person's character is thus constructed and
ever re-constructed according to the type and quality of relations
entered into.[51] Buber's conception of the evolving individual explains
how society, understood as the product of human relationships, should
also be dynamic and ever reinvent itself. The idea of static societies and
the reifications which help to perpetuate them is unacceptable to Buber
since it is not social structures and other reifications of subjective
thought which represent the true meaning of existence.

The I-It is an exclusive relationship and attitude to being in which
a distance is placed between oneself and the other in order to
experience and use. The I-It is thus 'the typical subject-object
relationship'[52] of 'natural separation'[53] in which the individual 'I'
distinguishes his or herself from the other by placing stress upon
difference rather than unity, upon apparent singularity and uniqueness
rather than fundamental similarity. 'Individuality in differentiating
itself from others is rendered remote from true being.'[54] In contrast, the
I-You is an inclusive relationship and attitude to being of 'natural
combination'[55] which is open and direct.[56] The 'I' of the I-You is one
that recognizes the primacy of relation in which self and other are parts
of unified being and creation.

Buber explains that the I-You and the I-It relations involve two
different kinds of movement. The first movement, which is generated
by an I-It attitude to being, is called 'primal setting at a distance' while
the second movement, generated by an I-You attitude to being, is called
'entering into relation'. This distinction explains the statement that

> the principle of human life is not simple but twofold, being built
> up in a twofold movement which is of such kind that the one
> movement is the presupposition of the other... That the first
> movement is the presupposition of the other is plain from the fact
> that one can enter into relation only with being which has been

set at a distance, more precisely, has become an independent opposite.[57]

By drawing attention to the distance that is required before one may enter into relation, Buber illustrates how 'every *Thou* in our world must become an *It*'.[58] However, while every *You* must become an *It*, every *It* may, but need not, become once again *You*. In this way, what was at one moment the *You* of an I-You relation must at the next become the *It* of an I-It relation. This I-It may once again become an I-You but will never remain as such. Furthermore, this I-It will not perforce return to the state of I-You. This continual potential for transition between the I-You and the I-It helps to explain how the I-You attitude is not 'the property of some superior person who has forever overcome the self-centred attitude to being indicated by the basic word I-It'.[59]

Buber was insistent that there is no 'spiritual elite' and that the I-You relation is available to all humanity including 'so-called idiots'.[60] While human beings may live for extended periods of time with an I-It attitude to being, Buber suggests that this is not true humanity and that the societies created thereupon will be replete with both alienation and conflict.[61] For Buber, the only way to escape from the prevalence of an I-It attitude to existence is through personal responsibility and the return of the I-You through dialogue with one's fellows.

Having considered Buber's conception of the I-It and the I-You relations, attention now turns to the character duality which results from individuals' way of relating to the world. Buber referred to this duality, which helps to provide a more complete understanding of the social construction of reality, as the Ego-orientation and the Person-orientation . The Ego-Person duality, in conjunction with the notion of personal responsibility, in turn provides the key to Buber's understanding of such social phenomena as national and ethnic conflict in modern society.

The Ego-oriented and Person-oriented 'I'

Buber explains that the 'I' of the I-It relation is that of individuality and is as such an 'ego-oriented I', conscious of itself as a subject which experiences and uses. In contrast, the 'I' of the I-You relation is a different 'I' and is that of a person, or 'person-oriented I', which is 'conscious of itself as subjectivity (without a dependent genitive).' While the individual, or 'ego-oriented I', exists by differentiating itself from other individuals, a person, or 'person-oriented I', exists by entering into relation with his or her fellows. The first attitude to humanity represents separation and difference, the second solidarity, combination and unity.[62] It is movement away from the presently dominant 'ego-oriented' attitude to being, which accepts difference, separation, and conflict as 'natural' phenomena, towards a 'person-oriented' attitude, that questions the factitious 'nature' of this conflict-provoking fragmentation, which would constitute the 'ontological shift' examined at length above. With this in mind, Dan Avnon suggests that, '[c]hange in perception of reality, in turn, leads to change in conduct',[63] in the sense that a human being's attitude toward being, and where the value of existence is located, has a practical influence upon social reality.

It is important to recognise Buber's insistence that the ego-person duality does not represent two kinds of human being but rather two poles of one's essential humanity. No human being is pure 'person' and none is pure 'ego'. 'Everyone lives in the twofold I.' However, while some are so person-oriented that they may be called persons, others are so ego-oriented that they may be called egos, or individuals. In this way, 'THE STRONGER the I of the primary word I-Thou is in the twofold I, the more personal is the man'.[64] This remark upon the relative strength of the I of the I-You is direct reference to the value attributed in society by human beings to the reified products of subjective thought that exist therein. It is in the knowledge that, for Buber, these subjective constructions are not always the valid representatives of reality that the following statement makes sense.

> The more a man, humanity, is mastered by individuality, the deeper does the I sink into unreality. In such times the person in man and in humanity leads a hidden subterranean and as it were cancelled existence – till it is recalled.[65]

The unreal, 'cancelled', social existence which is produced by a predominance of the ego-oriented attitude at the expense of person-orientation illustrates how every human being's attitude to being and social reality has implications far beyond him or herself. It is as a result of this observation that 'true history' is, for Buber, decided in the field between the ego-person duality.[66]

Avnon argues that the dominance of ego-orientation is most flagrantly manifest in modern society 'in the primary form of social organisation created by modern human beings – the nation state.'[67] This observation is corroborated by Buber's own understanding of the nation as man's 'expanded ego' to which he relinquishes responsibility in addition to belief in himself, God, being, and the primacy of relation.[68] According to Buber, at the root of any attempt to overcome both national and ethnic hostilities in a global society is the need to 'clear the (ontological) way' for the creation of communities distinguished by the prevalence of person-oriented, rather than ego-oriented, relationships.[69] In this sense, a shift in peoples' attitude to existence would give rise to an adjusted balance between the ego-person orientations in favour of person-orientation and the primacy of relation, thereby enabling the evolution of new forms of community.

The development of a global 'community of communities'[70] would, for Buber, represent humankind's overcoming of the alleged historical necessities of social life seen as conflict-causing exclusionary discourses.[71] A 'global commonwealth', the result of this community of communities, implies that, for Buber, the historical necessity, if ever there was one, of the nation-state has now run its course. For Buber, edification of global society therefore depends upon the development of new social structures which emphasise the primacy of relation and the fundamental unity of all humanity.

The conception of a global commonwealth, which 'will never build itself up out of individuals but only out of small and ever smaller communities', illustrates how the primal reality of the I-You relation exists, not in the subjects of the relation themselves, the I and the You, but rather, in the relation itself between them.[72] The same goes for the individual and the community, the true starting point for an understanding of both lies in the relation that occurs between them. In this way, just as the primal reality is represented by relation, so it is upon true I-You relationships that Buberian community is built.[73]

The Between

It is important to note that the above consideration of the relation 'between them' does not refer to Buber's concept of the 'between' which recognizes a quality in the interpersonal that belongs specifically to the sphere of the I-You relation. As recognized by Avnon,[74] this subtlety has been frequently misunderstood, not least in the interpretation of Buber's thought by Emmanuel Levinas.[75] Buber remarks that,

> The fundamental fact of human existence is neither the individual as such nor the aggregate [community] as such. Each, considered

by itself, is a mighty abstraction. The individual is a fact of existence in so far as he steps into a living relation with other individuals. The aggregate is a fact of existence in so far as it is built up of living units of relation. The fundamental fact of human existence is man with man. What is peculiarly characteristic of the human world is above all that something takes place between one being and another the like of which can be found nowhere [else] in nature. Language is only a sign and a means for it...[76]

The above, in addition to explaining Buber's position vis-à-vis the individual, community, and the relation between them, serves to clarify his position with regard to language, 'a sign and a means' of relation, and dialogue. While language is clearly a significant aspect of Buber's thought, it is relation and dialogue which hold centre stage.[77] As was made clear during consideration of the conscious 'I', while language constitutes an important aspect of relation and dialogue both can themselves occur without the use of language in its form as the spoken word. The evolution of the child and its pre-linguistic relation to, and dialogue with, its surroundings serve to illustrate this point.

In this way, while relation between people is the 'fundamental fact of human existence', Buber recognised the importance of the spoken form of language in facilitating relation though remained, according to Laurence Silberstein, sceptical of its arbitrary nature and its 'inadequacy in communicating human experience.'[78] Buber is insistent that the linguistic 'form of the words proves nothing' in the sense that when 'You' is said an 'It' is frequently being referred to. Likewise, when 'It' is said one is often referring to a 'You'.[79] It is because spoken language can be misleading in this way that Buber was at pains to emphasise the quality of physical relation and the unspoken aspect of dialogue that occurs between two people, and the attitude which is adopted toward the other, prior to the words used in communication.

The Eternal You

Despite the fact that this work is primarily interested in the sociological implications of his corpus, it is not possible to fully understand Buber's thought without reference to the eternal You which is perceived as the ultimate foundation for human relation. In this sense, it is the eternal You which provides the ultimate meaning for existence.[80] Though Buber was clear that there is no cogent proof for the existence of the eternal You or, as the phenomena may also be called, God, being, or the primal force of creation, he needed to elaborate his interpretation of the eternal You insofar as this was necessary for an understanding of his emphasis on the primacy and edifying qualities of true human relation. Since, as Dan Avnon remarks, 'the heart of Buber's philosophizing' is the 'distancing of self from the foundation of its being through the misplaced identification of self as thought (or as the images associated with and sustained by thought)',[81] it is clear that Buber owed his readers some explanation of what this foundation of being, the eternal You, might be.

Buber wrote that every I-You relation is a glimpse of the eternal You which can never itself become an It. While each individual I-You relationship reverts once again to It, the eternal You remains forever You.[82] God, says Buber, 'is that Being that is directly, most nearly, and lastingly, over against us, that may properly only be addressed, not expressed.'[83] Buber's insistence that the eternal You may only be 'addressed, not expressed' illustrates his fear that people feel a need to talk about the eternal You and experience God, as one would an 'It' in the hope of 'objective' knowledge, rather than enter into relation. This sentiment that people think about experiencing, rather than entering into relation with, the eternal You led him to suggest that '[i]f to believe in God means to be able to talk about him in the third person, then I do not believe in God. If to believe in him means to be able to talk to him, then I believe in God.'[84] It is because Buber's work considers God only in his relation to man that Buber refers to God as the eternal You, in other words, as relation.[85] The description of God as the eternal You, as a person, thus draws our attention to Buber's desire that God be considered only insofar as he represents the primacy of human relation. In this sense, man must approach the eternal You by 'becoming human'.[86] It is therefore wrong to view as religious the person who attempts to relate exclusively to God or who unerringly follows a religion's laws at the expense of true relation to his or her fellow human beings. To be religious is to 'become human' in true relation with one's fellow men and the eternal You.

In terms of 'becoming human' by approaching the eternal You, Buber suggests that it is a global human community or 'community of the human race' that would be worthy of God's countenance.[87] This conception of how it is only a global fellowship of humankind that may enter into true relation with the eternal You explains Buber's desire that conflict-causing identities and social structures in global society should be overcome in the knowledge that relation is the true ground of human existence. Such fellowship would value cultural difference insofar as it enriches this conception of global community but not to the extent that it serves as justification for physical conflict and aggression.

Existential Mistrust

Buber describes how, in the absence of genuine relation, human beings turn in one of two false directions, either inward in the search for self-affirmation of the Kierkegaardian variety or outward by immersing themselves in the seeming security of the collective, nation, or state. 'Individualism' and 'collectivism' are thereby criticized insofar as they prevent the development of true responsibility and genuine relation with one's fellow human beings.[88] Collectivism, for Buber, is typical of the modern age in the sense that it gives the appearance but not the reality of genuine relation.[89] In effect, humanity gives up true dialogical relations in the vain search for refuge and the illusory confirmation provided either by the self or by reified social structures. Buber illustrates, however, that the only lasting achievement of this circular reification is 'existential mistrust' of oneself, one's fellow human beings, and ultimately existence in general.[90] In the attempt to combat the prevalence of existential mistrust in modern society, Buber's post-I and Thou thought represents the idea that it is only those who are able to overcome mistrust in themselves and subsequently recognise the other in his or her primal reality as a human being, that is without any preconceptions about his or her background, who may re-establish genuine fellowship between men.[91]

When a plurality of different social groups, communities, nations, or states each seek refuge in the illusory security of the particular subjective values closest to them this multiplicity of reified securities inevitably leads to a feeling of general insecurity and existential mistrust in the relations between them. The 'other' group immediately puts one's own subjective, but apparently concrete, values into question. With reference to this multiplicity of subjective insecurities and in clear criticism of Hegel's 'absolute' conception of the state, Buber asks, '[b]ut how does it happen at all that the state can everywhere be absolutized when it exists in fact only in the plural, as 'the states,' each of them being continually reminded of its relativity through the existence of the others?'[92]

The question which these observations raise is whether the human need to belong to a particular group or culture may be reconciled with the attempt to encompass, and so create a fellowship of, all humanity. Since the capacity for devotion among human beings tends currently, with some exceptions, to stop at the level of the nation-state, this raises some very important questions about the potential for global social improvement. Is 'it the case that we can only escape the Hobbesian state of nature *nationally* (domestically)?' Further, can we do so 'only if the Hobbesian state of nature continues to exist *internationally?*' Finally, are 'ethnocentrism, racism, genocide, and war *necessary* parts of the price we pay for internal peace?'[93] Clearly Buber believed that not all of these conflicts are *'necessary'*.

Buber's meliorism resulted from his recognition that there is no such thing as a perfect society free of alienation, injustice and conflict. Such phenomena are inherent in social life and, as with the continual recurrence of I-It relationships, they are ever-present factors with which humankind must contend. Thus, insisting on a gradualist and peaceful approach to social renewal and the improvement of everyday relationships, Buber had to content himself with constantly reiterating the potential in humankind for the re-creation of genuine relation and community.[94]

Freedom Through Responsibility and Decision

For Buber, personal freedom and the ability to improve society are based upon decision and the avoidance of fatalism. Personal responsibility and the courage to make decisions underlie Buber's message. In their absence, so-called 'historical necessity' prevails. Buber argues that courage requires trust in the edifying nature of true human relation.[95] Recognizing the effects of social conditioning over time, Buber writes that it becomes evermore difficult 'to penetrate the increasingly tough layer' which hides humankind's true relation to being.[96]

For Buber, man is not naturally violent; violence and evil are the result of a particular attitude to reality.[97] Man, for Buber, is 'in an eminent sense good-and-evil' possessing a fundamentally twofold attitude to existence.[98] Evil is understood both as an absence of direction, in terms of 'directionlessness and decisionlessness', and as an absence of relation.[99] Relation and direction are therefore identified as being different aspects of the same reality. Human guilt is the result of an individual's perhaps unconscious awareness that he or she has failed to take the direction toward genuine relation with both humanity and the eternal-You.[100] Buber thus proposes that '[o]riginal guilt consists in remaining with oneself.'[101]

Returning to the notion of evil, for Buber no human being is either simply good or simply bad. It is man's very freedom to do evil that concomitantly enables him to redeem this evil by doing good.[102] Buber is clear that while all human beings share the capacity to decide against doing evil, it is not possible to be entirely good since humankind cannot presently be completely free from 'impulses of the passion.'[103] The recognition that humankind cannot escape entirely from 'impulses of the passion' illustrates how Buber's work is not a utopian plan for perpetual peace but rather a melioristic message as to how human society may be improved for the better.[104] Buber's work serves to illustrate how the good in society may be increased when human beings assume personal responsibility for creating true relationship in an effort to limit the potential evil which results when 'impulses of the passion' are not consciously refrained.

Buber's idea of an 'increasingly tough layer' which obstructs humankind from its true relation to existence thus provides a metaphor for the reifying effects of social conditioning over time and seems equally pertinent both to individual human beings and to the societies of which they are part. In this sense, a young child, who is less socially conditioned than adults from the same community, encounters less obstruction to what Buber locates as the true meaning of human being, namely relation. As a child grows older, he or she becomes ever more influenced by the norms and historical necessities of a particular society and therefore finds it increasingly difficult to locate humankind's true relation to being. Buber insists nevertheless that 'man as man' may yet redeem himself and it is for this reason that he placed such great emphasis in his work upon the role of education in society.[105] The true meaning of human existence may still be located by all human beings however 'natural' the norms of society have come to appear over time; it simply requires ever more effort since the layer of social conditioning that must be penetrated becomes increasingly tough.

The above analogy may also be applied to society. In temporal terms, the longer a particular norm has endured in society, the more 'natural' it will appear as an element of social life and the more difficult it will become to question its validity. In this sense, Buber's 'increasingly tough layer' serves not only to obstruct recognition of humankind's true relation to being but also to protect so-called 'historical necessity' from critique. It is due to the protection provided for historical social norms by the forces of social conditioning that Buber repeatedly draws attention to the need for personal

responsibility and the courage of decision in questioning the necessity
of preconceived opinions and social structures which frequently serve
as obstructions to humanity's true relation to existence. Yet again, it is
education which for Buber plays an important role in developing the
'creative powers' in human beings who may thereby learn to question
the (un)desirability of so-called historical necessities in society.[106]

The Melioration of Global Society

For Buber, what is crucial in terms of the edification of society is that
individuals are not deterred from assuming their role in social life due
to the present social and political conditions. Viewed as mere
reifications of subjective thought, human beings should not be
overawed at the idea of questioning historical necessities and societal
norms. In this vein, Buber suggests that the aim of the 'body politic...
[is] to realize in its genuine formations men's turning to one another in
the context of creation. The false formations distort but they cannot
eliminate the eternal origin'.[107]

Far from ignoring the political realm, Buber recognized its
importance in the social life of human beings. However, while accepting
the need for political institutions in society he wished to draw people's
attention toward the undesirable consequences of instances in which the
social sphere in society is weakened and thereby dominated by the
political.[108] Buber's writings suggest that the political realm should be
attuned to the harmonious needs of a global community of humanity
rather than to the justification and perpetuation of conflict-causing
fragmentation and division which frequently results between
contending nation-states. Avnon suggests that for Buber, '[t]he ultimate
goal of societal relations is the transformation of the person so that he
or she may participate in the meeting of fellowship and spirituality,
granted expression in conventional concepts – religion and socialism –
that are infused with new meaning. Only communities established with
this goal in mind stand a chance of developing into real expressions of
human fellowship.'[109]

Since Buber was emphatic that there is no objective proof of the
eternal You or of the I-You relation, all attempts to translate his insights
into rational discourse must fail.[110] It is clearly only belief or experience
that can support his suggestions. As Buber observes, if objective proof
of the eternal You did exist then, 'there would no longer be any
difference between belief and unbelief; the risk of faith would no
longer exist.'[111] Buber wrote on this issue that,

I give no guarantees, I have no security to offer. But I also demand of no one that he believe. I communicate my own experience of faith, just as well as I can, and I appeal to the experiences of faith of those whom I address. To those who have none, or imagine they have none, I recommend only that they do not armor their souls with preconceived opinions [and reifications]. I turn to those readers who either know from their own experience that of which I speak or are ready to learn it from their own experience. The others I must leave unsatisfied, and content myself with that.[112]

ACKNOWLEDGEMENT

The author wishes to thank Sasson Sofer, Dan Avnon and Sabine David for their comments on an earlier draft of this paper.

NOTES

1. In addition to the timely message which Buber's ideas contain *vis-à-vis* humanity's 'ontological crisis', a reintroduction of his thought is considered important following a recent article which ignored the fundamental importance of ontological issues in his work. See Daniel Warner, 'Levinas, Buber and the Concept of Otherness in International Relations: A Reply to David Campbell', *Millennium: Journal of International Studies* (Vol.25,No.1, 1996), p.112. 'Their [Buber's and Levinas'] primary concern is not with questions of ontology or Being, but with the space and character of interpersonality, and the ensuing responsibility.' Though not suggesting that ontological issues of being necessarily constitute the 'primary' concern in Buber's corpus, it is here argued that a prior understanding of Buberian ontology and its position *vis-à-vis* the dominant interpretation of Descartes' view is crucial to a comprehensive understanding of his message pertaining to humankind's 'postmodern condition'. For Buber's own view of the message represented in his work, a topic to be considered later in this study, see Martin Buber, 'Replies to My Critics', in Paul A. Schilpp and Maurice Friedman (eds.), *The Philosophy of Martin Buber* (La Salle, Illinois: Open Court Publishing, 1967), pp.692–3.
2. Dan Avnon, *Martin Buber: The Hidden Dialogue* (Lanham, Maryland: Rowman & Littlefield, 1998), pp.131–8.
3. As explained by Laurence Silberstein, 'The category of misreading, formulated by such contemporary literary critics as Paul de Man and Harold Bloom, refers to the fact that any act of reading is necessarily an interpretive act, and that one can never simply replicate a meaning that supposedly inheres in a text. It is related to Nietzsche's observation: 'No. Facts is precisely what there is not, only interpretations' (Nietzsche, *Will to Power*, 267)... The idea of 'strong misreading' and 'creative misreading' is argued by Harold Bloom... 'A strong reading can be defined as one that itself produces other readings' (Bloom, *Kabbalah*, 97)... [Richard] Rorty provides a philosophical context for the difference between 'strong

reading' and 'weak reading'... Referring to Bloom, Rorty describes strong
misreading as occurring when 'the critic asks neither the author nor the text about
their intentions but simply beats the text into a shape that will serve his purpose.
He does this by imposing a vocabulary – a 'grid', in Foucault's terminology – on the text
which may have nothing to do with any vocabulary used in the text or by its author,
and seeing what happens' (Rorty, *Consequences*, 151).' Laurence J. Silberstein,
Martin Buber's Social and Religious Thought: Alienation and the Quest for Meaning
(New York: New York University Press, 1989), pp. 276-277, note 2. See also,
Friedrich Nietzsche, *The Will to Power*, ed. and trans. Walter Kaufmann and R. J.
Hollingdale (New York: Random House, Vintage Books, 1967). Harold Bloom,
Kabbalah and Criticism (New York: Continuum, 1983). Richard Rorty,
Consequences of Pragmatism (Minneapolis: University of Minnesota Press, 1982).

4. Avnon, Martin Buber: *The Hidden Dialogue*, p.10.

5. Steven Kepnes, *The Text as Thou: Martin Buber's Dialogical Hermeneutics and
Narrative Theology* (Bloomington, Indiana: Indiana University Press, 1992), p.150.

6. Martin Buber, *I and Thou*, trans. Ronald Gregor Smith (Edinburgh: T&T Clark,
1994). There are two translations into English of I and Thou. The first is Smith's
which was first printed in 1937. The second is by Walter Kaufmann, *I and Thou*
(New York: Charles Scribner's Sons, 1970). Kaufmann replaced 'Thou' with 'You' in
the text as a result of the former word's formal and theological implications. For
Kaufmann's comment see his edition of I and Thou, pp.14–15. This work adopts
Kaufmann's alteration of the Thou since it seems to better represent the significance
of Buber's corpus. However, references in this work are to the original Smith
translation which, it is felt, is sensitive to Buber in other ways. Since Buber's work
was already well known, Kaufmann left the book's title unchanged.

7. J. F. Lyotard, *The Postmodern Condition: A Report on Knowledge*, trans. G.
Bennington and B. Massumi (Manchester: Manchester University Press, 1986).

8. Avnon, *Martin Buber: The Hidden Dialogue*, p.132.

9. Tom Rockmore, *Heidegger and French Philosophy: Humanism, antihumanism and
being* (London: Routledge, 1995), pp.6–8.

10. Martin Buber, *Eclipse of God: Studies in the Relation between Religion and
Philosophy* (New York: Harper & Brothers, 1952), p.28.

11. Rockmore, *Heidegger and French Philosophy*, p.9.

12. See Norman Hampson, *The Enlightenment: An evaluation of its assumptions
attitudes and values* (London: Penguin Books, 1990), pp.18–19 and 27–9. Hampson
notes that both 'Descartes and Spinoza were devout men who considered their
reason as enlisted in the service of God. The Roman Church put all Descartes' works
on the Index of prohibited books, but his influence permeated much of Christian
Europe to an extent that would have been impossible if he had been an adversary of
the faith.' p.29.

13. Rene Descartes, *The Philosophical Works of Descartes, Vol. 1*, ed. and trans.
Elizabeth S. Haldane and G. R. T. Ross (Cambridge: Cambridge University Press,
1970), p.105. Cited in Rockmore, *Heidegger and French Philosophy*, pp.193–4, note
40.

14. Descartes, *The Philosophical Works, Vol. 1*, p.224. Cited in Rockmore, *Heidegger
and French Philosophy*, p. 193, note. 38.

15. Jean-Luc Marion, *Questions Cartesiennes* (Paris: Presses Universitaires de France,
1991). See the chapter entitled 'L' argument releve-t-il de l'ontologie?', pp.221–58.

16. Hampson, *The Enlightenment*, p.28. Hampson notes that, 'Descartes, in his
revolutionary *Discourse*, announced his intention of beginning by accepting nothing
as true unless he himself had a clear and distinct perception of its veracity. What
mattered to the defenders of orthodoxy was not the motivation of the philosophers,

most of them – with the conspicuous exception of Hobbes – devout men who aspired to glorify God in their own way. From the viewpoint of the Christian churches their dismissal of the authority of the past was likely to bring down upon them the fate of Lucifer, as they presumed to weigh eternal truth in the balance of their own judgement. Such fears were, in fact, well-founded.'

17. Rockmore, *Heidegger and French Philosophy*, p.42.
18. Descartes, *The Philosophical Works, Vol. 1*, p.101. Descartes' emphasis. Cited in Rockmore, *Heidegger and French Philosophy*, p.43.
19. For a discussion of Buber's optimism despite numerous setbacks in life see Kepnes, *The Text as Thou*, p.140.
20. Buber suggests that his particular form of socialism 'is not a perfectionist but a meliorist one; what is decisive is what shall be and remain the *direction* of the always renewed melioration, ever adapting itself to the new historical conditions.' Sydney and Beatrice Rome (eds.), *Philosophical Interrogations: Interrogations of Martin Buber, John Wild, Jean Wahl, Brand Blanshard, Paul Weiss, Charles Hartshorne, Paul Tillich* (New York: Holt, Rinehart and Winston, 1964), p.76. In other words, Buber's meliorist vision is one that suggests that the constant requestioning of so-called historical necessities is required in order to retrieve true human relationships in the (re)construction of community. Buber recommends only that people 'do not armor their souls with preconceived opinions [and reifications]' in the hope that they will thereby locate the true value of human life in relation with their fellow men. Ibid., p.96.
21. Peter A. Bertocci, in Rome and Rome, *Philosophical Interrogations*, p.42. Buber (pp.43–5) subsequently criticizes Bertocci's misunderstanding of his thought. However, Bertocci's remark about Buber's desire to avoid some sort of totalitarian unity devoid of difference appears to constitute a fair reading of Buber's ideas.
22. Walter Goldstein, in Rome and Rome, *Philosophical Interrogations*, p.113.
23. R. B. J. Walker, *Inside/Outside: International Relations as Political Theory* (Cambridge: Cambridge University Press, 1993), p.64. For a discussion of the sovereign state as an exclusionary discourse see Richard Devetak, 'Postmodernism', in Scott Burchill and Andrew Linklater (eds.), *Theories of International Relations* (London: Macmillan Press, 1996), pp.179–209.
24. See Martin Buber, 'Replies to My Critics', in Paul A. Schilpp and Maurice Friedman (eds.), *The Philosophy of Martin Buber* (La Salle, Illinois: Open Court Publishing, 1967), pp.692–3.
25. See Martin Buber, *Pointing the Way: Collected Essays*, ed. and trans. by Maurice Friedman (New York: Harper Torchbooks, 1963).
26. Richard Rorty, *Philosophy and the Mirror of Nature* (New Jersey: Princeton University Press, 1979), p.12. See also Silberstein, *Martin Buber's Social and Religious Thought*, pp.10–13.
27. Rorty, *Philosophy and the Mirror of Nature*, p.361.
28. See Silberstein, *Martin Buber's Social and Religious Thought*, pp.104–7.
29. Buber's critique of Descartes goes as follows. 'When we hear him [Descartes] talk in the first person, we feel as if we were hearing the voice of direct personal experience. But it is not so. The I in the Cartesian *ego cogito* is not the living, body-soul person whose corporality had just been disregarded by Descartes as being a matter of doubt. It is the subject of consciousness, supposedly the only function which belongs entirely to our nature. In lived concreteness, in which consciousness is the first violin but not the conductor, *this* ego is not present at all. *Ego cogito* means to Descartes, indeed, not simply 'I have consciousness,' but 'It is I who have consciousness.' *Ego cogito* is, therefore, the product of a triply abstracting reflexion. Reflexion, the 'bending back' of a person on himself, begins by extracting from what

is experienced in the concrete situation 'consciousness' (*cogitatio*), which is not as such experienced there at all. It then ascertains that a subject must belong to a consciousness and calls this subject 'I'. In the end, it identifies the person, this living body-soul person, with that 'I', that is, with the abstract and abstractly-produced subject of consciousness. Out of the 'That' of the concrete situation, which embraces perceiving and that which is perceived, conceiving and that which is conceived, thinking and that which is thought, arises, to begin with, an 'I think that.' A subject thinks this object. Then the really indispensable 'That' (or Something or It) is omitted. Now we reach the statement of the person about himself: therefore I (no longer the subject, but the living person who speaks to us) have real existence; for this existence is involved in that *ego*... In this way Descartes sought through the method of abstraction to capture the concrete starting-point as knowledge, but in vain. Not through such a deduction but only through genuine intercourse with a Thou can the I of the living person be experienced as existing. The concrete, from which all philosophizing starts, cannot again be reached by way of philosophical abstraction; it is irrevocable.' Buber, *Eclipse of God*, pp.54–6.

30. Avnon, *Martin Buber: The Hidden Dialogue*, p.134.
31. Descartes, *The Philosophical Works, Vol. 1*, p.101. Descartes' emphasis. Cited in Rockmore, *Heidegger and French Philosophy*, p.43.
32. See George Herbert Mead, *Mind, Self and Society* (Chicago: University of Chicago Press, 1934). G. H. Mead, *Selected Writings*, ed. Andrew Reck (Chicago: University of Chicago Press, 1964). Jurgen Habermas, 'Individuation through Socialization: On George Herbert Mead's Theory of Subjectivity', in *Postmetaphysical Thinking: Philosophical Essays*, trans. William Mark Hohengarten (Massachusetts: MIT Press, Cambridge, 1992, pp.149–204). Paul E. Pfuetze, 'Martin Buber and American Pragmatism', in *The Philosophy of Martin Buber*, pp.511–42.
33. Buber, *I and Thou*, p. 16, pp.32, and 44.
34. Ibid., pp.36–9.
35. Ibid., p.40. See also p.46. Buber states, 'The man who has become conscious of I, that is, the man who says I-It...'
36. Buber, *The Philosophy of Martin Buber*, pp. 692-693.
37. Buber, *I and Thou*, p.40.
38. Ibid., pp.40–41.
39. With reference to the spiritual element in his ideas, Buber expresses his feelings with regard to the focus of his life's work as follows. 'If I myself should designate something as the 'central portion of my life work,' then it could not be anything individual, but only the one basic insight that has led me not only to the study of the Bible, as to the study of Hasidism, but also to an independent philosophical presentation: that the I-Thou relation to God and the I-Thou relation to one's fellow man are at bottom related to each other. This being related to each other is – if I may retain the expression – the central portion of the dialogical reality that has ever more disclosed itself to me. All my work on the Bible has ultimately served this insight...' Rome and Rome, *Philosophical Interrogations*, pp.99–100.
40. Buber, *I and Thou*, pp.42–3.
41. Avnon, *Martin Buber: The Hidden Dialogue*, p.9.
42. See Seyla Benhabib, *Critique, Norm and Utopia: A Study of the Foundations of Critical Theory* (New York: Columbia University Press, 1986), Chapter 5, 'The Critique of Instrumental Reason'.
43. Buber, *I and Thou*, p.15.
44. Ibid., p.32. Buber continues, 'except that situations do not always follow one another in clear succession, but often there is a happening profoundly twofold, confusedly entangled.'

45. Ibid., p.52.
46. Ibid., p.55.
47. This approach to Buber is supported by his statement that the 'central portion' of his life's work was a concern with the understanding that 'the I-Thou relation to God [Being] and the I-Thou relation to one's fellow man are at bottom related to each other'. Rome and Rome, *Philosophical Interrogations*, pp.99–100.
48. Benedict Anderson, *Imagined Communities: Reflections on the Origin and Spread of Nationalism* (London: Verso, 1991).
49. Buber, *I and Thou*, pp.15–16. See also Avnon, *Martin Buber: The Hidden Dialogue*, pp.39–41.
50. Ibid., p.85.
51. See Laurence Silberstein, *Martin Buber's Social and Religious Thought*, pp.127–8.
52. Maurice Friedman, 'Introductory Essay' to Martin Buber, *The Knowledge of Man: Selected Essays*, ed. Maurice Friedman (New Jersey: Humanities Press International, 1988), p.2.
53. Buber, *I and Thou*, p.40.
54. Ibid., p.86.
55. Ibid., p.40.
56. Buber, *The Knowledge of Man*, p.2.
57. Buber, *The Knowledge of Man*, p.50.
58. Buber, *I and Thou*, p.31.
59. Avnon, *Martin Buber: The Hidden Dialogue*, p.41.
60. Buber, *Philosophical Interrogations*, p.36.
61. Buber, *I and Thou*, p.52.
62. Ibid., p.85.
63. Avnon, *Martin Buber: The Hidden Dialogue*, p.152.
64. Buber, *I and Thou*, p.88.
65. Ibid.
66. Ibid.
67. Avnon, *Martin Buber: The Hidden Dialogue*, p. 154.
68. Martin Buber, 'The Spirit of Israel and the World of Today', in *Israel and the World: Essays in a Time of Crisis* (New York: Schocken Books, 1973), pp.183–94.
69. Avnon, *Martin Buber: The Hidden Dialogue*, p.154.
70. Martin Buber, *Paths in Utopia*, trans. R. F. C. Hull (London: Routledge and Kegan Paul, 1949), p. 136. Buber writes, 'An organic commonwealth – and only such commonwealths can join together to form a shapely and articulated race of men – will never build itself up out of individuals but only out of small and ever smaller communities: a nation is a community to the degree that it is a community of communities.' See also Rome and Rome, *Philosophical Interrogations*, p.71.
71. Rome and Rome, *Philosophical Interrogations*, pp.73–4.
72. Buber, *Paths in Utopia*, p.136. See also Avnon, *Martin Buber: The Hidden Dialogue*, p.153.
73. See Martin Buber, 'Nationalism', in *Israel and the World*, pp.214–26.
74. Avnon, *Martin Buber: The Hidden Dialogue*, p.39.
75. See Rome and Rome, *Philosophical Interrogations*, p.27.
76. Martin Buber, *Between Man and Man*, trans. Ronald Gregor Smith (London: Collins, Fontana Library, 1961), p.244.
77. Laurence Silberstein draws attention to the fact that, 'Although scholars such as Friedman and Horowitz speak of *I and Thou* as a philosophy of dialogue, this is not precise... The term *dialogue*... does not occur in *I and Thou*... The concept of dialogue... does not become central to Buber's writings until several years later... In contrast to the categories I-You and I-It, Buber's discussion of dialogue places greater

emphasis on action and movement.' Silberstein, *Martin Buber's Social and Religious Thought*, p. 305 note 7, p. 298 note 26, p. 143. Unlike Silberstein who traces the development of Buber's ideas, the present study refers simply to Buber's post- I and Thou thought thereby including consideration of both relation and dialogue as central elements in Buber's work.

78. Ibid., pp.299–300, note 37.
79. Buber, *I and Thou*, p.84.
80. See Silberstein, *Martin Buber's Social and Religious Thought*, p.220.
81. Avnon, *Martin Buber: The Hidden Dialogue*, pp.136–7.
82. Buber, *I and Thou*, p.99.
83. Ibid., pp.105–6.
84. Buber, *The Philosophy of Martin Buber*, p.24.
85. Buber, *I and Thou*, p.167. See also Rome and Rome, *Philosophical Interrogations*, p.91. Buber writes, 'That I proceed just from the relation between God and man, when I speak of God as the absolute Person and the eternal Thou, I have stated many times, most explicitly in the concluding chapter of the Postscript to the second edition of *I and Thou*.'
86. Buber wrote that, 'Adam [man] cannot approach the divine by reaching beyond the human; he can approach him through becoming human. To become human is what he, this individual man, has been created for.' Cited in Avnon, *Martin Buber: The Hidden Dialogue*, p. 129.
87. Buber, 'Three Theses of a Religious Socialism', in *Pointing the Way*, pp.112–14. See also Avnon's discussion of this issue in Avnon, *Martin Buber: The Hidden Dialogue*, pp.170–74.
88. Buber, 'The Question to the Single One', in *Between Man and Man*, especially p.106.
89. Maurice S. Friedman, *Martin Buber: The Life of Dialogue* (Chicago: University of Chicago Press, 1976), pp.125–32.
90. Buber, 'Hope for this Hour', in *Pointing the Way*, pp.220–29.
91. Buber, *Pointing the Way*, p.221
92. Ibid., p.215.
93. Dennis J. D. Sandole, 'The Biological Basis of Needs in World Society: The Ultimate Micro-Macro Nexus', in John Burton (ed.), *Conflict: Human Needs Theory* (London: Macmillan, 1990), p.75.
94. See Silberstein, *Martin Buber's Social and Religious Thought*, pp.185 and 202. Silberstein quotes Buber as follows, 'I am very far from thinking that 'there can be an ideal dialogic relationship if one could only 'restructure society.'' I never thought an ideal dialogic relationship possible in our world as it is. I am a meliorist and not an idealist, and so I want only as much dialogic element as can be realized in human life here and now.' p.185 (In Rome and Rome, *Philosophical Interrogations*, p.79).
95. Rome and Rome, *Philosophical Interrogations*, p.63.
96. Buber, *The Knowledge of Man*, p.68.
97. Interestingly, with reference to Hobbes, Buber agrees that humankind requires protection from itself under the supervision of a political body or what Hobbes refers to as the 'Leviathan'. However, where the thought of the two differs dramatically is in Buber's insistence that the political body or 'Leviathan' in question should represent the needs of all humanity rather than certain reified sub-groups therein. See Thomas Hobbes, *Leviathan* (Harmondsworth: Penguin Classics, 1985). See also Buber's consideration of Hobbes in 'Society and the State', in *Pointing the Way*, pp. 161-176, particularly pp.167–8.
98. Rome and Rome, *Philosophical Interrogations*, p.114.
99. Ibid., p.111.
100. See Maurice Friedman, *Martin Buber: The Life of Dialogue*, pp.103–6.

101. Buber, *Between Man and Man*, p. 203.
102. See Maurice Friedman, *Martin Buber: The Life of Dialogue*, p.65.
103. Rome and Rome, *Philosophical Interrogations*, p.114.
104. Paul E. Pfuetze, to name but one, has located perfectionism, 'even utopianism', in Buber's understanding of man and society, specifically with reference to his optimistic treatment of the Israeli Kibbutzim. However, a clear distinction must be made between Buber's philosophy and his perhaps overly idealistic interpretation of actual historical events. It is arguably due to his idealistic understanding of events that his philosophy is unjustly thought of as being both perfectionist and utopian in content. Familiarity with Buber's understanding of human nature illustrate that this is not the case. ibid., pp.75–6.
105. Buber, *The Knowledge of Man*, p.68. See Buber, 'Education', in *Between Man and Man*, pp.109–31.
106. Buber, *Between Man and Man*, p.109.
107. Ibid., pp.82–3.
108. See Martin Buber, 'Society and the State' and 'The Validity and Limitation of the Political Principle', in *Pointing the Way*, pp.161–76 and 208–19.
109. Avnon, *Martin Buber: The Hidden Dialogue*, p.174.
110. See Silberstein, *Martin Buber's Social and Religious Thought*, pp.220–21.
111. Rome and Rome, *Philosophical Interrogations*, p.84.
112. Ibid., p.96.

6

Derrida and Friendship

FRED DALLMAYR

For a considerable time now friendship has been under siege. Over a period of many centuries, self has been steadily removed or distanced from other selves – with the result that ancient notions such as 'concord' (*homonoia*) or 'communion' (*consensio*) have been increasingly problematised, if not entirely eclipsed. Several factors have contributed to this process in western civilisation. The rise of Christianity introduced a strong vertical thrust into human orientation, that is, an accent on salvation or the 'man-God' relationship, sometimes to the detriment of inter-human bonds. Modern western philosophy (as articulated chiefly by Descartes) erected the thinking ego into a bulwark of inner self-certainty, a bulwark segregated from the 'external' world comprising both nature and other selves. Subsequent liberal theory, from Thomas Hobbes to utilitarianism, placed the category of self-interest centre stage as the chief engine in politics and market economics, despite occasional (and narrowly circumscribed) concessions to inter-human sympathy and fairness. Even Kantian philosophy (arguably the noblest form of modern liberalism) sidelined or downgraded friendship and affection in favour of impartial rules of justice and the demand for rational respect. The same weighting of accents still continues in the most prominent western ideology or paradigm today, that is, procedural democracy – a paradigm privileging abstract and neutrally administered procedures over concerns with inter-human sympathy and lateral solidarity.[1]

The plight of friendship is particularly manifest in the area of (what is called) civic or political friendship. In classical philosophy, as articulated chiefly by Aristotle, friendship was treated as the ethical bond holding together a city or public regime, while its decay was seen as the harbinger of civil war or tyranny, or both. Adapting this thought to a specifically republican constitution, Cicero extolled the political significance of friendship, while simultaneously castigating a Stoic retreat into solitude as irresponsible and careless (devoid of *cura*). Here again, Christian theology brought serious complications. Although valuable as an antidote to corrupt politics, St Augustine's distinction between two cities also entailed a distinction between two kinds of citizenship and hence between two kinds of friendship: the one purely 'spiritual' and quasi-monastic, the other this-worldly and mainly defective or sinful.[2] Despite its secularising bent, modern philosophy largely preserved this division: namely, by further internalising and privatising friendship (and ethical life in general), while abandoning the public domain to the dictates of individual self-interest. Thus, while celebrating his intimate and 'perfect' friendship with Etienne de la Boëtie, Michel de Montaigne consigned social relations to the level of mere humdrum acquaintances, a level unable to generate genuine moral obligations. In a similar vein, though closer to a Kantian-style distance of respect, Ralph Waldo Emerson remarked a few centuries later: 'I chide society, I embrace solitude, and yet I am not so ungrateful as not to see the wise, the lovely, and the noble-minded as from time to time pass my gate,' and adding, 'In strictness, the soul does not respect men as it respects itself. In strict science all persons underlie the same condition of an infinite remoteness. ... What a perpetual disappointment is actual society, even of the virtuous and gifted!'[3]

The point here, to be sure, is not to relate a one-dimensional story of social decline, which would grossly truncate the intricate complexity of the process. The Christian, and later modern, turn to inwardness signalled also a deepening of human experience and of (what some call) personal 'authenticity'; as liberals are liable to stress, the same process also meant a growth of individual freedom, especially among previously submerged segments of the population. More importantly, the distantiation between human agents also entailed the possibility of a stronger recognition of the autonomy and separate integrity of other selves (although this point was hardly ignored by classical philosophical arguments). In the meantime, all these issues have gained a new and sharper profile through recent developments in western philosophy, especially by the stirring of self-critique occurring in the very bosom of modernist thought. In the wake of Husserl's relentless inquiries into self-other relations, a number of Continental thinkers have further problematised and 'decentred' the Cartesian ego (or subjectivity), thereby also placing friendship (including civil or political friendship) in a novel way on the intellectual agenda. Among these thinkers, Jacques Derrida deserves special attention, both because of his trenchant intellectual verve and because of his determined effort to rethink the meaning of friendship, including political friendship. The results of this rethinking have surfaced mainly in two texts: an essay entitled 'The Politics of Friendship' (1988) and a book-length study called *Politics of Friendship* (1994–97). In the interests of brevity and manageability, my focus will be placed here initially and mainly on Derrida's more succinct essay, although his longer book will also be invoked throughout in a supplementary fashion. In addition to the value of succinctness, the initial focus also allows me to comment on an instant rejoinder to the essay formulated by Thomas McCarthy. The presentation proceeds in three steps. While the first section recapitulates and gives a condensed overview of the main lines of argument of 'The Politics of Friendship', a second part recalls some of the central points of McCarthy's rejoinder (written largely from the vantage of Habermasian critical theory). By way of conclusion, I assess the cogency and significance of Derridean friendship in terms of both contemporary political philosophy and of political praxis.

I

Derrida opens his essay (and also his book) by citing an apocryphal statement attributed by Montaigne, without further reference, to Aristotle: 'O my friends, there is no friend.' The aporetic character of this statement (its invocation of friends whose lack is simultaneously affirmed) provides in many ways the keynote or tenor of the entire argument. In opening his argument with this phrase, one quickly detects, Derrida seeks to centre the light of attention not so much on its source, Aristotle, as rather on Montaigne, whom he describes as 'another reader of the country I come from'.[4] Apart from frequently repeating, almost ritualising, Montaigne's phrase or quotation, the essay in fact ascribes to Montaigne a pivotal role in the western understanding of friendship. This role emerges clearly toward the end of the essay, when Derrida offers what he calls a 'history of friendship' (to be sure, a history far removed from any traditional historicism). In many respects, this history resembles the sketch I offered at the beginning of these pages; but it also bears a distinctive Derridean imprint or trademark.

According to Derrida, the history of friendship gives evidence of 'two major ruptures' or transformative incisions. The first rupture occurred at the end or with the waning of the 'Graeco-Roman model', a model that Derrida describes as being shaped or marked 'by the value of *reciprocity*, by homological, immanentist, finitist, and politicist concord'. The post-classical incision is highlighted or exemplified by Montaigne who, despite certain borrowings from the past, 'breaks the reciprocity' of the classical model and 'discreetly introduces, so it seems to me, heterology, asymmetry, and infinity'. Derrida at this point raises some rhetorical questions (which seem to call for an affirmative response). 'Shall one say', he writes, 'that this fracture is Judaeo-Christian? Shall one say that it depoliticizes the Greek model or that it displaces the nature of the political?' A second fracture or rupture, the essay suggests, was introduced later by writers such as Nietzsche and Blanchot whose treatments of friendship 'defy both historicity and exemplarity'. In their diverse ways, these and other recent writers 'call the friend by a name that is no longer that of a neighbor, perhaps no longer that of a man'. Elaborating on the last part of this sentence, Derrida notes that the 'who?' of friendship now 'moves off into the distance beyond all these determinations'; in its 'infinite imminence', it exceeds 'the interest of knowledge, science, truth, proximity, even life and even the memory of life'. He also quotes Maurice Blanchot who, in an almost Emersonian vein, asserted that friendship involves 'the recognition of the common strangeness that does not allow us to speak of our friends but only to them' and that friends 'even in moments of the greatest familiarity keep their infinite distance'.[5]

Returning to the beginning and the opening phrase of Montaigne (quoting Aristotle), Derrida recalls the immediate occasion of his own essay: an address before a philosophical society to whose invitation he is responding (and whose members may in turn respond to him). Reflecting on this situational context, he asks whether this context has already any bearing on his chosen topic of friendship. 'Supposing', he states, 'that one can translate these Greek words today by "friendship", I still do not know if what exists between us is *philia* or *homonoia*, nor how one should distinguish here among us, among each of us, who together would compose this as yet quite indeterminate "us".' Remembering (or rather anticipating) the ending of his essay, one senses already that this contextual 'us' or 'we' is bound to be very complicated and elusive. Before sorting things out further, Derrida writes that in effect, 'we are already caught up in a kind of asymmetrical and heteronomical curvature of the social space, more precisely, in the relation to the Other prior to any organized *socius*, to any determined "government", to any "law"'. Distancing or 'rupturing' the classical Aristotelian legacy, Derrida here describes 'originary sociality' as a 'heteronomical and asymmetrical curvature', that is, as a relation which confounds and disrupts human autonomy and social reciprocity. Taking its bearings from some recent French literature, the essay does not hesitate to link this curvature with a kind of 'violence' or disruptive force, noting that what is happening is 'perhaps just the silent unfolding of that strange violence that has since forever insinuated itself into the origin of the most innocent experiences of friendship or justice'. What accounts for the violence or disjunction is the fact that sociality, in the sense of a responsibility to the Other (or to otherness), catches us unawares or by surprise, thus imposing on us a kind of 'responsibility without freedom' or autonomy. Derrida elaborates:

> This responsibility assigns us our freedom without leaving it with us, if one could put it that way. And we see it coming from the Other. It is assigned to us by the Other, from the Other, before any hope of reappropriation permits us to assume this responsibility in the space of what could be called *autonomy*.[6]

What emerges in these lines or arguments is the imposing influence of Emmanuel Levinas (whose name curiously remains unmentioned throughout the essay): all the key terms employed in the preceding passages, such as 'heteronomy', 'asymmetry' and responsibility instilled by the 'Other', are borrowed from the arsenal of Levinasian discourse (as articulated chiefly in *Totality and Infinity*). At issue here are the implications of this discourse for the theme of friendship – a point to which Derrida instantly turns. Reiterating his opening line, Derrida presents Montaigne's phrase as a kind of code-word or hidden passkey to his chosen theme. On the face of it, the phrase seems to be merely contradictory or to state a 'logical absurdity', namely, by joining a vocative apostrophe ('O my friends') with a predicative denial ('there is no friend'): 'The general truth of the *fact* would seem to contradict by an act the very possibility of the apostrophe, the possibility for it to be *serious*.' In an effort to unravel this paradox, Derrida construes the apostrophe and, indeed, the entire phrase as a transformative appeal or appellation, that is, an appeal calling forth a hidden potential: 'It resembles an appeal, because it makes a sign toward the future: be my friends, for I love or will love you. ... Accede to what is at the same time a desire, a request, a promise and, one could also add, a prayer' (where prayer means a performative utterance transgressing predication). Referring to the age-old quandary of whether friendship arises from insufficiency or completeness, Derrida resolutely opts for insufficiency and want: 'How could I give you my friendship where friendship would not be lacking, that is, if it already existed – more precisely, if the friend were not lacking?' Friendship here appears as a kind of transcendental-spiritual goal, and Derrida, in fact, speaks of the 'idea of friendship', of the 'ideality of its essence or telos' in the name of which we must conclude that, as yet, 'there is no friend'. Underscoring the futuristic eschatological accent of this outlook he insists: 'Friendship is never given in the present. It belongs to the experience of waiting, of promise, or of commitment' because its discourse 'is that of prayer and at issue there is that which responsibility opens to the future'.[7]

Yet, futurism does not fully exhaust the theme. Seemingly moving away or sideways from a Levinasian expectancy, Derrida also embeds friendship in an immemorial past. As he writes, 'the apostrophe "O my friends" turns us also toward the past'. It does so by alerting us to the 'always already' given presuppositions of being and discourse, by signalling toward that 'which must be supposed so as to let oneself be understood'. For Derrida, this presupposed matrix constitutes a kind of 'minimal friendship' or 'preliminary consent' without which people could not understand each other or be attentive to any appeal. As he elaborates:

> Without this absolute past, I could not, for my part, have addressed myself to you in this way. We would not be together in a sort of minimal community … speaking the same language or praying for translation within the horizon of the same language… if a *sort* of friendship had not already been sealed before any other contract: a friendship prior to friendships, an ineffaceable, fundamental, and bottomless friendship, the one that draws its breath in the sharing of a language (past or to come).

Remembering at this point the Aristotelian question of 'being' (*ti estin* or 'what is?'), a question vigorously and relentlessly renewed by Heidegger in our time, Derrida draws a parallel or connection between the fundamental questioning of 'philosophy' (rendered as the 'love of wisdom', *philein to sophon*) and friendship (*philia*): 'The very possibility of the question, in the form of "what is?", seems always to have presupposed this friendship prior to friendships, this *anterior* affirmation of being-together in the allocution.'[8]

In Derrida's presentation, however, this anterior affirmation (of minimal friendship) is not really operative or effective in the present, but rather strictly immemorial and hence inaccessible. As he insists, the affirmation 'cannot be *presented* as a being-present ... within the space of an ontology, precisely because it opens this space'. Hence, friendship construed both as futuristic promise and as immemorial past is not so much an actual experience, but rather a limit concept or an infinitely distant horizon. In fact, Derrida locates the 'very movement and time of friendship' in 'this surpassing of the present by the undeniable future anterior', a surpassing which opens up 'the absolute [vista] of an unpresentable past as well as future'. In this manner, the 'asymmetrical curvature' which was previously detected in Montaigne's phrase is now transferred or transcribed into an asymmetrical temporality which 'absolutely' privileges the future anterior and which envelops friendship within 'the performativity of a prayer'. To elucidate the character of this performativity, Derrida turns to the topic of 'response' and responsibility (a topic triggered by his own response to a professional invitation). Following again Levinas's lead, Derrida distinguishes between 'three modalities' of response: in the sense that one always answers 'for' oneself, 'to' a query or challenge, and 'before' a larger community or audience. As one can surmise, answering 'for oneself' does not imply here a Hegelian 'for-itself' and certainly not a self-identity or unity of the 'subject' which can never be secured 'as an empirical synthesis'; rather, it refers to the evocative quality of the 'proper name', an evocation which extends beyond self-presence and, in fact, 'beyond even life or presence in general'.[9]

The transgressive or transcendental quality of response is even more clearly evident in the other two modalities. 'Answering to' involves the need to answer to the 'Other', that is, to the Other's request, prayer, apostrophe or appeal. For Derrida, this need is primary and 'more original' than the other modalities chiefly for two reasons: first, because answering for oneself always occurs in response to the Other's challenge or insistence; and second, because even the proper name 'for' which one answers is always constituted (or co-constituted) by the Other. Hence, 'answering to' manifests the asymmetries noted above: it preserves the 'asymmetrical anteriority' even within the seemingly 'most inward and solitary autonomy of reserve', that is, in the heart of freedom. The third modality of 'answering before' inserts the second into a broader social context. In Derrida's account, 'answering before' indicates the passage to 'an institutional instance of alterity'; it is 'no longer singular, but is universal in its principle'. While 'answering to' refers to an Other who is singular and who 'must remain so' in a certain sense, 'answering before' places the response in relation to 'the law, a tribunal, a jury, some agency (instance) authorized to represent the Other legitimately, in the form of a moral, legal, or political community'. The source of this distinction is again unmistakable (though it remains again unnamed): it parallels directly Levinas's distinction between the singular encounter with the 'face' (of the Other) and the dimension of general or universal 'justice' in which the face is bracketed or submerged. Derrida's comments on the topic seem almost transcribed from Levinasian texts:

> Of these two dimensions of the relation to the Other, the one maintains the absolute singularity of the Other and of 'my' relation to the Other. ... But the relation to the Other also passes through the universality of the law. This discourse about universality which can find its determination in the regimes of morality, law, or politics, always appeals to a third party, beyond the face-to-face of singularities.[10]

Despite the clear division between the two dimensions (the stark opposition between singularity and universality), Derrida also acknowledges a certain interrelation or mutual implication of the two domains. In a move which perhaps oversteps the Levinasian model, he asks whether the two relations ('to' and 'before') do not 'imply each other at the moment they seem to exclude each other'? For does not the universality of the law in effect 'command me to recognize the transcendent alterity of the Other'? As it appears, however, the mutual implication of the two domains goes deeper than these comments suggest. The relation to the Other does not only 'pass through' the universality of the law, but shares with the latter a crucial trait: the remoteness of relationship (if that term is still applicable). Both the singular face-to-face and the general law are predicated not on close proximity or any kind of 'presence', but rather on respect, indeed, on the infinite distance of respect. Paraphrasing and in part modifying Kantian insights, Derrida describes answering 'to' and 'before' as 'two forms or two dimensions of the respect implied by any responsibility', a description which also carries over into the very 'heart of friendship'. One of the enigmas of friendship, he elaborates, 'comes from this distance or this respectful separation which distinguishes it, as a feeling, from love', and he calls at this point for 'a rigorous rereading of the Kantian analysis of respect in friendship', for 'there is no friendship without "respect of the Other"'.[11]

Venturing into broader historical-philosophical reflections, Derrida associates answering 'to' and 'before' with the legacy of traditional binaries or oppositions, such as those between singularity and universality, private and public, apolitical and political domains – oppositions which, in his view, have always divided 'the experience, the concept, and the interpretation of friendship'. On the one hand, he writes, from the angle of private singularity, friendship seems to be 'essentially foreign or unamenable to the res publica' and thus 'could not found a politics'. But, on the other hand, the 'great philosophical and canonical discourses on friendship', from Plato, Aristotle, and Cicero to Kant and Hegel, have tended to link friendship 'explicitly to virtue and to justice, to moral reason and to political reason'. Noting both the porousness and the remarkable resilience of traditional binaries, Derrida remarks that the latter tend to dominate 'the interpretation and the experience of friendship in our culture: a domination which is unstable and under internal stress, but therefore all the more imperious'. After providing some examples of the stubbornness and prejudicial character of traditional binaries (such as the exclusion of friendship between women and between man and woman), Derrida finally turns to the 'history of friendship' mentioned before, a history which revolves basically around a progressive rupturing and destabilisation of traditional models. To repeat the point made previously, the 'Graeco-Roman model' is portrayed as being marked specifically by reciprocity and the emphasis on politics ('politicist concord'), an emphasis which is later 'fractured' by Judaeo-Christian thought which 'depoliticizes the Greek model' or else 'displaces the nature of the political'. This displacement is continued and deepened by Montaigne in early modernity with his introduction of asymmetry and 'infinity', and later further radicalised by Nietzsche, Blanchot and others (presumably including Derrida) who call the friend by a name that is 'no longer that of the neighbor, perhaps no longer that of a man'.[12]

II

At the meeting of the particular philosophical society, Derrida's observations on responsiveness did not fall on deaf ears, but elicited instantly a response from one of its members, Thomas McCarthy. In his comments, McCarthy did indeed 'respond' to Derrida's address, though not by submitting simply to its appeal (or apostrophe), but by marshalling the resources of an alternative intellectual framework: that of modern critical reason. Basically, in terms of general orientation,

McCarthy was less intent on rupturing than on preserving a certain continuity of modern critical, especially Kantian, philosophy, though minus some of the latter's deeper 'metaphysical' premises. As he noted, Derrida's address exemplified a distinctive 'postmetaphysical' approach: one that enlists a 'deconstructive strategy' located 'at the level of metaphysics in order to disrupt and displace it'. By contrast, attention to recent sociology and critical theory yielded 'other, less metaphysically motivated, ways of thinking about social relations', possibly also about friendship. By pursuing this line of thought, it was possible to maintain critical alertness while avoiding deconstruction's rupturing bent. Hence, for McCarthy, a 'better way of being postmetaphysical in ethics, law, and politics' is to focus on concrete social relations and to 'stop doing metaphysics, even of a negative sort, when thinking about them'.[13]

Among recent social and critical theorists, McCarthy's response gave pride of place to George Herbert Mead and Habermas. Echoing distinctly Kantian teachings as filtered through Hegel's dialectics, Mead emphasised the parallelism of individual and society, and hence also of the processes of individuation and socialisation. To this extent, McCarthy was able to endorse (at least in part) Derrida's notion of a 'minimal friendship' or an immemorial insertion of humans in the 'curvature of social space' – a notion which seemed not so far removed from the phenomenological (and Habermasian) concept of the ordinary 'lifeworld'. However, contrary to Derrida's allegation, this lifeworld was not distantly recessed and unpresentable, but rather readily available in everyday life and continuously taken for granted; moreover, far from being elusive, it exhibited distinct structural features, including the features of an (embryonic) social agency and mutual accountability. As McCarthy writes (following Mead): 'At the level of our everyday interactions we normally believe ourselves to be, and take others as being, knowledgeable subjects confronted by real choices, for which we and they will be held accountable.' What is important to remember is that, for Mead, the network of social structures and expectations (what he called the 'generalized Other') was intimately connected with individuation or the rise of individual agency. Against this backdrop, Derrida's accent on 'asymmetry' was mistaken or at least greatly exaggerated, as was his emphasis on the disjunction between face-to-face relations and the universality of law. In McCarthy's words:

> It is not only in friendship, but in social interaction generally that the 'singularity of the Other' is intimately interconnected with

the 'generality of the law' (here: normative expectations). And although the individual is related 'asymmetrically' to the *generalized* Other, which is always 'anterior', the socially generalized patterns of behavior the latter comprises are themselves typically structured as relations of reciprocity with *individual* Others.[14]

Given this view of self-other relations, Meadian social theory could readily serve as a stepping-stone in the formulation of an ethical perspective, particularly one indebted to basic Kantian teachings. Strictly construed, McCarthy noted, the immemorial grounding or matrix of social ties should not be termed a 'minimal friendship' as rather a 'minimal ethics of reciprocity and accountability', one in which concern with personal integrity and identity is closely interwoven with the societal fabric of mutual recognition. This dual emphasis on individual dignity and societal norms has actually always been at the heart of 'traditional moralities', whose intuitive insights have been further refined and elaborated by modern philosophical ethics. In the Kantian tradition, in particular, respect for individual integrity has been grounded in the equal freedom or 'autonomy' of agents, while societal (and universalisable) morality has been tied to the 'impartiality of laws' which can be freely accepted by all participants. These Kantian accents have recently been both revived and reformulated by Habermas, who replaced Kant's 'noumenal' reflexivity with a stress on communicative rationality. Thus, in Habermasian discourse ethics, norms can be validated only by discursively testing their claims in the medium of the 'informed, uncoerced, reasoned agreement' of all individuals subject to their rule. In this (neo-Kantian) construal of the 'moral point of view', the principle of equal respect is reflected in the requirement of 'rationally motivated agreement' freely entered into by individual agents, while the concern for societal (and universalisable) norms is captured in the requirement of 'general and reciprocal perspective-taking' in which each agent takes 'the situations of others into account' and grants them 'equal weight'.[15]

Proceeding along these lines, McCarthy finds it possible to accommodate even one of Derrida's more unique and emphatic claims: that of the 'futurism' of friendships or the status of friendship as a future promise (encapsulated in Montaigne's apostrophe). Stripped of deconstructive hyperbole, the claim can readily be translated into the Kantian notion of a 'regulative idea' – a notion, he writes, that exhibits the same sort of 'promise' and 'responsibility to the future' that Derrida finds in 'friendships that are "the most perfect of their kind"'. In the Kantian tradition, regulative ideas are never fully actual and hence not 'present' or 're-presentable' in themselves; but they are effective in guiding our practices. In a similar vein, Habermasian communicative rationality is not empirically given, but must be 'counterfactually' assumed in the validation of moral standards. Summarising his observations, McCarthy locates the (limited) merit of Derrida's approach in its effort to counterbalance universalist abstractions, which are often 'unheeding of difference and in violation of singularity'; to this extent, Derridean thoughts on friendship provide 'an instructive antidote to the levelling, difference-denying tendencies of much moral and legal theory' (including the Kantian variety). Yet, properly construed, moral universalism (especially when couched as 'fairness') is necessarily also 'respectful of the Other and tolerant of difference', quite apart from the need to heed particular circumstances in the application of rules. Thus, even the limited benefits of Derridean deconstruction are in large part endemic to modern moral philosophy (reasonably interpreted); such benefits in any case cannot outweigh deconstruction's considerable disadvantages. The alternative outlook sketched in his rejoinder, McCarthy concludes, centres around the thesis that 'the curvature of social space' is not fundamentally 'asymmetrical and heteronomical' and that minimal friendship or 'originary sociality' is marked as well 'by relations of symmetry, reciprocity, and mutual recognition'. In any concrete social context, conduct of such relations belongs to 'the repertoire of competent social actors', which in turn implies an 'intuitive mastery of the moral point of view'.[16]

III

The above exchange of views (the sequence of 'response' and counter-response) is instructive and revealing in its profiled contrasts. In large measure, the encounter between McCarthy and Derrida illustrates and exemplifies the encounter between a basically 'modernist' perspective wedded to Kantian (or quasi-Kantian) premises and a loosely 'post-modern' or deconstructive outlook bent on rupturing these (and all other) premises. While demurring on the issue of metaphysics, McCarthy's arguments clearly preserve the continuity with earlier philosophical teachings; by contrast, Derridean formulations often are couched in a manner signalling a break with or exit from philosophical traditions. Despite their instructive counterpoint, however, the opposition of views is nevertheless circumscribed by several limiting factors. First of all, on a number of points, the two protagonists seemed to misunderstand or simply talk past each other. Thus, McCarthy's reference to individual integrity and its dialectical relation with generalised otherness (or normativity) seemed to bypass the Derridean (and Levinasian) meaning of 'singularity' – a term denoting a more radical uniqueness located beyond definition and hence also beyond the correlation of the particular and the universal. Likewise, McCarthy's invocation of the 'lifeworld' seemed to refer to a realm of mundane everydayness, a realm far removed from the original **arche-space** opened up by minimal friendship. Lastly, despite undeniable points of contact, the linkage between Derridean 'promise' and Kantian 'regulative ideas' should probably not be overstated. While Kantian ideas are postulates inherent in reason, Derrida's notion of promise or appeal appears to be more resolutely transgressive or eschatological in character, invoking coming events possibly located beyond reason.

Beyond such matters of detail, however, the encounter is circumscribed and limited by another factor: a subtle and nearly subterranean collusion of perspectives. As indicated above, both thinkers appeal explicitly and repeatedly to Kantian philosophy, though from different angles and for different purposes. McCarthy identifies morality, along Kantian lines, as the cultivation of 'equal respect for individuals' predicated on reciprocal autonomy. Derrida's essay places respect in the very heart of friendship, interpreting and equating respect with inter-human 'distance' or a 'respectful separation' sharply distinguished from 'love' as a feeling. Thus, both thinkers clearly pay tribute to the Kantian privileging of respect over feeling or sympathy, and both construe respect as a kind of goodwill across distance (in one case, between singularities, and in the other, between individual agents). This feature is closely linked with another, still more prominent collusion or convergence: their shared rejection or distantiation from the classical legacy, especially the Aristotelian conception of friendship as a social-political bond (*homonoia*) buttressing the common good. Habermas, whom McCarthy invokes, is well known for his dismissal of Aristotelian or neo-Aristotelian perspectives and for his staunch defence of the primacy of 'right over good' (that is, of moral principle over ethical goodness). Although acknowledging possible ties of fellowship or solidarity on the lifeworld level, such ties are entirely subsidiary to normative rightness and the operation of quasi-contractual public procedures. In turn, although quoting an apocryphal saying (reported by Montaigne), Derrida leaves no doubt about his critical stance toward Aristotle whose legacy represents for him pretty much the essence of western metaphysics. Thus, after citing (mostly without comment) some passages from *Nicomachean Ethics*, Derrida's essay concludes with his staccato narrative whose trajectory revolves basically around the rupturing exit from Greece and Rome. To repeat again the core of the indictment: the classical legacy is said to be marked 'by the value of reciprocity, by homological, immanentist, finitist, and politicist concord'.[17]

As illustrated by both critical theory and Derridean deconstruction, distantiation from Aristotle is surely a hallmark of modern western thought (since the time of Descartes and Hobbes), and unquestionably, his legacy is not immune from criticism or contestation. When, in the following, closer attention is given to Aristotle's arguments, the point is not to revive or rehabilitate his philosophy *in toto* or to endorse an Aristotelian orthodoxy, but simply to allow his voice to re-enter the dialogue about friendship, especially political friendship, on a more equal footing. As one may concede (and as I certainly would concede), there is probably no way in our time to embrace a full-fledged Aristotelian metaphysics, especially an emphatic notion of 'substance' or 'natural teleology'. On a political level, the same would hold for conceptions of commonality or the 'common good' seen as implying compact uniformity. Still, what seems questionable to me is that critique of Aristotle can proceed without close textual engagement, that is, through a simple mode of rupturing or exodus (presumably opening up a space 'outside' traditional philosophy). From this angle, Derrida's repeated invocation of his apocryphal motto seems at least puzzling, given the abundance of quotable phrases in Aristotle's available texts. Among many others, the following passage seems eminently worthy of reflection: 'If people are friends, they have no need of justice, but if they are just they need friendship in addition; and the justice that is most just seems to belong to friendship.'[18] Close exegesis of this and similar phrases might guard against reductionism and against a certain dismissive attitude prevalent in modern philosophy, and also in Derrida's rupturing indictment. For how, without reductive simplification, can one equate the classical legacy with such labels as 'homological, immanentist, finitist'? Clearly, terms such as 'immanentist' and 'finitist' bank on the metaphysical dichotomies between immanence and transcendence and between finitude (or totality) and infinity, dichotomies which, in Derrida's own account, were introduced by the 'Judaeo-Christian' rupturing of classical thought – with the result that the latter (antedating the rupturing) cannot possibly be identified with one side of these polar opposites. Only the imposition of later historical frameworks or 'pre-judgements' seems to allow the reduction of Greek thought to a simple unity (a unity which in any case is troubled by its Platonic strand).

Still more difficult and problematic is the ascription of 'homological' to classical thought – a term whose meaning is not further elaborated in the essay (beyond its counterposition to 'heterology'). Derrida's later book offers some clues regarding its sense or connotation. According to these hints, classical thought as a whole, and its conception of friendship in particular, approached everything from the vantage point of the self and, hence, invariably ended up by reducing the 'other' to sameness. This proclivity is said to be clearly evident in the case of Cicero, whose treatment of friendship, according to Derrida, 'leans sharply to one side – let us say *the same* side – rather than to the other – let us say *the other*' and who consequently reduced the friend to a replica of the self or to 'our own ideal image'. The discussion of Aristotle in the book is more roundabout and diffuse, but the finding is basically similar: by according primary emphasis to 'loving' over 'being loved', Aristotle is claimed (or intimated) to have incorporated the loved one into the inclination of the lover and hence to have truncated the calling or apostrophe of the 'other' in favour of the lover's activity (or *energeia*). Although posited as a premise of rupturing, this charge of 'homology' appears dubious and unpersuasive. What seems neglected in this charge is the self-transcending quality of friendship in classical thought: the aspect that real or 'complete' friendship means to love the other basically for the other's sake. This aspect is clearly underscored by Aristotle when he writes that 'those who wish good to their friend for the friend's sake are friends most of all; for they have this attitude because of (or for the sake of) the friend and not coincidentally'. Cicero seems to make a similar point when he comments that genuine friendship is to be desired not for any extraneous advantage, but 'because the whole of its profit consists in love only' and that those who only calculate their selfish utility 'are destitute of that most beautiful and most natural friendship which is desirable in itself and for its own sake'.[19]

Most problematic and difficult to disentangle is the charge of 'reciprocity' seen as a major failing of classical thought, standing in contrast to asymmetry and heteronomy. Here, one may note first of all a certain asymmetry or unevenness in Derrida's own presentation: namely, the disjunction between the 'asymmetrical curvature' of originary or immemorial sociality and the 'asymmetrical anteriority' of responsibility to the Other. Given that immemorial sociality (or friendship before friendship) seems to precede the very emergence of self and other, its asymmetry (if such it is) appears to be of a different sort than that between distinct singularities.[20] More important in the present context is the postulate of asymmetrical heteronomy viewed as basic moral yardstick. Although one may readily grant that the self is not 'self-constituting' in the sense of modern philosophy (from Descartes to Husserl), the turn to 'other-constitution' seems to perform a reversal fraught with equally troubling results. For one thing, the postulated primacy and anteriority of the 'Other' seems to reduce the self to a purely ancillary passivity – perhaps to passive subordination and even victimisation. On a more strictly philosophical plane, the very notion of the 'Other' and of the Other's radical 'exteriority' seems to presuppose, as its condition of possibility, the correlative notion of the self and the self's radical 'interiority' (a correlation only avoidable through a rupturing of sense). Thus, the radical turn to otherness seems to conjure up the very pitfall of self-enclosure which it is meant to redress. Some of these quandaries and concerns have been ably articulated by Paul Ricoeur in his *Oneself as Another*. There, addressing himself to Derrida's mentor, Ricoeur observes that Levinasian philosophy rests basically 'on the initiative of the other in the intersubjective relation' – an initiative which in effect 'establishes no relation at all, to the extent that the other represents absolute exteriority with respect to an ego defined by the condition of separation'. As he adds, the stress on heteronomy and anterior superiority seems to place the Other in the role of a 'master of justice', a master 'who instructs' and issues injunctions – thereby erecting a sharp and perhaps unbridgeable gulf 'between the reciprocity of friendship and the dissymmetry of the injunction'.[21]

Returning to classical thought, the 'charge' of reciprocity is of course undeniable, but it can be vindicated or defended on numerous grounds. According to Aristotle (as well as Cicero), friendship cannot simply be equated with unilateral goodwill or respect proceeding either from the self or the other; rather, it requires a mutuality of caring and affection of which friends are reciprocally aware. As Aristotle writes: 'Friendship is said to be reciprocated goodwill (*eunoia*). And perhaps we should add that friends are aware of the reciprocated goodwill.' Aristotle also adds that friendship usually involves a sharing of preferences as well as a sharing of practices or activities (a point to which I shall return later). The kind of distant respect extolled in Derrida's essay thus seems to fall short of friendship in several ways: apart from lacking the needed affection, respect can be extended to worthy people in far-off places and also to remote historical figures, with whom one could not claim to be linked through ties of friendship. The notion of reciprocity is also important for implying or suggesting a measure of equality among friends, although such equality should by no means be collapsed into sameness or uniformity. Aristotle speaks of friendship among unequals, such as friendship between parents and children or between people of higher and lower status, but insists that care must taken not to allow the distinction to decay into radical asymmetry or disjunction. Guarding against such decay requires the cultivation of a 'proportional' mode of loving and being loved, a proportionality sustained by the shared bond of love: 'This above all is the way for unequals as well as equals to be friends, since this is the way for them to be equalized.' By contrast, rupturing of the bond through radical separation conjures up ill will and discord, and above all the social-political evils of tyranny and slavery: 'In a tyranny there is little or no friendship, for where ruler and ruled have nothing in common, they have no friendship, as they have no justice either. ... Nor is there any towards a horse or cow, or towards a slave, insofar as he is a slave' (although friendship persists 'to the extent that a slave is a human being').[22]

To repeat again, the point here is not a wholesale retrieval of classical philosophy, but a caveat against its reversal. To all intents and purposes, Derrida moves in the opposite direction from that of Aristotle. His essay places the accent on separation and disjunction, and also on a 'strange violence' inhabiting human relations (or non-relations); it eventually affixes the term 'friend' to a figure that is 'perhaps no longer that of a man' (thus to a figure exiting the human condition, perhaps in the direction of a god or 'overman'). The accent on separation is still further expanded and radicalised in the book, *Politics of Friendship*. There, drawing primarily on Nietzschean teachings, Derrida stresses the 'incommensurability' between self and other, between 'lover' and 'beloved', and also the unilateral asymmetry prevailing among singularities. Opposing the symmetry of virtue postulated in Aristotle's 'complete' friendship he writes: 'How can we reconcile this first imperative, that of primary friendship, with what we have begun to uncover: the necessary unilaterality of a dissymetrical *philein* and the terrible but so righteous law of *contretemps*?' (the temporal rift 'disjoining the presence of the present'). Relying specifically on Nietzsche's *Human, All Too Human*, the book removes friendship from any sort of ready familiarity or commonality – asking whether friendship (meaning the 'friendship to come') does not lend itself 'inevitably, maddeningly, to madness'. The kind of friendship that emerges here, Derrida notes, is a relation 'without proximity, without presence, therefore without resemblance, without attraction, perhaps even without significant or reasonable preference'. To the extent that the term is still applicable, friends are, here, basically 'the friends of solitude', people who 'share what cannot be shared: solitude'. What comes into view are 'friends of an entirely different kind, inaccessible friends, friends who are alone because they are incomparable and without common measure, reciprocity or equality' – in Nietzsche's words, 'jealous friends of solitude'. Essentially heterogeneous, these 'friends' are necessarily 'dissociated, "solitarized", singularized, constituted into monadic alterites'; they remain solitary, although they may 'ally themselves in silence within the necessity of keeping silent together – each in his own corner'.[23]

This notion of a solitary or inaccessible friendship carries over (perhaps surprisingly) into the political domain, animating Derrida's views on what he calls the 'politics of friendship'. In his essay of that title, one may recall, classical thought was charged with favouring a 'politicist concord', while successive rupturing breaks were said to 'depoliticize the Greek model' or else to 'displace the nature of the political'. Yet, displacement in the essay was still far from complete. Thus, in his discussion of 'answering before', Derrida noted that 'one answers before the law', that is, before an agency 'authorized to represent the Other legitimately, in the form of a moral, legal, or political community'. Largely under Nietzsche's influence, displacement in the book takes a much more radical form, affecting the very meaning of 'the political' and 'political community'. Once human beings are seen as singular, solitary, and separate, the classical association of politics with concord (*homonoia*) and community becomes apocryphal or untenable. Opposing this classical legacy, Derrida explicitly advances his critique 'in the name of another politics'. Given the stress on inter-human distance, the 'other' politics 'to come' can only denote a 'community of solitary friends', inaugurating what he emphatically calls 'community without community, friendship without the community of the friends of solitude. No appurtenance, nor resemblance nor proximity'. In Nietzschean terms again, the new politics of friendship can be called a 'great politics', which must in no way be confused with 'the one with which the political scientists and the politicians entertain us'. What the friends of the coming politics insist on denouncing is a central traditional mistake: namely, 'the contradiction inhabiting the very concept of the *common* and the *community*' – a mistake challenged in the name of 'the incalculable equality of these friends of solitude, of the incommensurable subjects, of these subjects without subject and without intersubjectivity'. Derrida in this context advances the notion of a new 'anchoritic community', a network of those 'who love in separation (or love to be separate)', and also the concept of a 'good friendship' replacing Aristotle's primary type. Such good friendship 'supposes disproportion. It demands a certain rupture in reciprocity or equality, as well as the interruption of all fusion or confusion between you and me. By the same token, it signifies a divorce with love, albeit self-love.'[24]

With its accent on disjunction and non-communion, Derrida's argument, despite its rupturing efforts, inserts itself into a long tradition of western thought, a tradition which has tended to privilege transcendental verticality over lateral, inter-human bonds. As previously indicated, this tradition received powerful impulses from Augustinian Christianity with its separation of earthly from spiritual forms of citizenship and friendship (captured theologically in the subordination of *eros* and *philia* to *agape*). Seen in this light, Derrida's notion of an 'anchoritic community' is distantly reminiscent of quasi-monastic ideals, while his celebration of jealous solitude seems to align itself both with Pascalian anti-humanism and (in a more secular vein) with the remote (non-)communion of New England transcendentalists. No doubt, in our late modern (or post-modern) era, there are good and weighty reasons speaking in support of this non- or anti-communitarian stance. In an age of rampant consumerism and commodification, when primary attention everywhere is focused on commodity production and appropriation, nothing seems indeed more urgent than the insistence on a certain human non-availability, that is, on the prohibition to treat humans (and the world at large) as simple commodities or means to ends. In many ways, this insistence runs counter to a powerful strand in modern metaphysics which construes the entire world as the target or 'project' of a designing and infinitely appropriating (individual or collective) subject – a construal undergirding modern processes of industrialisation and capital accumulation. Derrida is eloquent in denouncing this metaphysics. Postulating a 'new justice' beyond calculation and equivalence, he asks readers to envisage an equity placed 'beyond proportion, beyond appropriation'. Taking a leaf from some pages in Nietzsche's *Gay Science*, he elaborates:

> This 'disappropriation' would undoubtedly beckon to this other 'love' whose true name, says Nietzsche in conclusion, whose 'just name' is friendship. ... [This] little two-page treatise on love denounces, in sum, the right to property. This property right is the claim of love (at least, of what is thus named). The vindictive claim of this right can be deciphered throughout all the appropriative manoeuvers of the strategy which this 'love' deploys. It is the appropriating drive (*Trieb*) par excellence. 'Love' wants to possess; it wants the possessing. It is the possessing – cupidity itself (*Habsucht*).

As opposed to this 'drive', friendship as non-community challenges 'the very value of proximity, the neighbor's proximity as the ruse of the proper and of appropriation'. Its goal is 'not to give in to proximity or identification, to the fusion of you and me', but rather 'to place, maintain or keep an infinite distance within "good friendship"'.[25]

Although appreciating the denunciation of instrumental appropriation or *Habsucht*, one can still wonder about the extreme character (and hence the justice) of Derrida's proposed antidote. For clearly, friendship may be jeopardised not only by egocentric appropriation, but also by a radical 'disappropriation' celebrating inter-human remoteness and infinite distance. As experience teaches, retreat into solitude may occasionally lead to 'vertical' overtures, but it may also (and perhaps more frequently) be the gateway to an unabashed narcissism (which is the most prominent character flaw of our age). In the case of Derrida's presentation, one may puzzle how non-communicative remoteness can at all be reconciled with the postulated (Levinasian) responsibility or responsiveness to the 'Other'. More sharply phrased: how can self-transgression happen or how can self at all be transformed without the steady and 'timely' intervention of an 'other', that is, without the difficult labour involved in undergoing the challenge or 'apostrophe' of an 'other' located concretely in time and space? These and similar considerations are prone to introduce at least some question marks into the celebration of solitude and splendid aloofness – question marks which classical writers abundantly attached to this theme. As is well known, Aristotle saw friendship as a remedy for isolation and solitary life; he even argued that very good and 'blessedly happy' people still cultivate friendship and, in fact, 'desire to spend their days together, since a solitary life fits them least of all'. Following Aristotle's lead, Cicero likewise presented humans as sociable beings whose character development is likely to be impeded by solitude. Turning against certain Greek philosophers who rejected social ties as a threat to inner peace, Cicero chided their aloofness or self-security (*securitas*) as a moral failing, stating:

> Wonderful wisdom indeed! For they seem to take the sun from the sky who withdraw friendship from life. ... For what is that freedom from care or caring (*cura*) they talk about? In appearance it is flattering, but in truth it is in many cases to be disdained. ... For if we fly from care, we must fly from virtue also.[26]

What is troubling here is not the praise of solitude as such (which remains valuable in many respects), but rather its contemporary social-political context: the upsurge to undisputed global dominance of the ideology of liberal individualism (or libertarianism) in its conjunction with market imperatives. This upsurge can be traced back to the dismantling of the Soviet Union (and perhaps still further to the after-effects of 1968). Since the time of these events, all the major intellectual trends in the west have tended to conspire to one end: the debunking of any social commonality or 'community' (terms resonating loosely with socialism and communism) in favour of the celebration of individual separateness or the non-relation of singularities. As a corollary of these trends, notions such as the 'common good' or public concord (*homonoia*) have tended to be summarily dismissed as crippling or restraining (forgetful of the possibly empowering effects of public life). Despite obvious differences of accent, this dismissal or at least devaluation is shared by a number of theoretical perspectives, from traditional liberalism to recent critical theory and deconstruction (notwithstanding the fact that separation proceeds sometimes from the self, sometimes from the primacy of the other). The costs or negative side-effects of this dismissal (thematised under such labels as 'anomie', 'world-alienation', and '*trahison de tous par tous*') are not entirely ignored, and occasionally even deplored, but without any effect on the general orientation. To some extent, Derrida tries to assuage or accommodate such concerns by talking not simply about non-community, but about a 'community without community' or a 'friendship without friendship'. However, in view of the overall stress on remoteness and separation, such phrases seem to be more like wordplays covering up a basic non-community.[27]

A major drawback of this accent, especially with regard to political friendship, is the lack of praxis or shared social practices. On this point, of course, classical writers were emphatic, insisting that friendship in the proper sense had to be shown not only in words (or the inner mind), but in deed. Aristotle, as indicated, held that even happy people still like to 'spend their days together', adding that friendship ultimately amounts not only to a sharing of views, but a 'sharing of life' manifest in the willingness to 'share the friend's distress and joy'. In turn, Cicero emphasised the broad range of friendship, extending from enjoyment of ordinary pleasures to mutual character formation to practices in the public realm. Importantly, for both writers friendship, although initially preferential and intimate, was destined to spread or fan out into public life (hence their shared concern with public or political friendship).[28]

Viewed against this background, Derrida's postulate of remoteness and the perennial absence (or non-presence) of friends appears oddly disabling – and also humanly implausible. (Michel de Montaigne, so frequently invoked in his writings, seems to have happily ignored the postulate when enjoying the company of Etienne, although he did not allow his fondness to percolate into the larger community.) Similarly disorienting is Derrida's persistent critique of steadfastness, and especially of Aristotle's emphasis on the need of friends to remain faithful and reliable (*bebaios*) to each other. But how, without a measure of faithfulness and reliability, can friendship at all be cultivated and even conceived? How, without attentive care and reliable helpfulness (a help often required promptly or 'presently'), can friendship be kept from deteriorating into a chance encounter or simply a mode of self-indulgence? Can one still speak of friendship if 'friends' are always safely elsewhere, promising something in the indefinite future (perhaps on a transcendental plane)? At this point, it may be helpful to invoke some biblical passages (an apostrophe not unprovoked by some 'messianic' allusions in Derrida's texts). One such passage is the story of the 'good Samaritan' – a story, one may recall, in which the vertical spirituality of some priests is put to shame by the instant helpfulness of a stranger passing by. Another pertinent passage is to be found in some lines from Micah (6:8) in which the prophet, in succinct terms and without rhetorical flourishes, summarises basic rules of human conduct: 'He has shown you what is good; and what does the Lord require of you but to do justice, and to love kindness, and to walk humbly with your God?'

NOTES

1. The above account is no doubt sketchy and simplified in many ways – though the general direction of the development can scarcely be doubted. Some facets of this direction are well pinpointed by Gilbert Meilaender when he writes: 'There can be little doubt that friendship was a considerably more important topic in the life and thought of the classical civilizations of Greece and Rome than it has, for the most part, been within Christendom. With the possible exception of the literature of monasticism, friendship has never been a central concern of Christian thought. ... It would be difficult, if not impossible, to find a contemporary ethicist – whether philosophical or theological – who in writing a basic introduction to ethics would give friendship more than a passing glance. Indeed, having been for a time in the modern period the province of essayists (such as Emerson), friendship now appears to have fallen to a still lower estate: a book on friendship now means, quite often, a collection of little sayings, attractively illustrated, meant as a gift, and sold in a drugstore.' Meilaender is also quite emphatic about the difference between modern liberalism and classical friendship: 'There is a qualitative difference – a moral difference perhaps – between the liberal understanding of politics as activity necessary simply to leave the individual free for his or her private concerns, and the ideal of a participatory-communal polity' (anchored in friendship). See Meilaender, G. C. 1981. *Friendship: A Study in Theological Ethics*, pp.1, 70–71. Notre Dame (IN), University of Notre Dame Press.

2. An illustrative example of this division can be found in the booklet on 'Spiritual Friendship' by the Cistercian abbot Aelred of Rievaulx (around 1150), who sharply distinguished between pure or 'spiritual' friendship, on the one hand, and merely 'carnal' or 'worldly' forms of friendship on the other. See Pakaluk, M. ed. 1991. *Other Selves: Philosophers on Friendship*, pp.129–45. Indianapolis, Hackett Publishing Co. Accentuating and further radicalising the abbot's point, Meilaender writes: 'I want to suggest, hesitantly but firmly, that a Christian ethic ought to recognize the ideal of civic friendship as essentially pagan, an example of inordinate and idolatrous love.' Meilaender, G. C. 1981. *Friendship: A Study in Theological Ethics*, p.75. Notre Dame (IN), University of Notre Dame Press.

3. In his essay 'Of Friendship', Montaigne wrote: 'Common friendships can be divided up: ... but this [true] friendship that possesses the soul and rules it with absolute sovereignty cannot possibly be double. ... A single dominant friendship dissolves all other obligations.' For his part, Emerson in his essay on 'Friendship' asserted: 'It is foolish to be afraid of making our ties too spiritual, as if so we could lose any genuine love. ... Let us feel if we will the absolute insulation of man. We are sure that we have all in us.' See Pakaluk, M. ed. 1991. *Other Selves: Philosophers on Friendship*, pp.195, 221–2, 224, 231. Indianapolis, Hackett Publishing Co. On the other hand, though largely sharing Emerson's outlook, Henry David Thoreau expressed more sociable sentiments: 'A base friendship is of a narrowing and exclusive tendency, but a nobler one is not exclusive; its very superfluity and dispersed love is the humanity which sweetens society, and sympathizes with foreign nations; for though its foundations are private, it is, in effect, a public affair and a public advantage, and the friend more than the father of a family, deserves well of the state.' See Thoreau, H. D. 1925. Friendship. In *A Little Book of Friendship*, eds. Morris, J. and Adams, St. Clair, pp.109–110. New York, George Sully & Co.

4. Derrida, J. 1988. The politics of friendship. *Journal of Philosophy*, Vol.85, p.632.

5. Ibid., pp.643–4. The reference is to Blanchot, M. 1971. *L'Amitié*, pp.326–7. Paris, Gallimard. Also as Blanchot, M. 1997. *Friendship*. Trans. Rottenberg, E. Stanford, Stanford University Press.

6. Derrida, J. 1988. The politics of friendship. *Journal of Philosophy*, Vol.85, pp.633–4. (As published in the *Journal of Philosophy*, the essay uses *homonomia* as a translation of 'concord', which is clearly a mistake. The Aristotelian term is *homonoia*.)
7. Ibid., pp.635–6. See also Levinas, E. n.d. *Totality and Infinity: An Essay on Exteriority*. Trans. Lingis, A. Pittsburgh, Duquesne University Press.
8. Derrida, J. 1988. The politics of friendship. *Journal of Philosophy*, Vol.85, pp.636–7. The notions of future and anterior friendship are further elaborated in Derrida, J. 1997. *Politics of Friendship*, pp.235–7. Trans. Collins, G. London, Verso.
9. Derrida, J. 1988. The politics of friendship. *Journal of Philosophy*, Vol.85, pp.637–8. See also Derrida, J. 1997. *Politics of Friendship*, pp.250–52. Trans. Collins, G. London, Verso.
10. Derrida, J. 1988. The politics of friendship. *Journal of Philosophy*, Vol.85, pp.639–41.
11. Ibid., pp.640–41. For Derrida's ambivalent relation to Kant, see also Derrida, J. 1997. *Politics of Friendship*, pp.253–62. Trans. Collins, G. London, Verso.
12. Derrida, J. 1988. The politics of friendship. *Journal of Philosophy*, Vol.85, pp.641–4.
13. McCarthy, T. 1988. On the margins of politics. *Journal of Philosophy*, Vol.85, pp.645, 648.
14. Ibid., pp.645–6.
15. Ibid., pp.646–7.
16. Ibid., pp.647–8. Somewhat more extensive concessions to Derridean deconstruction, as an antidote to universalist abstractions, have recently been made by other thinkers equally indebted to Habermas. See especially Honneth, A. 1995. The other of justice: Habermas and the ethical challenge of postmodernism. In *The Cambridge Companion to Habermas*, ed. White, S. K., pp.289–323. Cambridge, Cambridge University Press.
17. Derrida, J. 1988. The politics of friendship. *Journal of Philosophy*, Vol.85, p.644. For Habermas's critique of Aristotelian or neo-Aristotelian views, see, for example, Habermas, J. 1990. Discourse ethics: notes on a program of philosophical justification. In *Moral Consciousness and Communicative Action*, trans. Lenhart, C. and Nicholson, S. W., pp.98–108. Cambridge (MA), MIT Press. For his privileging of the 'right' over the 'good', see Habermas, J. 1990. Morality and ethical life: does Hegel's critique of Kant apply to discourse ethics? In *Moral Consciousness and Communicative Action*, trans. Lenhart, C. and Nicholson, S. W., pp.195–215. Cambridge (MA), MIT Press. Compare also Dallmayr, F. 1991. Kant and critical theory. In *Between Freiburg and Frankfurt*, pp.105–31. Amherst, University of Massachusetts Press.
18. Aristotle. 1985. *Nicomachean Ethics*, 1155a25, Book VIII, 9.11., p.208. Trans. Irwin, T. Indianapolis, Hackett Publishing Co.
19. Derrida, J. 1997. *Politics of Friendship*, pp.4, 7–10. Trans. Collins, G. London, Verso; Aristotle. 1985. *Nicomachean Ethics*, 1156b10, Book VIII, 9.35., p.213. Trans. Irwin, T. Indianapolis, Hackett Publishing Co; Cicero. 1990. *On Friendship and the Dream of Scipio*, pp.43 (IX, 31), 63 (XXI, 80). Ed. and trans. Powell, J. G. F. Warminster, Aris and Phillips Ltd. The charge of the reduction of friends to sameness is particularly strange in the case of Cicero, whose friend Atticus was in so many ways unlike him (he abstained from politics and leaned toward Epicureanism).
20. The first anteriority might perhaps be called ethical or 'ontological', while the second pertains to the field of morality. It is perhaps not accidental that the discussion of immemorial friendship ends with a long footnote devoted to Heidegger and to (what Derrida calls) the 'incessant meditation on friendship in the path of Heidegger's thought'. See Derrida, J. 1988. The politics of friendship. *Journal of Philosophy*, Vol.85, p.637, note 5. For more critical comments on Heidegger, chiding him for an insufficient break with Aristotle, see Derrida, J. 1997. *Politics of Friendship*, pp.240–44. Trans. Collins, G. London, Verso.

21. Ricoeur, P. 1992. *Oneself as Another*, pp.188–9. Trans. Blamey, K. Chicago, University of Chicago Press.

22. Aristotle. 1985. *Nicomachean Ethics*, 1155b30, 1159a35, 1161a34–1161b10, pp.210 (Book VIII, 9.22), 223 (Book VIII, 9.53), 229 (Book VIII, 9.66). Trans. Irwin, T. Indianapolis, Hackett Publishing Co. Aristotle also includes in radical separation the process of divinisation in which a person is elevated above humans to become a 'god'; for as a god, 'he will no longer have friends'. See ibid., 1159a5–10 (Book VIII, 9.52). Aristotle's views are echoed by Cicero when he writes: 'This is indeed the life of tyrants where undoubtedly there can be no good faith, no affection, no steady confidence of another's goodwill; all is perpetual mistrust and vexation – there is no room for friendship. ... It is of the greatest importance in friendship to treat inferiors as equals. ... This conduct should be adopted and imitated by all, so that if a person has attained to any outstanding quality, either in character or intellectual gifts or wealth, he should communicate and share it with his friends.' See Cicero. 1990. *On Friendship and the Dream of Scipio*, pp.53 (XV, 52), 59–61 (XVIII, 69–70). Ed. and trans. Powell, J. G. F. Warminster, Aris and Phillips Ltd.

23. Derrida, J. 1997. *Politics of Friendship*, pp.10, 14, 23, 28–9, 35, 54–5. Trans. Collins, G. London, Verso.

24. Ibid., pp.6, 35, 37, 42–3, 62. In stipulating a 'community without community', Derrida deliberately radicalises and moves beyond the more moderate notions of an 'unavowable community' or of an 'inoperative (or un-managed) community' proposed respectively by Maurice Blanchot and Jean-Luc Nancy. He writes: 'There is still perhaps some brotherhood in Bataille, Blanchot, and Nancy, and I wonder ... if it does not deserve a little loosening up and if it should still guide the thinking of the community, be it a community without community, or a brotherhood without brotherhood.' See ibid., p.48, note 15. That classical thought established a parallel between other-love and self-love is, of course, undeniable, but also plausible and defensible (seeing that people who hate or corrupt themselves do not usually qualify as friends). On this point, Paul Ricoeur seems again on the mark when he writes that 'between the two extremes of the summons to responsibility, where the initiative comes from the other, and of sympathy for the suffering other, where the initiative comes from the loving self', friendship appears as 'a midpoint where the self and the other share equally the same wish to live together'. See Ricoeur, P. 1992. *Oneself as Another*, p.192. Trans. Blamey, K. Chicago, University of Chicago Press.

25. Derrida, J. 1997. *Politics of Friendship*, pp.64–5. Trans. Collins, G. London, Verso. The reference is to Nietzsche, F. 1974. *The Gay Science*, pp.1, 14. Trans. Kaufmann, W. New York, Vintage.

26. Aristotle. 1985. *Nicomachean Ethics*, 1157b21, 1169b18, pp.216–7 (Book VIII, 9.44), 257 (Book IX, 11.64). Trans. Irwin, T. Indianapolis, Hackett Publishing Co.; Cicero. 1990. *On Friendship and the Dream of Scipio*, p.51 (XIII, 47). Ed. and trans. Powell, J. G. F. Warminster, Aris and Phillips Ltd. At another point, Cicero presents even the majestic beauty of the universe as stale and insipid unless it is shared in company: 'Thus nature leaves nothing solitary and, as it were, always reaches out to something as a support – which in the dearest friend is most delightful.' See ibid., p.67 (XXIII, 88). Somewhat annoyed with the extreme subtlety of some philosophers, Cicero adds: 'We must not, then, listen to persons who overflow with self-indulgence when they argue about friendship, of which they have no real knowledge either in theory or in experience.' See ibid., p.53 (XV, 52).

27. Derrida's verbal artistry is, of course, part of his acclaim. In addition to postulating a 'community without community', his book also advances such notions as 'decision without decision (or decisionism)' and an 'enmity without enmity' (or an exchangeability of friend and enemy, which, of course, can only happen if both are

equally respected and esteemed). See Derrida, J. 1997. *Politics of Friendship*, pp.58–9, 67–8, 249. Trans. Collins, G. London, Verso. The labels 'anomie', 'world-alienation', and '*trahison de tous par tous*' (betrayal of all by all) are associated respectively with the names of Durkheim, Hannah Arendt, and Gabriel Marcel.

28. See Aristotle. 1985. *Nicomachean Ethics*, 1157b22, 1166a7, 1172a1, pp.216–7 (Book VIII, 9.44), 245 (Book IX, 11.11), 265 (Book IX, 11.92). Trans. Irwin, T. Indianapolis, Hackett Publishing Co.; Cicero. 1990. *On Friendship and the Dream of Scipio*, p.73 (XXVII, 103). Ed. and trans. Powell, J. G. F. Warminster, Aris and Phillips Ltd. Despite his own accent on a rarified anchoritic (non-)relation, Derrida repeatedly criticises both Aristotle and Cicero for their stress on the rarity of close or genuine friendship, charging them with fostering a kind of preferential oligarchy (*oligophilia*). See Derrida, J. 1997. *Politics of Friendship*, pp.3, 71. Trans. Collins, G. London, Verso. This criticism, however, neglects the lateral extension of friendship into social and political life. Thus, Aristotle regarded friendship as a cornerstone of politics and wrote: 'Certainly it is possible to be a friend of many in a fellow-citizen's way, and still to be a truly decent person.' Even more emphatically Cicero states: 'Among the good a liking for the good is, as it were, inevitable ... But the same kind of disposition extends also to the multitude; for virtue is not inhuman or cruel or arrogant, being accustomed as she is to watch over whole peoples and to provide the best measures for their well-being – which assuredly she would not do did she shrink from the affection of the many.' Aristotle. 1985. *Nicomachean Ethics*, 1160a22, 1171a17, pp.225 (Book VIII, 9.62), 263 (Book IX, 11.73). Trans. Irwin, T. Indianapolis, Hackett Publishing Co.; Cicero. 1990. *On Friendship and the Dream of Scipio*, p.53 (XIV, 50). Ed. and trans. Powell, J. G. F. Warminster, Aris and Phillips Ltd.

7

The Virtue of Solitude and the Vicissitudes of Friendship

HORST HUTTER

If we would understand the natures and functions of friendship in modernity, we need to grasp the configurations of self and soul peculiar to modern societies. Forms of human relatedness express in an outward and visible manner the invisible orders, conflicts and disorders within. The various types of human character condition the different forms of relatedness, and characters in turn are shaped and limited by social institutions and political practices. Neither can be fully appreciated without a consideration of the other. Such consideration would see the trends of culture and society as indicative of the deeper flows of the currently dominant dispositions of the psyche. Any one-sided, merely sociological approach would thus remain on the surface of the phenomena of friendship and would not make visible its spiritual significance. But a similar, one-sided concern for the deep structures of modern selves, without an understanding of their social contexts, would be blind to the limited actualities and possibilities of friendship. My approach in the following discussion will be guided by the above ideas. It will focus on the structure and functions of the modern self and show how these actualities inform the theory and practice of friendship. Although friendship is always to be considered as a universal human phenomenon, the way in which this phenomenon manifests itself is inevitably shaped by cultural factors. Specifically, my discussion will be limited to the appearance of friendship in advanced modern societies. By this I mean those societies that have fully experienced the deep-going changes brought on by industrialism and the concomitant factors of disintegration, disenchantment and partial reintegration. In these societies, now frequently engaged in a post-modern revision of the tenets of modernity, the problems of community show themselves with particular poignancy. The more or less permanent crises that afflict these societies have brought to the fore the roots of such problems in processes of psychic and spiritual disintegration.

My remarks are inspired by the insights into the nature of friendship first expressed in the teachings on friendship of the philosophical schools of classical antiquity.[1] One thought that is common to the two major, distinct teachings on friendship of these schools (that is, the Platonic-Aristotelian and the Stoic-Epicurean) is that a human being's capacity for loving others is closely defined and conditioned by the modalities of self-love.[2] The quality of friendship for others is dependent on the quality of self-friendship. This essay, hence, has two focuses of analysis: an intuitional analysis of the experiences of modern self-hood and a conceptual distillation of some aspects of classical thought.[3] Specifically, I shall proceed in three steps.

1. The first of these consists of an exploration of the deconstruction of the subject of Christian metaphysics. Orders of self had been organised around an orientation and structuring of human striving toward the attainment of eternal salvation. The means-end relationships thus constituted had favoured the containment of affects, especially negative ones such as anger and hatred, fear and resentment. It had thus permitted an integration of natural egoisms into a vision of service to the public good. This ultimate end of striving, now no longer credible to many, has largely disappeared, which in turn has liberated negative affects and made visible the inner war that now threatens both psychic and political identity. With a schizoid condition being the normal condition, all intimate bonds, such as friendship and love, are severely strained.[4]

2. The lack of beneficial psychic integration has led to the creation of new forms of quasi-friendship groupings around the fault lines of psychic conflicts. Among these communities, the 'new age' religious sects, the various hate and resentment groupings and the communities of ideological mendacity would seem to be politically most important. Modern societies, thus, are forms of spectacle in which the principles of enmity (or enmity-friendship) and difference (or difference-sameness) serve as focuses of identity. Psychic and social identities are established through processes of negative 'othering'.

3. Identities based on negative 'othering' may be seen as defective forms of friendship. Simultaneously, the processes of disintegration have permitted new forms of friendship. In various ways, these

new forms are adaptations to the features of finitude, mobility, solitude and uncertainty so characteristic of modern life. Two forms may chiefly be distinguished, namely, what has been called 'friendship-in-mind'[5] and 'stellar friendship'.[6] These forms indicate that of the two philosophical paradigms of friendship, the Stoic-Epicurean would seem most appropriate to our age.[7]

Nihilistic Souls and 'the war that they are'

Taken in its largest possible sense, the concept of friendship defines and describes a relationship between a Self and Other by means of a Third that permits and enables the bond. The mere co-presence in time and space of two persons, even their frequent dealings with each other, does not constitute them as friends. Nor, for that matter, does such co-presence make them enemies. It is the presence of a Third in the intentional structures of strivings, which are their selves, that links a Self and an Other in either friendship or enmity, or in both simultaneously. Friendship and enmity are thus both constituted by relation to this Third.

Traditionally, this Third has been called the Good.[8] This notion is shared by the otherwise quite divergent models of friendship provided by Greek philosophers. As suggested above, these models may be divided into two major types. On the one hand, both Platonic and Aristotelian teachings, despite their differences in regard to the logical and ontological status of the Good, see two persons united in friendship or set apart in enmity as the result of common or divergent visions of the Good. On the other hand, for the Stoics and Epicureans, it was a person's striving for wisdom (defined differently, to be sure, by these two schools) that enabled a self to recognise the value of friendship and so to become united with an other.[9] These four schools, moreover, agreed with one another on the fact that the true Good for human beings was difficult to discern and that most humans did not know the true Good and, hence, were disunited in folly and at variance in enmity due to the pursuit of partial or merely apparent goods. Moreover, the fact that the many were living in a 'cloud of unknowing' in regard to the Good, as it were, had important political implications. Unwilling ignorance about these most important matters in the public mind made it possible for equally deceived, but clever, tyrannical natures to achieve political dominance. Powers established in this manner, then, had a vested interest in continuing the structures of ignorance, to which end they adopted the creation and management of mythologically contrived falsehoods.

The dialectic of the human self, however, whether in a state of ignorance or of enlightenment, ensured the universal operation of the dynamics of friendship and enmity. Ignorance would tend toward enmity, which could only be transformed into friendship through insight into the Good or guidance by those who had such insight. The Third defined as the Good was a term necessary not only for relating a Self to an Other in friendship, but was also indispensable for forging the bond of psychic unity. For the soul itself, especially in the Platonic-Aristotelian model, was conceived as a field of tensions, struggles, contradiction and warfare that required a 'political' ordering.[10] Friendship between two persons was possible only to the extent to which the inner war had been resolved. Only those who had become friends of themselves and had ceased to be enemies of themselves could truly be friends of others. The regimes of civic and personal friendship, hence, depended for their existence and quality on the psychic regimes of the selves involved. The Platonic Republic defines in broad outlines the various modalities of orderings of the conflicts of the soul and shows the conditions under which self-friendship may arise. Aristotle also sketches the connections between self-friendship and friendship for others in his discussion of short-sighted and egoistic self-love in contrast to philosophical self-love.[11]

Similar theories may be derived from the teachings of the Epicureans and the Stoics. These exhorted humans to a proper scale of goods to be achieved through striving for self-perfection, which to them was the essence of philosophy.[12]

In all four schools, the sage was seen to be the person in whom true self-friendship had been realised. Sages had achieved inner concord through complete orientation to the Good, and by the attainment of this variously defined condition of the soul (as *eudaimonia*, *Ataraxia* or as *apatheia*) could serve as the transcendent, yet still 'empirical', norm to be set before the strivings of all persons.[13] Even though few humans might actually realise sage-hood, striving for this condition could nevertheless serve as the ultimate focus of all strivings, ordering all manner of human goods in a ranked order of values, and thus unifying the direction of willing and desiring. Indeed, what is usually called 'will' could only be conceived as such a unification of desire. There is in this vision no independent faculty of will.[14] Self-enmity would thereby be transformed into self-friendship and the inner war would be resolved into a condition, if not of peace, then at least of a lifelong truce under the rule of a perceived Good.

One of the remarkable things about the philosophical discourses about the Good is that there is no unified vision of it, no one definitive definition. Instead, we find a great variety of accounts; it appears that the Good can only be approached elliptically in a continuous process of dialectical approximations.[15] To be sure, some philosophers insisted on the unambiguous knowability of the Good, defining it as pleasure, as in the case of Hedonists and Epicureans, or as utility or knowledge, as in the case of some Platonists and Aristotelians or Stoics. But none of these definitions were universally and unequivocally sustainable. Each definition seemed at some point to get mixed in paradoxical circularity; the Good appeared to be always just out of reach and to be a kind of 'beyond'. The philosophical struggles in this seemed to mirror the political controversies arising in and from the search for the Good. The pursuit of self-interest, either in the form of individual or collective egoisms, never seemed to result in the certain knowledge and attainment of a common good. (As an aside, one might remark here that this condition does not seem to have changed in the modern age.)

It was perhaps the chief political virtue of dogmatic Christianity to attempt to fix the Good in a universally valid and politically effective vision. Much labour, effort, blood, sweat and tears were expended in the pursuit of this Christian good. If the effort had succeeded, then indeed the contentiousness arising from different visions of the Good might have been muted. The cooperation of temporal and spiritual 'powers' might have sustained a quasi-permanent sort of truce and an abatement of the natural condition of enmity-friendship. But dogmatic Christianity in its attempted union of faith and reason has failed, both politically and even more, on grounds of dialectical reason. It is our fate to live amid the shambles of this noble dream. The self-destruction of this ideological edifice, including the now evident failure of its secularised successors, such as Marxism, capitalism and liberalism, has had profound political repercussions in the form of fierce and bitter wars and revolutions on a hitherto unimagined scale. But it also has even deeper effects on the regimes of the soul that underlay dogmatic Christianity. But an understanding of the psychological ramifications of this loss requires some clarification of the nature and functions of a philosophically inspired or revelation-based regime of the soul.[16] Its absence shall clarify for us the current dangers for and from the human spirit.

The wars of the soul have usually been seen to occur between the two sides of reason and passion. But this is a simplified understanding of what is actually a much more complicated situation.[17] For 'passion' is a unified entity in name only; there is war among the different passions also: fear against anger, desire against aversion, love against hate. Furthermore, reason itself does not seem to be a unified tendency, but self-contradictory in its aspect of discursivity, and obscure for the most part in its aspect of insight and vision. There does not seem to be any sun-like clarity in this domain either. We have come to suspect that reason, reputedly the greatest of human powers, may itself be a kind of higher and subtler passion, as easily led astray as are anger and fear, vengeance and envy. Reason seems infinitely capable of supplying to the fiercely struggling passions a great variety of 'reasons' that justify the aims to which they tend anyhow.

The chief benefit of the classical and Christian regimes of the soul had lain in their ability to contain the so-called 'negative' passions of fear, anger, envy, vengeance, resentment and hatred.[18] These regimes aimed to transform the psychic energies that were liberated in the occurrence of these passions into the emotional bases of the virtues. The flow of these energies could be diverted by the ruling element in the soul into the socially safe channels of virtues such as courage, hope, justice, patience and humility. Such channelling would deprive these energies of some aspects of negativity, such as their automatism and their tendency to crystallise into politically destructive actions. As automatisms they are at all times obstacles to personal autonomy. Individuals are also naturally driven by them into developing personality systems that are little more than emotional conglomerates of short-sighted egoisms. In the development of the virtues, the ruling element counteracts these tendencies by utilising their negative elements of automatism and egoism to create psychic dispositions beneficial both for personal autonomy and public civility. Their 'negativity' could thus be transformed into political 'positivity', and 'vices' be changed into 'virtues' under the rule of law and custom. Education and philosophical re-education of selves are instrumentalities designed to achieve these ends.[19]

This process of gradual civilising of an originally barbarian human nature depends on the establishment in the soul of a distinction between ruling and ruled elements, as already indicated. The natural diversity of the human soul, its strange multiplicity, facilitates and requires the establishment of a hierarchy which assigns to each element its proper functions and rewards. Function, reward and punishment integrate diverse and contradictory tendencies into an artificial whole, which as such has some possibility of autonomy.[20] The hierarchically structured whole, in turn, is integrated on the basis of some principle which permits the distinction between 'better' and 'worse', 'higher' and 'lower', and 'sooner' or 'later'. It is this principle that permits value distinctions which are the 'Good' of the philosophical schools. This Good sets up a general means-end scheme in which all actions and strivings are integrated into a teleological edifice in which each good striven for by either a part or by the whole soul becomes a means to a still higher good, and so forth, ending in an ultimate aim, a *summum bonum* that lies 'beyond' the life span of each individual. Thereby, the soul becomes a well-ordered commonwealth in which the 'higher' parts persuade or constrain the 'lower' parts to cooperate in servicing the whole.[21] Persuasion and constraint here are equivalent to the intra-psychic processes of sublimation and repression.

The overall disposition of the whole soul depends on the mix of persuasion and constraint peculiar to an individual self. The greater the amount of repression, the higher is the level of psychic instability and the lower is a self's quotient of self-friendship. Conversely, the greater the amount of persuasion, the higher is the level of psychic stability and the lower is the self's quotient of self-enmity. Self-friendship consists then in the harmony and agreement between the higher and the lower selves. This bond of agreement is facilitated by an individual's understanding of the inner Third, the ultimate Good, and the ordering vision to which it gives rise for the establishment of a hierarchy of goods. We may think of the appropriate mix between persuasion or sublimation and constraint or repression as resulting from an individual's capacity for waging war with himself. The highest capacity in this warfare would belong to those for whom repression approaches zero and in whom inner discourse approximates free discussion among friends. It is easy to see that given the above paradigm of the human soul, the capacity for self-friendship and the spiritual quality of the inner war would be directly proportional to a self's capacity for friendship toward an other. Friendship would both confirm and enhance an individual's capacity for spiritualising the inner warfare. Hence friendship would also serve as a powerful tool for the establishment of a given mix of persuasion and constraint.

A further conclusion to be drawn from the above model of the soul is that human selves are greatly diverse in the manner in which they handle the 'enemy' within. The more reconciled they become to their inner 'enemies' in friendship, the more likely they are to be friends to other friends with the whole soul and not merely with a part. Conversely, friendship may occur between any part of one self with the corresponding part of the other. Not only the 'positive' aspects and passions of individuals, but also their 'negative' passions may become allies and friends of similar passions in others. Individuals may be friends that are whole-heartedly linked by a shared vision of the Good in a proper hierarchy of goods. But they may also be united by shared hatreds, shared resentment and envies, and a common object for the discharge of the affects of vengeance, or yet by a mixture of both. To be sure, the latter friendships may occur primarily between those who are defined largely by repression and only slightly by sublimation. They would also be friendships that are partial, unstable and self-contradictory. A person linked to someone by a shared hatred for a common 'enemy' would remain in a friendly link to the Other only so long as the accumulated negative energy could be safely diverted outward toward an 'outer' Third, instead of being channelled toward the Other. Many such relations are mixed relations of friendship and enmity, love and hate, and peace and war (sometimes called *philos* **and** *aphilos* in some Greek tragedies). They are as unstable as the selves involved in them are unstable, and they are partial and defective. They are defective in so far as the self is never linked to the Other wholly and whole-heartedly. These partial selves linked partially to others contain, moreover, identity formations which derive, whatever stable identity they have, from the repression of the Other excluded in enmity. This excluded Other is inside both selves thus linked in defective friendship, as well as exterior to both selves. It functions as the Third, the focus of integration around which identity is crystallised. This positive friendship side of identity, however, is based on the 'enemy' Other. Hating, envying, resenting and fearing the same objects in common, the persons so linked are linked primarily by their negativity. Whatever positive affects there are, are either neglected or repressed, or stand in the service of the identity of negativity. Furthermore, the whole soul is split apart in a schizoid duality. In a society such as ours, in which contact with the Good 'beyond' is largely lost and in which the general teleology of action with its scale of goods is disintegrating, defective friendships are the order of the day. The schism in the soul cannot be overcome, because the vision of the unifying Third has been suppressed into the subconscious. Inferior and mediate goods are postulated as ultimate ends of action, and human selves lose awareness of the negativities that drive them. They hate, envy, resent and fear, and blinded by these, know not what they do, nor do they understand themselves. Since the mediation between negative emotions and the intellect, usually effected by the higher, positive emotions, is also disrupted, the intellect becomes like a ghost driving a machine. It serves the destructive aims of negativity, becoming the primary tool for the fabrication of falsehoods. Base motivations are masked by high-minded ideological rationalisations. The emotions of love and friendship reinforce the identities of vengeance and hate; they become spurious and frequently manifest themselves hypocritically as a shared form of moralistic grandstanding. But in a society characterised by such relations, the true basis of morality in a shared vision of the Good has already been lost.

The Power of Negativity in the Politics of Difference

Discontinuity, weakness of will and bad faith appear to be the fundamental features of political orders experiencing nihilistic disintegration. These features characterise both selves and politics. As has been stated, they are the result of the loss of a vision of the Good shared by all elements of a composite whole, such as a Self or a polity.

The elements of a composite whole need to be integrated around a distinction between ruling and ruled parts. This distinction permits the establishment of a hierarchy of parts and their specific goods and aims. Any composite whole, hence, contains potentially the dynamic conflict of a friend-enemy relationship, an ordering of sameness and otherness. The Other may be conceived as either a friend or an enemy. Hence, composite structures may be defined as such wholes either as relations of self-friendship or self-enmity, or both. The necessary othering may be positive or negative, or both. A friendship relationship by a Self with an Other would, hence, also be based upon either positive or negative othering, or both.

Friendships based on negative othering are inherently defective. They are discontinuous, because there is no continuity of the part of the whole involved in a structured hierarchy. Similarly, the lack of organisation of parts around an ultimate aim implies weakness of will. Individuals and polities are unable either to recognise their true good, or if they recognise it, are unable to muster the strength for its pursuit. Lastly, negative othering necessarily falsifies the positive features of others and represses awareness of inner negativity. The public stance is one of massive bad faith. In addition, discontinuity, weakness of will and bad faith in the polity reinforce similar characteristics in individual selves.

Aristotle had conceived of two inferior forms of friendship between persons, that is, friendship established either for the sake of utility or for the sake of pleasure.[22] But pleasure and utility are still positive aims, based on positive othering. The negativity of a Self and an Other so united stand in the service of positive emotions such as limited love and sympathy. Relations are still formed by the ability to recognise and accept the specific individuality of others. In relationships based on negative othering, however, the order of positivity and negativity is reversed. Defective friendships are defined by negative aims in which the emotions of fear, hatred, envy and resentment for an 'enemy' other constitute a common bond.

Nihilistic societies seem to give rise to two distinct forms of bonding of this kind, which may be conceived as communities of hate and communities of mendacity. Persons in such relations are primarily united by negative emotions and only secondarily by an appreciation of the positive qualities of the Other. The specific psychic characteristic of the community of mendacity would seem to be bad faith. Individuals in them are unaware of large parts of themselves that are split off from waking consciousness. Their existence seems to be largely the lying pursuit of false aims. Moral indignation and an inability to see one's own faults are combined with monumental self-deception and an honest eagerness to reform and forcibly convert others. This honesty, however, is an extension of self-deception. It is frequently combined with a punitive moralism that revels in the misfortunes of others. Righteous indignation is unable to embrace forgiveness and seeks to supplement and reinforce supposedly divine punishment of sinners with human punishment. The 'enemy' other evokes in the punitive moralist a denying response to his own suppressed other. Hence there must be punishment, lest the repressed content of selves be made conscious and visible. Righteously indignant persons thus maintain their own repression, by visiting punishment on those who openly permit themselves what they secretly may also desire. Lastly, punitive moralists frequently mask their own subconscious self-divisions and inner misery with vast metaphysical systems of interpretation of the world and their own suffering.

Modern societies are characterised by a proliferation of fundamentalist sects and new-age religious groups, the members of which seem to share the characteristics detailed above. To be sure, not all of these are groups of friendship united by punitive moralism. There are undoubtedly groups animated by genuine religious striving and realistic spiritual regeneration. But many of these groups are characterised by bizarre and wildly speculative interpretations of the world. The distinction between genuine and mendacious groupings, however, is defined more by the type of othering they practise: positive and inclusive or negative and exclusive.

Mendacious friendship groups, however, do have many characteristics of genuine friendship, hence meriting their appellation. They may be based on confused and partial interpretations of the human condition, but they provide warmth, support to members in need, close fellowship, often heroic altruism and the possibility for overcoming narcissism and isolation. These features counteract their persecutorial and punitive tendencies.

But even the relationship to the close Other, the one that is included in the in-group, is fraught with ambiguity. In such relationships, each self is defined by an attitude of mixed self-friendship and self-enmity. The interior 'enemy' Other is repressed and not acknowledged. The attitude adopted by a Self toward an Other is hence fraught with an equal ambiguity of knowledge and ignorance and of friendship and enmity. The friend is never adequately understood, and accepted, nor is the Self adequately understood and accepted. In addition, the relationship toward the excluded Other is a mirror image of the relationship to the included Other: it is a relationship to an enemy-friend.

Friendship groupings that appear to be considerably more dangerous to the excluded others are the quasi-religious and political hate groups. Their identities, and the self-identities of their members, are derived almost entirely from negative othering. The association comes into being around the will to subjugate or destroy the 'enemy' Other. The latter functions as the scapegoat for the frustrations, humiliations and the general insufficiencies and sufferings of all existence. Considerable intellectual resources may be invested, and often by highly intelligent individuals, in the construction of an image of the hated enemy. The 'enemy' is invested both with the ridiculous qualities of a bumbling fool and the diabolical cleverness of an evil spirit bent on conquest and destruction. Every wicked deed, every falsehood, every murderous act becomes justifiable and righteous for the cause of defeating the 'enemy'. The most horrendous acts by members of such groups directed against the 'enemy' come to be seen as the performance of sacred duties. This may go so far as the 'moral' justification of genocide.

The emotional energies invested in such groups are primarily negative. It is fear, anger, impotent rage, envy and resentment which induce individuals to join such groups. Thereby they search for a meaning to their suffering by being related to others. Under the sway of such emotions elaborate historical and metaphysical narratives are constructed and accepted as truths, 'truths' which are grossly at variance with what is the case; the picture of the 'enemy' bears little and only superficial resemblance to his actuality. The world-views propounded are quite elaborate systems of falsehood, mixed with real insights, that serve, however, to define and fortify both group and ego identities. When murderous deeds are committed, the complicity in them further reinforces the bonds of the hate group and verifies the interpretation.

These negativities, however, also evoke positive bonding emotions. The more intense are the negativities, the further advanced in complicity in wicked deeds, the more intense are also the positive feelings that unite. Camaraderie in danger, common and cathartic discharges of violence, and glorying in the courageous overcoming of individual insignificance are some possible experiences. To these we may add the experiences of sharing in need, kindness to one's associates, fellowship in the conduct of life and the elation produced by participating in battles of presumed metaphysical significance. Induction into such groups often assumes the aspects of a religious conversion with the adoption of significant symbols and emblems of membership. Special greetings and rituals of commonality confirm participation. Even profound thinkers may then be seduced into perceiving such groups, when they achieve the level of mass movements, as momentous. Indeed, whole nations have come and may still come under the sway of such movements. Then the destructive energies released are truly frightful.

The two above-sketched forms of modern friendship groups are animated by the power of negativity. They thrive in an age of chaotic confusion, economic insecurity and spiritual disintegration. While at any time the human Good is only dimly visible to most, it becomes especially obscure under the reign of nihilism. Then social life is characterised by inversion; in the general loss of values and their reduction to the lowest common denominator, the sense of 'better' and 'worse', of 'noble' and 'base' as well as of excellence is almost lost. Difference, subjectivity and equal self-assertion are prized, not only in popular culture, but have also become the defining principles of philosophy, in so far as it is its epoch comprehended in thought. But as I have attempted to show, the search for the higher and for relatedness that transcends narcissism continues even in the perverted forms of these defective friendships, for it is not possible for human beings not to search for relatedness and meaning.

The Fragility of Modern Existence

It may be considered odd and unwarranted to see in mendacity and hate groups any of the characteristics associated with the noble form of association called friendship. However, lest we ourselves fall into the structures of negative othering, we need to understand and appreciate the positive elements of these dangerous groups, for in such understanding we may find the political strategies needed for overcoming these dangers. Human beings need to search for relatedness and meaning, the two primary goods of friendship. Relatedness and meaning in turn constitute the foundations of trust, without which civil society disintegrates.[23] Now the trends of modern, urban life are such as seriously to threaten precisely these goods. These trends are the increasing isolation of individuals; the disintegration of the family; an increasing disordering of erotic life; increasing competitiveness for access to the scarce means of life and labour; increasing economic insecurity and pauperisation; an enormous rise in the enslavement of many to the world of work with its corollary of the abolition of leisure; and a general atomisation of society.[24] Competitiveness erodes trust and relatedness. Enslavement to long hours of work threatens leisure time and the ability to form friendships, and atomisation increases psychic instability and mental illness. Trust becomes a victim of anger, fear and hatred, produced by the dissatisfaction of the basic needs for warmth, loving acceptance and recognition. The unchaining of negative passions in such conditions, then, provides one of the few emotional bases upon which individuals may search for relatedness and meaning, and, hence, for avenues by which to achieve trust, or at least the ability to trust one's partners in hatred, fear and anger.

It is not yet certain how far the atomisation and deconstruction of civic orders can and will go. The limits to the progress of loss of insight into the good life and its necessary, communal prerequisites have not yet been reached. Furthermore, there are important counter-tendencies produced by the revolution in information technologies. These make accessible information about what is happening to large numbers of people. This available information has led and is leading to knowledge and understanding of the terror of the situation in large numbers of concerned persons, who then may form voluntary associations to combat the negativities. The cause of friendship hence does not seem entirely lost.

Yet the ability to establish deep and lasting friendships seems to be adversely affected by the above features of modern life. In particular, there were two aspects which the philosophical paradigms of friendship had specified as essential. These are lastingness and the desire of friends to maintain continuous, lifelong and close contact. Both of these seem natural in societies with low social mobility and a fairly static order of class, status and residence. Modern societies, however, know very high degrees of geographical as well as upward and downward status mobility. These tend to render all relationships fleeting and counteract the requirements of equality between friends. The consequent individual isolation may often be experienced as quite painful; it is certain to be a major factor behind weakness of character and all manner of neurotic disorders. It also may induce individuals to seek company at any price in associations that rarely go deep enough to permit a real opening of selves to one another. In such conditions, the practice of solitude may have to become a virtue.[25] Techniques of self-care may have to be devised, and are being devised, that enable persons to make creative use of the possibilities of isolation and whatever ways of being related do exist. In addition to practising the virtue of solitude, friendship would require the further virtue of honesty with oneself. Honesty is indeed a prerequisite for forming essential relations as such, which, however, may be especially difficult in present circumstances. The mendacity and deceitful nature of public discourse joins forces with the oppressive rule over many of mixtures of true and false opinions passionately held. Indeed, the maintenance of schizoid personality structures requires precisely such public and private ideologies. Divided egos can maintain their strength and identity only by continuously lying to themselves. Large parts of the self are split off and remain in the darkness of ignorance. The opening to an Other which permits relatedness and insight into meaning requires a prior overcoming of self-ignorance in a condition of resolute honesty. Like the ability to use solitude creatively, honesty has to be practised in a process of self-care and self-transformation.

Meanwhile, we may conceive of new ways of conceptualising friendship that take into account the factors of fleetingness and mobility. Two very interesting notions suggest themselves. One is the idea of the 'friend-in-mind' recently proposed by a sociologist of friendship.[26] The other is Nietzsche's idea of 'stellar friendship'.[27] The very existence of these two types of modern friendship would seem to indicate the presence of the virtues of solitude and honesty. Let me now turn to a specification of these categories.

Friendship-in-mind arises in societies characterised by high degrees of geographical mobility in which many individuals experience frequent displacement. This, however, does not abolish the intention toward friendship in the psychic fields of the persons concerned. Openness to the Other is continuous, and close contact may be renewed when the opportunity presents itself. Such contact may be infrequent and may be interrupted by periods of intermission that last years. Such friendships are 'model relationships of an on-going living past-present'. They are defined by 'extremely pleasurable memories of past encounters that do repeat themselves when these friendships are renewed'.[28] They are relationships maintained in the psychic realm of persons which help maintain personal identity and meaning structures. It would also seem that the development of modern information technologies facilitates the development and cultivation of this kind of friendship. While they are not characterised by spatial propinquity, they nevertheless are lasting relationships in the intentionality of the souls of the persons concerned. Hence, they must be based on essential connections between Self and Other, involving orientation to a Third in the vision of a common Good.

Not all modern friendships, however, last for a lifetime. We have to accept not only geographical mobility, but also changes in status and class or conversions to different life tasks. Above all, the vicissitudes of modern life force upon us the recognition that a great part of what happens in our lives is something that befalls us. Our likes and dislikes, our characters and ways may be changed, but not beyond an irreducible element in us which is what is given to us. What is given may be those elements of human existence that merely happen, even against our best intentions and volitions (which does not require the assumption of a giver). These givens being our portion and lot, self-friendship would imply that we learn to love also this, even if it should estrange us from those we once loved. We might then say to one another:

> We are two ships, each of which has its goal and its course; we may, to be sure, cross one another in our paths, and celebrate a feast together, as we did before, and then the gallant ships lay quietly in one harbor and in one sunshine. But then the almighty strength of our tasks forced us apart once more into different seas..., and perhaps we shall never see one another again – or perhaps we may see one another, but not know one another again.[29]

The ultimate solitude of our existence always forces a final separation. Human fragility makes us realise both the value of friendship and the impossibility of its perfection. These things are not altered but perhaps made more human by the thought that our lives may be thought to be trajectories of an 'immense, invisible curve and stellar orbit … in which our courses and goals may be comprehended as small stages of the way – let us raise ourselves to this thought. But our life is too short and our power of vision too limited for us to be more than friends in the sense of that sublime possibility.'[30] Even Plato and Aristotle had acknowledged that no friend is to be preferred to the disclosures of our givens. Each of us has to confront his own truths, that is to say, to understand that part of reality which defines us by its ineluctability.[31] The most fundamental of these ineluctable elements is the finitude of all human things.

The limitations of modern societies circumscribe the friendships occurring in them in the domain of 'private' life. Political friendship in the sense in which Plato and Aristotle had understood it, is possible only in the type of small political order contained in a *polis*. The bond that unites the greatly diverse individuals of large mass societies is not civic friendship, but at best a kind of benign indifference. The model of friendship most appropriate for us would, hence, seem to be the one proposed by Epicurus.

Epicurean friendship is not tied to human beings in their capacity as citizens, but is oriented to a cosmopolitan ideal. Friendship in this sense is 'a dance that circles the world proclaiming to us all to awake to the praises of a happy life'.[32] It faces many obstacles today, especially from what in a narrow sense is called the 'political' sphere. This sphere seems to be largely dominated by the passions of anger, greed, resentment and fear. It favours, hence, only what has been called above defective friendships. It further encourages betrayal of real friendship. Success in politics almost seems to require bad faith. Fundamental dishonesty with oneself makes friendship unstable, because the links between dishonest people are established as much by the forces of enmity as they are by those of friendship. They are not linked essentially and authentically, because they lack an orientation to the ideal of an inclusive good. The struggle for power and interest is inherently inimical to this inclusive good. In such circumstances, friendship can only flourish among those who orient their intentionalities to something higher than and 'beyond' the individual self, in a continuous struggle for self-overcoming. For us moderns, the best guide in this struggle is in accordance with the human wisdom of Epicurus. *Homo amicus. Magis amica veritas.*

NOTES

1. Of particular relevance for my arguments here are: Aristotle. *Nicomachean Ethics*, VIII, IX; Plato. *Lysis*; Bailey, C. 1970. *Epicurus. The Extant Remains*. New York, George Olms; Rodis-Lewis, G. 1975. *Epicure et son Ecole*. Paris, Gallimard; Price, A. W. 1989. *Love and Friendship in Plato and Aristotle*. Oxford, Clarendon; Hadot, P. 1987. *Exercices Spirituels et Philosophie Antique*. Paris, Etudes Augustiniennes; Hadot, P. 1995. *Qu'est-ce que la philosophie antique*. Paris, Gallimard; Hutter, H. 1978. *Politics as Friendship*. Waterloo (Ontario), Wilfred Laurier Press; Mailaender, G. 1980. *Friendship: A study in Theological Ethics*. Indiana.
2. Compare Aristotle. *Nicomachean Ethics*, 166a1–30, 1167a27–1169b2; Hutter, H. 1978. *Politics as Friendship*, pp.92–132. Waterloo (Ontario), Wilfred Laurier Press; Price, A. W. 1989. *Love and Friendship in Plato and Aristotle*, pp.105, 107–114, 197. Oxford, Clarendon; Hadot, P. 1987. *Exercices Spirituels et Philosophie Antique*, pp.28–9. Paris, Etudes Augustiniennes; Hadot, P. 1995. *Qu'est-ce que la philosophie antique*, pp.192, 195. Paris, Gallimard.
3. A full substantiation of my arguments in this essay would require a book. I have restricted myself to the bare outlines of a thesis which is, I believe, sustainable. I ask for 'the reader's' indulgence and willingness to judge my train of thought on its merits, independent of its detailed scholarly support.
4. This section is inspired in a major way by Nietzsche's *Beyond Good and Evil* (especially Part V) and *The Will to Power*, Books I and II. Compare Deleuze, G. and Guattari, F. 1972–80. *Capitalisme et Schizophrenie*, two Vols. Paris, Editions de Minuit. See especially Vol.I.
5. Gurdin, J. B. 1996. *Amitie/Friendship*, pp.70–79. London, Austin and Winfield.
6. Nietzsche, F. *The Joyful Wisdom*, Part IV, No.279.
7. I am grouping Plato and Aristotle on one side, and the Stoics and the Epicureans on the other. The difference between the two sides that is most important for my argument concerns the source of friendship. For Plato and Aristotle, friendship was an integral part of the life of a *polis*, for the Stoics and Epicureans, by contrast, friendship was a cosmopolitan and universal human phenomenon. Compare Hutter, H. 1978. *Politics as Friendship*, pp.116–32. Waterloo (Ontario), Wilfred Laurier Press.
8. My remarks on the Good, here, largely follow the discussion of it in the middle portion of Plato's *Republic*, with its emphasis on the dimness of human vision of the Good, its contentiousness and the consequences of human ignorance.
9. On the philosophical schools as schools, see Hadot, P. 1995. *Qu'est-ce que la philosophie antique*, pp.91–264. Paris, Gallimard.
10. On this point, see the following illuminating study of Nietzsche's psychology: Parkes, G. 1994. *Composing the Soul. Reaches of Nietzsche's Psychology*. Chicago. On orientation to the Good, see Plato. *Lysis*, 216c–18c, 219c–20c.
11. Aristotle. *Nicomachean Ethics*, 1168a27–1169b2; Hutter, H. 1978. *Politics as Friendship*, pp.113–7. Waterloo (Ontario), Wilfred Laurier Press.
12. The view of philosophy propounded here is based on Hadot, P. 1987. *Exercices Spirituels et Philosophie Antique*, pp.9–74. Paris, Etudes Augustiniennes; Hadot, P. 1995. *Qu'est-ce que la philosophie antique*, pp.91–226. Paris, Gallimard; Hutter, H. 1989. Philosophy as self-transformation. *Reflexion Historiques (Historical Reflections)*, Vol.16, Nos.2 and 3, pp.171–98.
13. Compare Hadot, P. 1995. *Qu'est-ce que la philosophie antique*, pp.46–87. Paris, Gallimard; Hadot, P. 1987. *Exercices Spirituels et Philosophie Antique*, pp.77–116. Paris, Etudes Augustiniennes.
14. See, for example: Wood, M. H. 1907. *Plato's Psychology in its Bearing on the Development of Will*. London, Oxford; Dihle, A. 1982. *The Theory of Will in Classical*

Antiquity. Berkeley, University of California Press; Zeitler, W. M. 1983. *Entscheidungsfreiheit bei Platon*. Munchen, Beck; Nietzsche, F. *Beyond Good and Evil*, Nos.19, 188, 200, 225, 257.

15. On the difficulties associated with any simplistic account of a 'theory of the Good', for example, in Plato, see: Wieland, W. 1982. *Platon und die Formen des Wissens*, pp.95–224. Goettingen, Vandenhoeck and Ruprecht; Rosen, S. 1969. *Nihilism. A Philosophical Essay*, pp.140–97. New Haven, Yale University Press.

16. Compare Parkes, G. 1994. *Composing the Soul. Reaches of Nietzsche's Psychology*. Chicago.

17. Compare Hutter, H. 1997. Thumos and psyche. *Etudes Hellenique* (*Hellenic Studies*), Vol.5, No.l, spring 1997, pp.81–97.

18. Compare Rabbow, P. 1954. *Seelenfuhrung. Methodik der Exerzitien in der Antike*. Munchen, Kosel; Rabbow, P. 1960. *Paidagogia. Die Grundlegung der abendlandischen Erziehunqskunst in der Sokratik*. Goettingen.

19. Compare Hutter, H. 1989. Philosophy as self-transformation. *Reflexion Historiques* (*Historical Reflections*), Vol.16, Nos.2 and 3, pp.171–98.

20. Compare Zeitler, W. M. 1983. *Entscheidungsfreiheit bei Platon*, pp.54–88. Munchen, Beck.

21. Compare Wieland, W. 1982. *Platon und die Formen des Wissens*, pp.263–80. Goettingen, Vandenhoeck and Ruprecht.

22. Aristotle. *Nicomachean Ethics*, 1155b–1157b; Hutter, H. 1978. *Politics as Friendship*, pp.107–9. Waterloo (Ontario), Wilfred Laurier Press.

23. This is one of the main points of the excellent study on friendship by Eisenstadt, S. N. and Roniger, L. 1984. *Patrons, Clients and Friends: Interpersonal Relations and the Structure of Trust in Society*, pp.21–3, 40. Cambridge, Cambridge University Press. See also Gurdin, J. B. 1996. *Amitie/Friendship*, pp.374–7. London, Austin and Winfield.

24. Ibid., pp.433–7.

25. Compare Nietzsche, F. *Beyond Good and Evil*, Nos.284, 286.

26. Gurdin, J. B. 1996. *Amitie/Friendship*, pp.70–76. London, Austin and Winfield.

27. Nietzsche, F. *The Joyful Wisdom*, Part IV, No.279.

28. Gurdin, J. B. 1996. *Amitie/Friendship*, pp.70, 71. London, Austin and Winfield.

29. Nietzsche, F. *The Joyful Wisdom*, Part IV, No.279.

30. Ibid.

31. See the famous passage in which Aristotle, seemingly echoing Plato, states that the truth is to be honoured above friends. Aristotle. *Nicomachean Ethics*, 1096a16; Plato. *Republic*, 595c2–3.

32. Bailey, C. 1970. *Epicurus. The Extant Remains*, 114, Fragment 52. New York, George Olms. See also the discussion at Rodis-Lewis, G. 1975. *Epicure et son Ecole*, pp.362–9. Paris, Gallimard.

8

Reviving Greco-Roman Friendship: A Bibliographical Review

HEATHER DEVERE

The resurgence of interest in friendship as a philosophical concept in the past decade has seen a burgeoning in the literature of collections and commentaries. Prior to the late 1980s, the topic of friendship was covered sparsely in the literature. Reference to the importance of friendship in the Greek and Roman context was very limited. An early work is **Carpenter** (1915), a collection of excerpts arranged in roughly chronological order which includes 'modern' writers on the subject of Greek and Roman friendship, as well as passages from Plato, Xenophon, Plutarch, Homer, Sappho, Ovid and Virgil. Two important works published in the 1960s were **Singer** (1966) and **Cleugh's** translation of **Flacelière** (1962). Singer argues that modern concepts of love and the philosophy of love stems from two principal sources – Plato, his followers and his critics on the one hand, and Christianity and Judaism on the other. A large section of the book is devoted to 'Love in the Ancient World' and deals with Platonic *eros*, friendship in Aristotle, philosophic love in Plotinus, sex in Ovid and Lucretius, which leads on to the section covering religious love in the Middle Ages. Flacelière covers different aspects of love in Ancient Greece including Homer, mythological references to love, homosexuality, marriage and family ties, courtesans, philosophers of love and romantic love. The philosophers to whom he refers include Heraclitus, Socrates, Plato, Xenophon, Aristotle, Epicurus, Lucretius and Plutarch.

A focus on friendship rather than love is evident in two studies in the 1970s. A very comprehensive commentary on the topic in English is **Hutter** (1978) who makes the point that moderns are suspicious of the intrusions of friendship into politics, and have regarded affective emotions as a threat to the smooth functioning of the social order. He argues that 'at the present moment in the Western tradition of thought

... the idea of friendship has receded into the background and has been supplanted by the idea of market exchange as the major principle for the intellectual ordering of the political world' (2). This is contrasted with the high regard for friendship in Ancient Greek and Roman society. Hutter discusses the social and political context of Greek theories of friendship, the psychodynamics of Greek friendship, gives an overview of the various theories of friendship based on the writings of Aristotle, Plato, the Epicureans, and the Stoics, and then looks at Roman friendship by concentrating on the life and times of Cicero. A final chapter covers friendship in modern society. Another important contribution on classical friendship, and the French equivalent of Hutter, is **Fraisse** (1974). Fraisse's introduction refers to studies on friendship as 'research into a lost problem' and the need to 'rebuild the path' from Homer to Plutarch. In the first section, Fraisse gives a chronological account of references to friendship by early poets, dramatists and historians, including Homer, Sophocles, Euripides, Herodotus, Lysias and Xenophon. The second section concentrates on a philosophical study of the concept of friendship, and covers Plato, Aristotle and Epicurus. The third section deals with the Stoics, and finishes with Seneca and Plutarch.

In the past ten years, numerous collections, anthologies and commentaries on love and friendship have appeared. Some deal specifically with the ancient world. **Price** (1989) looks in some detail at the works of Aristotle and Plato which deal with friendship, desire and love. He focuses on Socrates' philosophy of love and friendship in the *Lysis*, the *Symposium* and the *Phaedrus* and Aristotle on varieties of friendship, perfect friendship and civic friendship in the *Eudemian Ethics* and the *Nicomachean Ethics*. The aim of the book he states is 'to display that their approach is reflective and fertile, well-conceived in theory and pregnant in practice; to respond to it briskly with the cliches of modern thought is to prefer the pleasures of the parrot to the pains of the philosopher' (1). **Fitzgerald** (1997) comprises papers presented in 1991 to the Society of Biblical Literature Annual meeting in Kansas City. Included are essays on friendship in the Greek world prior to Aristotle, in works by Aristotle, Cicero, Plutarch, Dionysius, and in the Neopythagorean writings, the philosophy of Alexandria, in Greek romances, in the *Toxaris*, in Greek documentary papyri and inscriptions, and New Testament evidence for the Greco-Roman topos on friendship and useful bibliographical references. This edition complements another Fitzgerald collection on friendship in the New Testament world (1996), one section of which also deals with the

Greco-Roman world. **Konstan** (1994) looks at five 'romantic' prose fictions from Greek antiquity. He argues that the Greek novel is the locus of a special construction of *eros* which is symmetrical, unlike the asymmetry of power and passion that characterises instances of homoerotic love of other Greek writings.

Konstan (1997) supplies a history of friendship from the Homeric epics until the Christian empire of the 4th and 5th centuries AD. Konstan's analysis challenges the dominant interpretations in current scholarly literature on friendship in the ancient world, especially Greek friendship. Konstan argues that there was an 'anthropological turn' in classical historiography, which emphasised systems of exchange in pre-modern societies where obligatory reciprocity was seen to outweigh sentiment in personal relations. The concept of friendship was then interpreted as being quite different to modern ideas of friendship. Konstan gives a detailed analysis demonstrating how terms such as *philia* and *amiticia* have been misinterpreted and claims that Greek and Roman friendship has a comparable status to the status it enjoys in modern life (5). The book is divided into five chronological sections – archaic Greece, the classical period, the Hellenistic world, Rome and Christian and pagan friendship, and the writers discussed include Homer, Hesiod, Sappho, Theognis, Epicurus, Aristotle, Plato, Xenophon, Cicero, Plutarch, Philodemus and Themistius. Konstan discusses the relationship between morality and friendship, friendship and politics, public and private, male and female friendships, and friendship and inequality. There is also a brief bibliographical essay.

Thornton (1997) writes about 'what the literary remains from 700–100 BC say about sex' in Greece, and focuses on the primary texts with references to secondary texts in English (7). Part 1 traces the depiction of sex and sexual desire as a 'controlless love' and covers imagery used to characterise *eros,* the goddess of sex, the Greek distrust of women's sexual power, and homosexuality. Part 2, entitled 'fancied sway', analyses the means or 'technologies' used by the Greeks to control and exploit the energy of *eros* and explores rituals, philosophy, religion, marriage and pederasty.

Pakaluk (1991) is an anthology of writings on friendship which he claims includes 'almost all of the central philosophical writings on friendship produced in the West'. His introduction discusses the reasons for a renewal of interest in the topic of friendship. Each entry is preceded by a two-page commentary by Pakaluk. The works from the ancient world which he includes are Plato's *Lysis;* Aristotle's *Nicomachean Ethics (Books VIII and IX) and Rhetoric (Book II:4);*

Cicero *De Amicitia;* Seneca 'On Philosophy and Friendship' and 'On Grief for Lost Friends' from *Epistulae Morales.* Although there are several writings from the canon which are omitted, it is, as he suggests, a collection which 'provides a kind of standard, which needs to be met, before it can be surpassed'.

Several recent edited collections of contemporary writings also include contributions on ancient friendship and love. Soble (1989) presents extracts from Plato's *Symposium* as an example of *eros,* Aristotle on *philia* and St. Paul as an exponent of *agape*-style love, and a section on 'Exploring the Classics' introduced by himself. Contributors in this section include Gregory Vlastos on 'The individual as an object of love in Plato', John A. Brentlinger on 'The Nature of Love' and L.A. Kosman on 'Platonic Love'. Porter and Tomaselli (1989) includes a chapter by Pat Easterling on 'Friendship and the Greeks' which looks at the various aspects of friendship such as kinship, sexual love, comradeship, guest friendship. In Badhwar (1993) Nancy Sherman writes on 'Aristotle on the Shared Life', and the contribution of another respected Aristotelian scholar, John Cooper, concerns Aristotle's ideas of 'Political Animals and Civic Friendship'. Rouner (1994) offers more commentaries on Aristotle. Jurgen Moltmann in 'Open Friendship: Aristotelian and Christian Concepts of Friendship' argues that the concept of freedom is necessary in these models of friendship. John E Smith's 'Two Perspectives on Friendship: Aristotle and Nietzsche' is a comparative approach which discusses friendship as a relationship between elites concerned primarily with autonomy. Gilbert Meilaender sees marriage as the model of true friendship between women and men in his essay 'When Harry and Sally Read the Nicomachean Ethics: Friendship between Men and Women'. Michael Pakaluk discusses the need for civil fraternity in the body politic in his analysis entitled 'Political Friendship'. Goicoechea's (1995) tribute to Singer is a compilation of papers delivered at the 1991 conference of the Brock Philosophical Society of St. Catharines, Ontario which was a three-day colloquium on the work of Singer. The collection includes two interviews with Singer, one on the history of love, and an essay by Paul Gooch 'A Mind to Love: Friends and Lovers in Ancient Greek Philosophy' in which Gooch compares his views on Aristotelian and Platonic love to those of Singer.

In addition to these edited collections are commentaries by sole authors on love and friendship. Bloom (1993) writing on love and friendship laments what he calls the 'de-eroticization' of the world and attempts to revive an interest in love by providing 'the most eminent examples of rich descriptions of love to which we can have immediate access'. Almost half the book is devoted to the works of Rousseau and Plato which he regards as 'the two greatest philosophical teachings about *eros*'. The final section of his study is a detailed analysis of Plato's 'Ladder of Love' in the *Symposium*. The recent English translation by George Collins of **Derrida** (1997) looks at the political history of friendship as conceived by writers such as Cicero, Montaigne, Kant, Nietzche and Carl Schmitt. Derrida uses the address attributed to Aristotle "O my friends, there is no friend" as the focus and keynote for each of the ten chapters of his book. In deconstructing the concept of friendship, he wonders about the implicit politics of the language used to describe and talk about friendship. In particular, he questions the biblical and Greek lineage of equating friendship and fraternity which has served to exclude 'the feminine or heterosexuality, friendship between women or friendship between men and women.' (279) **Wagoner** (1997) is an introductory text which assumes no previous knowledge of philosophy and covers erotic, Christian, romantic, moral and mutual love, and love as power. The chapter on erotic love deals with Plato's *Symposium* and *Phaedrus* and the chapter on mutual love compares Aristotle with Luce Irigaray. There are also special issues devoted to a discussion on friendship. The winter 1998 issue of *South Atlantic Quarterly* includes comparisons of friendship in Aristotle and Derrida by Heller; Plato and Nietzsche by Dwight David Allman; and Epicurus and Marx by Constantinou. Aristotle on friendship is discussed by Aubenque and the idea of heroic friendship in Homer, Sophocles, Plato and Aristotle is examined by Ruprecht.

Interpretation of terms

Nomenclature and interpretation of conceptions of friendship are examined by several authors. **Fraisse** documents the use of the term *philia* through the historical and philosophical writings of antiquity, from Homer's concentration on *philos, philein* and *philotes*, the possible invention of the term by Pythagoras, the idea of philanthropia in Eschytes, the concept of guest-friendship in Herodotus, the political sense of the word *philia* as used by Thycydides, the sense of *philia* in Plato, Aristotle, Epicurus and the Stoics. There is a debate among commentators about the correct interpretation of *philia*. For some *philia* is contrasted with *eros* and is considered to be a less intense, less emotional, non-sexual relationship or feeling. **Dover** (1973) argues that *philia* is used to refer to love but denotes milder degrees of affection, rather than obsessive desire. **Singer** contrasts Plato's use of *eros* with Aristotle's use of *philia*, with *philia* being a feeling which is asexual, rational and unemotional. For **Flacelière** (1962), *philia* is seen by the Greeks as a deep respect and affection uncontaminated by desire, somehow purer or superior to *eros*. Commentators such as **Easterling, Blundell** (1989) as well as Dover and Flacelière extend the idea of the non-sexual nature of *philia*, and argue that the concept is broader than our concept of friendship and includes relationships with blood relatives and describes family ties. Blundell also extends *philia* to cover a complex web of relationships which can be political or business in nature. Other commentators are anxious not to exclude a passionate component from *philia*. **Nussbaum** (1986) claims that *philia* does not exclude passion, physical desire or sex and can refer to love affairs too. **Price's** interpretation of *philia* is very broad, and covers the range of relationships from those between lovers to very casual but agreeable acquaintances.

Konstan has written extensively on nomenclature with reference to ideas of friendship. Konstan (1996a) challenges what he considers to be conventional interpretations of *philos* and *philia*. He traces the history of the terms used for the concepts, and finds that in the earliest Greek texts *philos* was used to describe something which was 'dear' or a comrade. In the Classical period, *philos* was generally restricted to intimate associates, not closely related by blood or marriage. He claims that the noun *philos* is equivalent to the English word 'friend', but there is no corresponding word that specifically designated the relationship of friendship. *Philia* has a broader semantic range, and includes relationships between parents and children as well as, more rarely, solidarity among fellow-citizens. He argues that the 'ambiguity has caused difficulties for modern scholars, but the Greeks themselves were, like us, quite clear about the difference between friends, relatives, and countrymen' (92).

Included in the literature on friendship is reference to the Greek concept of 'guest friendship' represented by the Greek word *xenia*, which describes the complex duties and obligations due to visitors or strangers. The idea of *xenia* is portrayed in Homer's epics the *Odyssey* and the *Iliad*. **Herman** discusses the possible conflict between the commitment to one's citizen duty and the moral obligations to a guest-friend, which is a bond between citizens of different cities, and contrasts the concept of this ritualised friendship with ideas of kinship and normal or civic friendship. Easterling also discusses the concept of *xenia* and contrasts it to *philia*.

There is much less discussion of the Latin terminology. But the debate centres around whether *amicitia* is equivalent to our understanding of friendship or whether it is more commonly used to refer to the patron-client relationship. **Hutter** defines *amicitia* as describing the moral and customary relationship in Rome between patron and client. **White** writing on patronage in poetry in early Imperial Rome also argues that the relationship between patrons and clients is described by the term *amicitia* with the patron being the *amicus*. However, **Saller** believes that it is misleading to discuss these bonds as friendship and that *amicitia* and *patronatus* are 'quite separate categories in the Roman mind' (56). **Spielvogel** looks at the class structure of Rome and the patron-client relationships which work within a theme of *amicitia*. **Epstein** whose interest is in enmity rather than friendship contrasts *inimicitiae* to *amicitia*, claiming that *amicitia* confers sacred obligations in the public and political arena. However, **Konstan** (1995) challenges these interpretations of the notions of *amicus* and *amicitia*. He argues that *amicus*, is used distinctively to refer to friends rather than being a synomym for client and patron. **Powell** (1995) considers both *philia* and *amicitia* and concludes that the concept of friendship in the works of ancient society 'contains nothing essentially unfamiliar to the modern reader' and 'that the reason for this is that friendship in its essence is much the same for human beings in all societies' (45).

Historical Background of Traditions and Values

There is a range of sources which give background on the topic, describing the historical context, the traditions and values of the era and there is concensus about the important role played by friendship in the societies of classical Athens and Rome. Works which examine the history of the different philosophical traditions, and the social and political context invariably have references to or sections on friendship. For example, **Arnold** on Roman Stoicism treats friendship in the chapter on 'Counsels of Perfection'. A more recent work, **Macintyre** on moral theory, includes chapters on heroic societies, Athens, Aristotle, and a comparative look at Homer, Aristotle, the New Testament, Benjamin Franklin and Jane Austin, which refer to the place of friendship and its distinctive role in different communities, and its relationship to the other virtues. **den Boer** is concerned with the code of personal behaviour in every day life in Greece and Rome. Included in this private morality is love of neighbour, and den Boer, like

MacIntyre, sees the concept of friendship as having a distinctive role in different communities, with the Greek concept of friendship or *philia* being limited to feelings for one's fellow Greeks, and the Roman idea of friendship representing a loyal association of citizens.

A major theme covered in the historic literature is that on sexual traditions, mainly of the Greeks. One of the most detailed and comprehensive is **Licht**. The contents include erotic rituals and literature, homosexuality and heterosexuality, marriage, masturbation, prostitution and 'perversions'. Most useful for our topic is his chapter on 'Erotic in Greek Literature', which gives a chronological summary of literature on *eros* from the epic and lyric poetry and prose of the classical period through to the love poetry and prose up until AD 530, by which time the Greco-Roman culture had become overwhelmed by the Goths and Christianity. **Winkler** uses a less systematic methodology, described as 'desultory science' and 'equestrian academics', to present a variety of perspectives from different approaches about sexual practices in ancient Greece, which includes erotic protocols, men's sexual behaviour, erotic magic spells, and chapters on Penelope in the *Odyssey,* and on Sappho's lyrics. **Dover** (1973) looks at the regulations and traditions governing sexual behaviour in the relatively uninhibited Greek culture, including segregation of the sexes, adultery, homosexuality, prostitution, chastity and self-control. A special issue of the journal *Differences* in 1990, edited by **Konstan** and **Nussbaum,** covers 'Sexuality in Greek and Roman Society' includes an article by Halperin which looks at 'The Democratic Body: Prostitution and Citizenship in Classical Athens'.

The issue of homosexuality is dealt with specifically in two important works. **Dover** (1978) looks at the extent and status of homosexuality in Ancient Greece using as his sources the literature of the period and the visual arts. **Buffière** focuses more on pederasty. He covers the difference between pederasty and homosexuality, attitudes of the Athenian intelligentsia to the phenomenon of pederasty, and the place of *eros* and pederasty in Plato and Aristotle, treatises on love of the Peripatetics, the writings of the Cynics, the Stoics, and Plutarch. Both refer to these ideas as being acceptable in certain sectors of Greek society, but certainly not uncontroversially. Buffière, for example, claims that Socrates and his entourage were the first in Athenian philosophical circles to manifest an interest in pederasty, but that Socrates' relationship with young men were argued to be pure as opposed to carnal. **Dover** (1973) discusses the taken-for-granted nature of homosexuality in Classical Greece, but also refers to the 'dual standard of morality' where an older Greek was congratulated if he found a boy to love, whereas the boy was praised if he managed to retain his chastity (59-73). The issue of homosexuality and pederasty is also dealt with in most of the literature which refers to friendship and love. **Hutter** refers to the disagreement among Classical scholars about the extent of social acceptance of pederasty and the date of its appearance as a wide-spread practice in Greece. **Flacelière** (1962) believed that pederasty was probably confined to the leisured nobility of Athens and that it was not introduced to Greece before the Dorian invasions. An era in which there was a concentration and sensitivity to physical beauty, combined with the rise of the gymnasia and the arenas in which boys practiced their athletic pursuits, he claims, encouraged the development of homosexual relations, and in particular pederasty. **Babut** discusses the change in attitude towards pederasty evident in the later Stoics who emphasised marriage rather than homosexual love. However, pederasty was not wholly condemned. Rather the Stoics interpreted the relationship between sage and young boy as spiritual rather than physical. **Eglinton** uses the model of Greek love to look at 'boy-love' in historical context. **Foucault** in his major work on *The History of Sexuality* also deals with this issue in Volume III, 'The Care of the Self'. He refers to the way Roman culture posed the question of boys as objects of pleasure, and the 'valorization of marriage' which contributed to a lessening of focus on the love relation between men in theoretical and moral discussions (190). He cites one of the most important ideas of Plutarch's *Amatorius* as being 'that the woman is just as capable as the man of inspiring amorous passion.' (182n).

This changing role of women in antiquity is another topic dealt with extensively in the literature. There is a debate regarding both Greek and Roman women about the extent of the freedom enjoyed by them in the classical era. Women in Rome played an important part in public and social life as sacred priestesses, were accorded high status within the family and some wealthy women were able to exercise a degree of political power (**Bell; Fau; Balsdon; Hallett** in Perandotto and Sullivan; **Fantham et al**). However, Roman women were subject to many legal restrictions such as no legal control over their children, no right to vote, and male guardianship (**Gardner** 1993). Most commentators acknowledge the ambiguity of the role of Athenian women. Women took part in some business activities, had an important role in ritual activity and were responsible for the prosperity of the household. However, Greek women were not legally permitted to transact much important business, had no political rights and were excluded from much of Athenian activity (**den Boer; Pomeroy; Flacelière** 1962; **Bell; Fantham et al; Wright**). Flacelière argues that as Greek women were unable legally to act independently, and did not receive the same education as men, they were therefore unable to act as the intellectual or spiritual companion of males.

It was the increasing independence and education of women which enabled them to be considered to be capable of friendship with men and the literature of the period increasingly focussed on the possibility of friendship between female and male, particularly within marriage. There is a paucity of literature which deals with the idea of friendship between women themselves, and very little which looks at friendship or love from a woman's perspective. There is some historical evidence which indicates that women formed friendships and loving relations with other women. **Hutter** argues that the female friendship groups formed in Sparta, Mytilene and Doreic and Aeolina Greece were possible because these were cultures where women enjoyed more public freedom (59). **Fantham et al** find some epitaphs which describe the love of women for other women. But the main written source for information about women's relationships in the period are the poems of Sappho. Hutter suggests that the group of women surrounding Sappho was regarded in antiquity as comparable to the group of men surrounding Socrates, that both groups were inspired with a mixture of *philia* and *eros,* and that the fragments of the poems of Sappho which sing the praises of female friendships 'were reminiscent of the praise of male friendship to be found in a number of Greek poets generally' (60).

Xenophon

Morrison's bibliography gives a comprehensive list of all the works by or about Xenophon published up until 1988 in Latin, German, French, English, Italian, Spanish and 'Other'. Much of the secondary material on Xenophon concentrates on his reliability as a witness to the teachings of Socrates. **Alline** discusses the debate about Xenophon's accuracy as a reporter of Socrates which has some commentators believing Xenophon to be objective, persuasive and measured, and others challenging the validity of Xenophon as a witness. Alline himself believes that Xenophon's reports are contradictory and inaccurate and reflect Xenophon's romantic and vain personality and his tendency to moralise and embellish. **Edwards** argues that because Xenophon was simple-minded, unimaginative and had no philosophic system of his own, it is likely that his accounts of Socrates would be a faithful description of his teaching and character, although they might be somewhat naive and commonplace. **Chroust** agrees with Alline that Xenophon's accounts of Socrates 'may contain a nucleus of historical truth around which a complex fabric or fictions has been woven by Xenophon.' (16). However, **Strauss** gives a different picture of the value of Xenophon's account of Socrates' teachings. Strauss devoted himself to a detailed textual analysis of all of Xenophon's works and argues that Xenophon should be regarded as a vital source for 'our precise knowledge of Socrates' thought'. **Bonnette's** translator's note refers to the sentiments voiced by the more recent generation of translators who express respect for Xenophon and she credits Strauss with giving translators more reason to treat Xenophon carefully. **Higgins** also acknowledges 'an enormous debt' to Strauss for challenging the scholarly tradition of berating Xenophon. Higgins attempts a 'close reading' of Xenophon which also looks at the 'total oeuvre'.

Another related topic of debate in the literature is the comparison between the *Symposium* of Plato and the *Symposium* of Xenophon. There is disagreement among commentators as to which *Symposium* or Banquet was written first, although most credit Plato with providing the model followed by Xenophon. The date of Plato's, about 385, is known, but the exact date of Xenophon's Banquet is not. **Flacelière** (1961) believes that Xenophon's came after Plato and that Xenophon's Socrates is portrayed as being more convivial and more moralistic about homosexuality (105). Xenophon's Socrates is seen by **Ollier** to be diminished by Xenophon's portrayal. He agrees with Flacelière that it is likely that Xenophon followed Plato. There are striking and numerous similarities between the two works, and it seems highly unlikely that Plato would need to imitate Xenophon. Ollier argues that it is more plausible that Xenophon's *Symposium* is derived more or less from Plato's, but is a more personal account aimed at rectifying some of the criticisms of Socrates. **Tredennick and Waterfield** (1990) also believe that it is 'extremely likely that Xenophon is dependent on Plato rather than the other way round.' (220). **Tredennick** (1970) points out that although there are differences in the two portraits of Socrates, they both depict 'a man eager for goodness' (7). **Gemoll** contrasts the way in which Xenophon and Plato treat pederasty and **Feuerstein** believes that Xenophon rendered Socrates' teaching more exactly, whereas Plato wanted to go a step further than Socrates. **Gallardo,** whose article compares the Symposia of Plato, Xenophon and

Plutarch, also sees Plato rather than Xenophon as the initiator of the philosophical tradition of symposia which continues a tradition of erotic literature.

There is very little in the English language specifically on Xenophon and friendship or *eros*. One reference which has friendship in its title is **Hirsch** *Friendship of the Barbarians: Xenophon and the Persian Empire*. However this concentrates on Xenophon's attitudes to the Persians and his reliability as an historian. It is not really about friendship, but uses a quote from the Anabasis for the title.[2] **Tredennick's** 1970 translation of the *Memorabilia* and *Symposium* also discusses the distinction between celestial and common love, which Plato's Socrates emphasises, as well as the more practical love for the ordinary man (22). **Higgins** does not concentrate on friendship but he does touch upon such matters as Xenophon's treatment of the similarity between friends and kin (27) and there is a discussion of the role of friendship in citizenship, and Socrates' relationship with his friends (38). **Strauss** gives a detailed commentary on the *Memorabilia* and the *Symposium* and refers to the *Symposium* as having three themes of 'beauty and love', 'laughter' and 'wisdom' (145). He believes that Socrates shows through selected myths 'that gods and heroes too esteem the friendship of the soul more highly than the enjoyment of the body' (174). However, there is little more specifically on friendship. **Bruell** discusses briefly whether there is an attempt by Socrates to transcend justice with acts of friendship (267) and there is also a brief reference to the relationship between marriage and *eros* (290). However, the article concentrates on the *Oeconomus* and household management rather than Xenophon's writings on love or friendship. **Konstan** (1991) writes of *eros* and *philia* in Xenophon's novel *Ephesian Tale* where he contrasts Xenophon's attitude to homoerotic and heteroerotic relationships and sets these in the context of the classical Greek novel.

Plato

By contrast with Xenophon there is a vast literature on the dialogues of Plato, and in particular on those associated most closely with the themes of love and friendship - the *Lysis,* the *Phaedrus* and the *Symposium.* Apart from commentaries which relate specifically to one or other of these three dialogues, there are debates in the literature about how much Plato's theory reflects the ideas of Socrates, how the Greek terms relating to love and friendship should be interpreted, what constitutes Platonic love, the role of women in Plato's dialogues and the historical sequence of the dialogues.

Although Plato is more generally accepted as being Socrates's mouthpiece, there is nevertheless, as there is with Xenophon, a debate about how closely Plato reflects the teachings of Socrates. **Cobb** refers to the discussion about whether Plato's version is an accurate portrayal of Socrates' views, whether Socrates is only a spokesperson for Plato's ideas, and whether Plato actually challenges Socrates' ideas. **Graham** refers to the theory that the Socrates of the early dialogues is a more faithful representation than the Socrates portrayed later on, and attempts to distinguish between Plato and Socrates. **Cornford** also claims that Plato and Socrates had contrasting views (75). **Dawson** discusses the relationship between Socrates and his followers and the impact of his teachings on the writings of Aristotle, Cicero, Marcus Aurelius, Epictetus and others.

Commentators on Plato include discussion on the interpretation of the Greek terms for love and friendship. **Gonzalez** surveys the commentaries on the *Lysis,* many of which refer to the debate initiated by Pohlenz and von Arnim about the distinction between *eros* and *philia* in Plato. **Levin** in Anton and Kustas looks at the way in which the terms *eros* and *philia* are used in the dialogues to throw light on the 'progression of meaning from a less inclusive to a broader usage' (xxviii). **Grube** distinguishes between *philia* and *eros* with *philia* being a more general term for love, including the love of parents or between youths as well as passionate love. Because *philia* is an inclusive term, the development of *eros,* he argues, can be traced through the dialogues, including the *Lysis* (92n). On the other hand, **Hyland** argues that the terms *eros* and *philia* are distinct and not used interchangeably by Plato. *Philia* is more closely connected with reason, *eros* with desire. For **Irwin** (1995), *eros* is associated with sexual desire, with one sort of *eros* being rational, but also sharing some of the intensity and apparent irrationality of non-rational appetites (306). **Nehamas** and **Woodruff** also distinguish between *eros,* which refers to a particularly intense attachment and to desire generally, and *philia,* which 'applies indifferently to the feelings of friends, family members and lovers'(xiii). **Cobb** agrees that *eros* can refer to desire, primarily sexual desire, whereas *philia* is concerned with a relationship of 'mutuality and sharing between friends and between members of a family and would not ordinarily imply sexual desire.' (6). **Halperin** (1985) further claims that Plato's *eros* is concerned with desire 'in the sense of passionate longing for a beloved or cherished value' rather than simple sexual desire which is aimed at a particular object (170). **Santas** (1988) provides a 'chart on love' referring to *Philia, Eros* and *Agape,* where he places 'friendship' somewhere between *philia* and *eros.* **Brentlinger** contrasts Platonic *eros* with Christian *agape* and argues that they are not easily distinguishable from each other (123).

There is also a controversy in the literature about quite how personal is the love which Plato describes in his dialogues. **Vlastos** argues that Plato's love is more concerned with passion for abstract objects rather than a sexual love for another individual. **Price** (1981) disagrees and claims that Plato's theory of love includes both 'personal and intellectual aspects' (27). **Kosman** (1976) also opposes Vlastos by arguing that Plato does value interpersonal love, love of the beloved and love of 'humanity incarnate' within the beloved (67). The interpretation of love proposed by **Nussbaum** (1986) is based on her idea that Plato is writing about passion 'out of a particular experience of his own' and is a response to personal individuality (212). **Gill** in Loizou and Lesser summarizes the debate, and ends up agreeing with Kosman and Price 'that one needs to explore ways of thinking about personal love that are not centred on the notion of unique individuality if one is to do justice to the nature, and the cogency, of Platonic thinking about love' (83).

The role of women in Plato's dialogues has been the subject of both feminist and mainstream writers. Much of the debate centres around whether or not Plato was a 'feminist' and why he referred to philosophy as a woman. There is a substantial amount of commentary on Plato's treatment of gender in Book V of *The Republic,* but the writings which are more relevant for our purposes are those which explore why Plato used Diotima in the *Symposium* to act as Socrates' mouthpiece in his teachings on love. **Tuana's** edited collection includes some of the major contributions to the debate - Vlastos, Saxonhouse, du Bois, Brown, Irigaray, Nye. There is reference to the debate in **Cobb** on the *Symposium.* **Irigaray** has contributed to the debate and a special issue of *Hypatia* on French Feminist Philosophy produced in 1989 includes articles which debate Irigaray's interpretation of the role of Diotima in the *Symposium* and a book by **Chanter** is a further interpretation of Irigaray's 'rewriting of the philosophers'. **Halperin's** (1990) chapter 'Why is Diotima a Woman' proposes several possible interpretations.

That Plato's references to women indicate a negative attitude is argued by several commentators. **Wender** discusses whether Plato was misogynist, paedophile or feminist and concludes that Plato 'did not

like or admire us. But he felt it would be just and expedient to give us
a chance' (90). **Cobb** suggests that using a woman to act as Socrates'
teacher might be interpreted as a comic device, not to be taken
seriously, because of the common attitude towards women that they
lacked balance and were excessive (72). **Irigaray** argues that Diotima's
message of universal love is undermined by the fact that there are no
women present at the *Symposium*. **Brown** argues that Plato personifies
philosophy and truth as female because this will make them seem
difficult, unattainable, and more inaccessible to men. However, she
claims that Plato ends up 'reinforcing Athenian constructions of
politics as male and corrupt while glorifying philosophy as female,
powerless, and pure'. **Halperin** (1990) also makes the suggestion that
Diotima is not there to represent or speak for women, but rather to
represent the other – an alternative identity for the male.

Several commentators argue that Plato demonstrates a respect for
women which might be considered feminist. **Cobb** finds it significant
that in the *Symposium* Socrates depicts himself as philosophically
inferior to everyone else and that, consistent with this, his superior
should be a woman. **Nye** (1989) takes issue with Irigaray whose
ahistorical analysis does not recognise Diotima's authority, thus missing
the significance of Diotima as the 'hidden host' at the Banquet. Nye
claims that in classical times women priestesses, such as Diotima,
would have been accorded great respect. Diotima therefore, cannot be
said to be speaking from a marginalised position. **Saxonhouse** (1984)
argues that Plato uses Diotima in the *Symposium* to raise questions
about the 'arrogance of the male world that would exclude the female
and bring to itself death and sterility' (24). She claims that Plato did
not care for women as such but was able to overcome the misogyny of
his culture and incorporate the female into his work in recognition of
their difference and creativity in order to criticize the contemporary
structures of his own society (25).

Three Dialogues – the Lysis, the Symposium and the Phaedrus

Most commentaries on Plato's dialogues deal with each of them
separately, but there are some which treat the three primarily
concerned with love and friendship in a comparative way. **Grube** gives
a summary of these dialogues, discusses how they are interrelated and
traces the development of *eros* through the three dialogues. **Robin** sees
the *Symposium* as a continuation of the *Lysis* and the *Phaedrus* as a
clarification of the *Symposium*. He examines the part each of the
dialogues play in the constitution of the theory of love (39). He argues

that the *Lysis* is mainly negative, demonstrating the insufficiency of the popular notion of friendship, that the *Symposium* is positive addressing the questions that the *Lysis* leaves unresolved; and that the *Phaedrus* develops those points left unexplained in the *Symposium*. The *Phaedrus*, he argues, makes us see that the desire for immortality is part of the nature of the soul, which is aroused by beauty and liberated by love. **Santas** (1988) has separate chapters on each of the dialogues and also considers the *Republic* in tracing what he claims is Plato's thesis of 'the unity of love'. Santas believes that we need to take seriously the distinction between a generic and a specific *eros* and to think of *philia* as another species of desire for the good (94). **Price** (1989) also has separate chapters devoted to the different dialogues. Like Robin he argues that the *Lysis* sets the scene for Plato's investigation into love and friendship, the *Symposium* discusses it further, but the *Phaedrus* concludes with a more realistic description of feelings of love and the personal interest in another person. **Vlastos** devotes a chapter to 'Love in Plato'. He discuses the *Lysis, Symposium,* and *Phaedrus* as well as the *Republic* and by means of these compares Plato to Aristotle. Vlastos concludes that Plato's theory 'does not provide for the love of whole persons, but only for love of that abstract version of persons which consists of the complex of their best qualities' (31).

The *Lysis* and the *Symposium* are discussed together by **Kosman** (1976) who deals with questions such as whether Plato's theory of love is basically egoistical and selfish; and whether it is concerned with the love of an individual person, or with the love of beauty or of beautiful qualities. Kosman, as indicated earlier, concludes that the vision to which Diotima alludes is 'the mystery of loving being itself incorporated in the world, of loving in my very beloved himself humanity incarnate' (67). **Hyland** explores the *Symposium* and the *Lysis* and argues for an hierarchical distinction between *eros*, desire and *philia*, based on the degree of reason in each. **Kelson** recounts the *Lysis* and the *Symposium* and deals with the issue of homosexuality in a psychological analysis of Plato.

More common are comparisons between the *Symposium* and the *Phaedrus*, called by **Cobb** 'Plato's Erotic Dialogues', which deal 'with both the earthly origins and the spiritual heights of erotic love' (1). Cobb comments in detail on these two dialogues and also lists references to *eros* in other dialogues – *Charmedes, Lysis, Republic, Laws, Theatetus* and *Phaebus*. The focus of **Nussbaum** (1986) is the contrast between two central preoccupations of ancient Greek thought about the human good – the pursuit for self-sufficiency, control and choice; and the place of luck and love of riskiness. She has separate chapters on the speech of Alcibiades in the *Symposium* and the idea of 'madness, reason and recantation' in the *Phaedrus*. Although her emphasis is not on love and friendship, she does refer to the personal love expressed in these dialogues which she argues is evidence that Plato writes about passion 'out of a particular experience of his own' (212). **Gill** in Loizou and Lesser refers to Nussbaum's contribution to the debate. Gill also concentrates on the *Phaedrus* and the *Symposium* and disagrees with Nussbaum, seeing Kosman's and Price's interpretations as more convincing. He argues that 'Like Kosman and Price, I think that one needs to explore ways of thinking about personal love that are not centred on the notion of unique individuality if one is to do justice to the nature, and the cogency, of Platonic thinking about love' (83). **Irwin** (1995) in a chapter on Platonic love discusses the different aspects of *eros* covered by Plato in the *Phaedrus*, the *Symposium* and the *Republic*. He argues that Plato insists that one sort of *eros* belongs to the rational part of human thought, but shares some of the intensity and apparent irrationality of non-rational appetites. **Rist** examines the *Phaedrus* and the *Symposium* in detail and claims that what Plato was talking about was a rarified kind of love which demanded 'an emotional response beyond the range of most of even the greatest of his admirers...' (23). **Kraut** (1973) looks mainly at the *Republic* but also discusses the *Symposium* and the *Phaedrus*. Kraut argues that Plato has been misread as an egoist because he sometimes uses the concept of self-interest in a broader way than we do. **Stannard** discusses the *Symposium* and the *Phaedrus* and argues that Plato's formulation of the dialectic was the outcome of his reflection on the role played by Socratic *eros* in philosophical inquiry (120). **Morgan** in a book for 'beginners' recounts some of the different readings regarding Plato's attitudes to sexuality.

Aristotle

The main issues that arise in connection with Aristotle on friendship are types of friendship, meaning of terms, egoism and self-love, self-sufficiency in friendship, politics and friendship, and Christianity and friendship.

Two works devoted to Aristotle on friendship are **Stern-Gillet** (1995) and **Schollmeier** (1994). Stern-Gillet discusses the neglect of the topic of friendship, until relatively recently, by commentators on

Aristotelian ethics. She argues that 'Aristotle's conception of friendship, far from being a mere appendix to his ethics, constitutes an integral and crucial part of it' (4). In addition, she claims that it is important for modern day readers to be shaken from their complacency by exposure to Aristotle's views on friendship which are often in sharp contrast to modern notions. Her book concentrates on the ideas of relationship between self and others and includes chapters on selfhood, selves and other selves, for the sake of others, self-love, egoism, self-sufficiency, and friendship, justice and the state. Schollmeier places more emphasis on the political component of Aristotle's philosophy. However, he agrees with Stern-Gillet that philosophers have been negligent in not seeing the integrity of Aristotle's theory and incorporating his philosophy on friendship. Schollmeier offers some useful schematic diagrams categorising different types of friendships and relationships, and his chapters cover topics such as happiness and virtue, a definition of friendship, a motivation for friendship, political friendship and political justice.

Other authors whose works contain chapters on Aristotelian friendship include **Price** (1989), **Nussbaum** (1986) **Wadell** and **Singer**. The numerous translations of Aristotle's ethical writings often include commentary on his theory of friendship. **Rees'** translation is accompanied by a detailed commentary on each book of the *Nicomachean Ethics* by Joachim who considers the role of friendship in the ideal life. The link between Aristotelian ideas of friendship and Christianity is examined by several writers commenting on the works of St. Thomas Aquinas. There is a 1964 translation by **Litzinger** of Aquinas' commentary on the *Nicomachean Ethics*. The connection between friendship and charity is further explored by **Jaffa** in his study of Aquinas' commentary. **Jones** looks at the theological transformation of Aristotelian friendship in the thought of Thomas Aquinas and makes a contrast between Aquinas' account of the moral life, which emphasises friendship with God or charity, and Aristotle's account which, he claims, sets up a contradiction between friendship and contemplation, particularly related to the gods (380).

Commentators on Aristotle also discuss the definition of terms related to the debate on friendship. **Tracy** provides a comprehensive list of the various kinds of *philia* distingushed by Aristotle, including the pleasurable, profitable, erotic, marital, filial, parental, companionable and civic, before focusing his discussion on '*philia* par excellence' or perfect *philia*. **Cooper** (1993), in Badhwar, discusses rhetoric and the passions and claims that the art of rhetoric includes speaking from the heart motivated by *eunoia*, which he interprets as good will, and *philia*, which he calls 'friendly feelings'. A chapter on Aristotle and relationship goods in **Nussbaum** interprets *philia* as including not only relationships between friends, but also close family, strong affective relationships and relationships that have a sexual component (354). However, Nussbaum does acknowledge that in Aristotle's account of friendship, sexuality and sexual attraction do not play a major part (369). **Hadreas** looks at the translation of the terms *eunoia* which he sees as an essential condition of friendship and suggests that it should be rendered as either 'recognition of another's worthiness' or 'to think favorably of'.

Much of the commentary focuses on Aristotle's three categories of friendship. Do the inferior types of friendship – utility and pleasure – count as true friendship? Assuming the virtuous are self-sufficient, can they have any need for friends? These and other dilemmas are raised by Aristotle's analysis. **Cooper** (1980) and **Alpern** debate the issue of the two inferior kinds of friendship. Cooper argues that both these types of friendship include well-wishing and concern for the friend himself, but that perfect friendship is less self-seeking and the well-wishing is both broader and deeper. However, Alpern believes that there are difficulties with this position and he claims that 'a strong case can be made that inferior friendships do not involve disinterestedness' even though he admits that these relationships 'can be seen to exhibit cooperation, trust, commitment, and other virtues of interpersonal relationships' (304). **Price** (1989) discusses Cooper's views in detail and argues that he is 'correctly understanding the structure of Aristotle's treatment, but applying it against the grain of the text' (154).

Cooper also contributes to the debate on the self-sufficiency of perfect friendship. He suggests that the need for friends does not imply a defect in the person, but means that having friends 'is a necessary constituent of a flourishing life' (318). **Sherman** also claims that Aristotle sees self-sufficiency as not merely living but flourishing. Self-sufficiency is possible in the material sense, but a person without friends would not be self-sufficient with regard to good activity. **Stern-Gillet** argues that Aristotle's ideal of self-sufficiency 'is anything but constraining or mean-spirited' (130). **Adkin** compares the concepts of friendship and self-sufficiency in Homer and Aristotle. He discusses the 'degree of selfishness of the different types of Aristotelian *philia*' and argues that the essentials of the concept in Aristotle remain as in Homer. His reference to self-sufficiency is discussed in terms of the survival of the social unit. **Aubenque** argues that friendship is essential for self-knowledge, as man strives for an imitation of the divine.

The most extensive and complex debate on Aristotle concerns the egoism in friendship he advocates and whether self-love and altruism are compatible. **Price** (1989) sees this as a paradox 'into which Aristotle has stumbled' (p112) and cites earlier commentators, such as W. D. Ross (1954), G. C. Field (1921) and W. F .R. Hardie (1968) who argue that Aristotle's theory is egoistic. However, most recent commentators dispute this view, although the debate continues about the relationship between self-love and altruism. **Stern-Gillet** discusses the issues of self-love, altruism, and egoism, including an exegesis of Aristotle's pronouncements on self-love and its relation to friendship. Stern-Gillet argues that Aristotelian self-love 'would not necessarily carry the egoistic connotations that we have come generally to associate with this notion, and it would co-exist with or even ground disinterested love for others' (80). **Schollmeier** suggests that 'Aristotle's political philosophy might turn out to be both altruistic and pluralistic and that these properties would make his theory more sophisticated and more feasible than usually supposed' (15). **Rogers** claims that altruism is not a helpful concept to use for interpreting Aristotle's doctrine of friendship.

Kraut (1975) argues that Aristotle cannot be interpreted as an egoist because for Aristotle 'being loved is secondary to loving' (313). **Annas** (1988), looking at the role of self-love in Aristotle's ethics, is not satisfied 'with the way Kraut brings in restrictions from outside in order to mitigate the apparent self-centredness of Aristotle's conclusion' and she also disagrees with Kraut on his interpretation of the role of competition in Aristotle (10). In **Kraut's** (1988) response to Annas, he agrees with much of her discussion and admits that she is right to be puzzled by Aristotle's description of the self-sacrificing agent. But he disagrees that an excellent person should take no account of the fact that the heroic action he is about to perform would be good for him, and suggests that if one is aware that one is acting for one's own sake as well as for the sake of others, this mixed motivation is not incoherent or morally questionable (22).

Dziob also disagrees with Annas that 'the issue is really the person's reasoning part' (13) when considering self-love. Dziob concurs with Kraut's conclusion that each friend is better off for having competed and argues that Annas agrees with her (Dziob's) conclusion that the moral rivalry of friends 'yields mutual victory... hence neither contestant is deemed selfish or unselfish' (799). **Kahn** agrees with

Annas 'in recognizing the doctrine of the other self as the nerve of the argument..., the crucial concept which permits Aristotle to pass from virtuous self-love to an altruistic concern for the interests of others' (29). However, he believes that she does not emphasise enough Aristotle's doctrine of *nous,* or the way the intellect 'plays an implicit role in the derivation of altruism from self-love' (29). **Benson** argues that Annas' interpretation is too meagre and that Kahn's 'imports unneeded metaphysical baggage' (58). He suggests a third interpretation. In considering whether Aristotelian friendship is altruistic, Benson refers to Nagel's distinction between two standpoints for considering value questions. According to this theory there are two kinds of altruism – viewed from either an objective or a subjective standpoint. Benson claims that Aristotle's account makes no reference to the objective viewpoint and that 'the altruism of the objective viewpoint is not appropriate to friendship.' (62). Objectivity is one way to escape from the narrow confines of self-concern, but the other way is to 'expand the boundaries of the self by incorporating the personal viewpoints of others within one's own.' (63) and so friendship becomes the way in which one can be altruistic.

Cooper (1980) in Rorty also argues in defence of altruism. He concludes his chapter by saying that 'Aristotle's argument, in short, is that in loving and valuing the other person for his own sake, one becomes able to love and value oneself.... There is no reduction here of friendship to narrow self-love' (333). **Millgram** agrees with Cooper to an extent but admits that his own interpretation of Aristotle does not allow for genuine altruism and claims that Aristotle's explanations of friendship 'are uniformly self-oriented...' (376). **Schoeman** claims that Cooper emphasises the good for one's character and life of having friends, whereas Schoeman wants to emphasise why it is good to be a friend and how this can reveal 'an important way in which friendship is a virtue for Aristotle' (271).

The impartialist claim that we should give the interests of others the same weight as our own is discussed in **Sherman** who contends that Kantian theory gives insufficient weight to intimacy and friendship in his moral scheme (612). Sherman also contrasts ideas of attachment and altruism, arguing that friendship goes beyond this attachment to a specific person and that 'through friendship happiness becomes extended to include the happiness of others'. **Politis** suggests that there is a more complex question than whether altruism is compatible with self-love. '[G]iven that self-love is compatible with some kind of altruism, what kinds of altruism is it compatible with, especially if the self-love in question enjoys priority over love for others?' (159).

The role Aristotle assigns to friendship in state and society is an important theme in the literature. Aristotle's concept of friendship has been used to contribute to the modern communitarian debate. Some commentators such as **Stern-Gillet** and **Annas** (cited in Stern-Gillet) claim that the concept of civic friendship was not regarded as particularly important for Aristotle. Stern-Gillet devotes a chapter to 'friendship, justice and the state' and points out that the term civic friendship has become a semi-technical expression used by recent commentators, although it was in fact used 'economically' by Aristotle. However, Stern-Gillet acknowledges that Aristotle was not unconcerned with civic friendship, and saw it as a reflection of the constitution of the state 'which, to a large extent, determines not only the nature and the extent of the civic bond, but also its moral worth' (154).

Cooper (1977, 1980, 1993) on the other hand, claims that Aristotle sees civic friendship as an essential component, in addition to personal friendship, for a flourishing human life. He claims that Aristotle rejects the commercial model for a city and identifies friendship explicitly as the bond between fellow citizens in the city community. Plato's and Aristotle's views of 'the city' are compared in **Price** (1989) who sees Aristotle's civic friendship as 'an extended variety of friendship of the good' (204). Price writes that although he and Cooper have attached 'different labels to civic friendship (he of "utility", I of virtue), we are trying to make sense, in overlapping ways, of what is in substance the same conception' (205 n36). **Bickford** takes issue with commentators such as Cooper who view Aristotle from a unitary perspective. She argues that although Aristotle does stress the role of community and friendship in politics, he understood 'politics as a realm of conflict and interaction among imperfect, diverse, and sometimes unequal citizens' (419). **McIntyre's** account of Aristotle's view of the community opposes Bickford's interpretation. According to McIntyre, Aristotle treats conflict as 'an eliminable evil. The virtues are all in harmony with each other and the harmony of individual character is reproduced in the harmony of the state' (157). **Schollmeier** on civic friendship refers back to the debate about altruism. He contends that both personal and political friendship can be either altruistic or egoistic. The forms of government based on altruistic friendship are kingship, aristocracy or polity, whereas egoistic friendship produces oligarchy, tyranny or democracy (see Figure 7, 115). **Derrida** also discusses the relationship between friendship and the political and how the 'living together' aspect of Aristotle's friendship makes it political (200).

Comparing the Eudemian Ethics and the Nicomachean Ethics

The relationship between the *Nicomachean* and the *Eudemian Ethics* and the logical forms of analysis used by Aristotle are debated in the literature. **Kenny** takes a very technical look at textual and philosophical differences, but refers to friendship only sparsely. **Fortenbaugh** discusses the use of focal analysis in the *Nicomachean Ethics* and the *Eudemian Ethics*. He claims that the *Nicomachean* shows Aristotle at his logical best by the use of function, analogy and resemblance analysis. The richness of the analysis in the *Nicomachean*, Fortenbaugh suggests, is evidence of its superiority to the *Eudemian Ethics*. **Walker** takes issue with some of Fortenbaugh's interpretation and he argues that in the *Nicomachean Ethics* Aristotle relates the three types of friendship 'not by appeal either to the notion of analogical or to that of focal homonymy, but in terms of the third and little noticed form of homonymy' (180). **Pakaluk** (1992) uses narrow textual analysis to explore the nature of Aristotle's description of friendship and argues that this needs to be considered with reference to the *Eudemian Ethics*. According to Pakaluk, Aristotle's division of friendship into three kinds is a 'rejection of and alternative to a Platonic understanding of friendship and love, according to which goods are beautiful and things are "harmonious"' (129). **Price** (1989) argues that Aristotle uses the two works on Ethics to explore in different styles the issue of friendship, '*the Eudemian Ethics* being more abstract and metaphysical, the *Nicomachean* the more concrete and empirical' (121); the *Eudemian Ethics* more logical and the *Nicomachean Ethics* more detailed. Price discusses both Walker's and Fortenbaugh's analyses and adopts an interpretation 'quite close to Walker's' (139) and finds some parts of Fortenbaugh 'useful' (144). He concludes that 'ideally... Aristotle would have combined the rigor that is an aim of the *Eudemian* treatment with the greater amplitude of the *Nicomachean*' (148).

Cicero

Much of the commentary on Cicero and friendship focuses on translations and interpretations of Cicero's *de Amicitia* (or the *Laelius*) but also on Cicero's political thought more generally. Themes debated are Cicero's personal friendship, the originality of his thought and whether *amicitia* was concerned with personal or public relationships. **Powell's** translation includes substantial commentary on the *Laelius*. **Fiore** includes commentary on the *Commentariolum Petitionis* which in its practical outlook contrasts with the more idealistic discussion of friendship in *Laelius*.

Rawson, one of the few works in English which focuses specifically on Cicero and friendship, is more biographical than philosophical, recounting the friendship between Cicero and Pompey. Cicero's accounts of friendship among the Roman elite illustrates the way in which *amicitia* operated in practice. **Spielvogel** discusses Cicero's relationship with various members of the nobility, patron-client relationships and relationships among the ruling class. **Hutter** makes the connection in Cicero's life between politics and friendship and the conflict of loyalties to friends or the state.

How original was Cicero's work? How influential were the Greek sources? Earlier commentators such as **Allcroft** and **Masom** (1895) claim that 'there is probably very little original thought in the *Amicitia*' (95) and that Cicero's ideas were merely adapted from Greek writers such as Theophrastus, Plato, Aristotle and Xenophon. They suggest that his lack of acknowledgement of his sources is because it was embarrassing for a Roman writer to show too close an acquaintance with Greek literature. However, more recent writers play down the influence of Greek authorities and point to the originality of Cicero's interpretation. For **MacKendrick,** Cicero 'stands out as the first serious, original expounder of Hellenistic philosophical positions' and 'enhanced and enriched intellectual history and gave it dialectical vitality' (4). The chapter in MacKendrick 'On Friendship', by Karen Lee Singh, claims that there is no proof that Cicero borrowed directly from Plato or Aristotle and that 'the most important source for *On Friendship* was certainly Cicero himself – his own writings and experience' (220). She sees him as coming from a 'purely Roman perspective that gives the work its originality.' (221). **Powell** (1990) acknowledges that while most of the ideas in the *Laelius* derive from Greek sources, 'the composition and arrangement is Cicero's own' (5). **Brunt** says that Cicero was obviously influenced by the Greeks although his sources cannot definitely be identified. He recommends, however, that Cicero's *Laelius* be taken seriously 'as an expression of Roman experience' (4). **Konstan** (1994/5) refers to the claim by Gellins that Cicero borrowed freely from Theophrastus and also to the consequent dispute among critics about the amount of influence by Theophrastus (3-4). **Fiore** refers to the extensive analysis conducted on the source of Cicero's *Laelius* and concludes that 'the prevailing view is that Cicero cannot be tied to any particular sources or schools of thought for his views on friendship but that the treatise rather represents an eclectic sampling of views as well as ideas prevalent in the popular culture of the day' (60). **Grant** argues that if Cicero had copied the Greek philosophers he would have demonstrated more rigor and logic in his writings, instead of the inconsistency he displays (13). His originality, for Grant, consists in adapting Greek philosophy to the Roman environment (14).

Grant also discusses the extraordinary influence which Cicero's work has had and claims that Cicero 'has been the greatest of all conservers and transmitters of cultural values, the greatest unifying force of Europe, the shaper of its civilised speech' (31). Grant gives a chronological account of those influenced by Cicero's writings on love and friendship who include Caesar, Virgil, Seneca, Jerome, Augustine, Abelard, John of Salisbury, Guillaume de Loris, Jean de Meun, Boethius, Chaucer, Petrarch, Erasmus of Rotterdam and Montaigne. **Powell** (1990) also traces the influence of the *Laelius* on Seneca, Plutarch, Epictetus, Lucian, Maximus of Tyre, Libanius, Themistius, Aelred of Rievaulx, Peter of Blois, Marbod of Rennes and Montaigne. Was friendship (*amicitia*) in the Roman world a personal or a political relationship? **Hutter** finds that in ancient Rome there was nothing to equal the Greek cult of friendship and that 'Roman thinkers seem never to have seen *philia* mixed with *eros*' (138). **Brunt** uses Cicero to show that *amicitia* involved more than just the relationship between political colleagues. These political connections 'were often fragile and ties of private friendship could transcend their bonds'(20). **Konstan** (1997) agrees and argues that *amicitia* included mutual fondness and commitment which in Roman society also carried weight in political situations. **Powell** (1990) also warns against using the term *amicitia* as a technical term for any alliance between Roman aristocrats. He claims that the word has essentially the same meaning as friendship involving genuine feelings of goodwill and affection, but often occurs in political contexts. Cicero was referring essentially to personal friendship, although Romans on the whole were 'more prone than we are to mix personal and political considerations' (22). **Lee Singh** (in Mackendrick) says that *amicitia* can be employed loosely as a courtesy address, to describe personal relationships based on common interests as well as to refer to the highest level where friends, such as Cicero and Atticus, are in complete accord in all things without exception (219).

Seneca

Despite a Senecan revival in the twentieth century, work directly relating to Seneca on friendship remains rare. Motto has been responsible for several sourcebooks and bibliographies which chronicle Seneca's life, work and influence. The annotated bibliography in **Motto and Clark** (1989) bears witness to the twentieth century renaissance in Senecan studies. Works published between 1900 and 1980 are listed with some commentary. Items cited include bibliographies, editions, translations, manuscript studies, textual criticism, studies of Seneca's life, philosophy, language and style, influence and sources. **Motto** (1970) uses keywords to list all references made by Seneca to specific concepts. So Seneca's reference to 'friend' and 'friendship' are all listed, as well as passages which refer to Seneca's own friends. **Motto** (1985) includes forty of Seneca's letters plus commentary. Designed as a textbook, with Latin text, notes and vocabularies, the book also includes an introduction which covers Seneca's life, work, philosophy and style. An historical chronology of his extant works and a selected bibliography are also included. Seneca's Epistle III 'On Friendship' is presented with commentary about the relationship between the bond of friendship and his appeal for the rights of women. **Motto and Clark** also collaborate in *Essays on Seneca* (1993). Although there is nothing specifically on friendship in this work, there is a chapter entitled 'Seneca on Women's Liberation' where Seneca is acknowledged to be 'well in advance of his time regarding granting women equal opportunity at the banquet table, equal place at the feast of human endeavour.' (p177). More general discussions on friendship or love which make reference to Seneca include **Foucault, Fraisse** and **Hutter**.

Brief reference to friendship is made in some of the translations of Seneca's works. **Gummere** lists early English translations and identifies Theophrastus' work on friendship as an influence on Seneca. Gummere refers to Seneca's striking plea 'for the equality of the sexes and for conjugal fidelity in the husband to be interpreted no less strictly than honour on the part of the wife.' (xi) **Campbell** refers to the 'not uncommon choice of consolation or friendship as a theme' (21). Several of the translated selections of Seneca's 'Moral Epistles' omit those related to friendship. **Lipsius** and **Costa** (1988) do not include any of the letters on friendship.

Scholars have concentrated on Seneca's philosophical influence. **Campbell** refers to his influence among early Christians, in medieval times, the late Elizabethan age and the early seventeenth century. He lists those who have quoted Seneca, including Jerome, Lactantius, Augustine, Dante, Chaucer, Petrarch, Calvin, Montaigne, Pasquier, John of Salsbury, Emerson, Baudelaire, Erasmus, Sir John Harrington, Descartes, Corneille, La Fontaine, Poussin, Rousseau, Diderot, Balzac and Sainte-Beuve. **Cooper** and **Procope** (1995) refer to Seneca's influence on Plutarch as well as later writers such as St. Martin, archbishop of Braga in Portugal, Erasmas and the Belgian philosopher and scholar Lipsius. **Palmer** traces the influences of Seneca and Cicero from the birth of Christianity and includes those writers mentioned by other commentators as well as Boethius (sixth century), Alcium (eighth century), Lupus the Abbot of Ferrières (ninth century), Pope Sylvester II (tenth century), Otto Bishop of Freising, William of Conches (twelfth century), Vincent of Beauvais (thirteenth century), Master Robert Rypon (fifteenth century), Lyle, Marlow (sixteenth century), Bacon, Thomas Sutton and John Dunne (seventeenth century). **Reynold** comments that it was only the eighteenth century which was marked by non-contribution to Senecan studies. Seneca's contribution to English drama is discussed in **Mendell**. **Costa** (1974) believes that 'no other single writer of the ancient world has exercised a comparable influence on both the prose and the verse of subsequent literatures' (vii).

A substantial part of the discussion of Seneca's influence relates to his links to Christianity. The debate about the relationship between St. Paul and Seneca includes some medieval evidence, subsequently shown to be false, that these two thinkers had corresponded with each other (Costa 1988 and Reynolds). **Sevenster** discusses the one-hundred year debate in which some scholars have claimed personal contact between Paul and Seneca, others that Seneca was instrumental in shaping Christian thought, and others have compared their ideas without claiming any contact or influence. Sevenster compares the ideas of Paul and Seneca, drawing exclusively from their own writings and includes an examination of the difference in the attitude between the two to social relations and enemies. Seneca believed that people are bonded by nature to help each other. Friendship is highly esteemed. For St. Paul, men are bonded through God and fellowship between them is through Christ. The words *philia* or *philos* are never used in Paul's letters and he speaks rather of fellow-workers in Christ or fellow sufferers. Seneca argues that we should not waste time by devoting ourselves to quarrels, the preservation of serenity is important and we should help our enemies. Paul's position is that we should love our enemies and leave vengeance to God. For Paul, love is fulfilment of the law, and love is therefore a Christian duty.

Plutarch

Plutarch is famous for his personal friendships with many prominent people, for his influence on later writers and for carrying further Socrates' ideas on love (*philia*). He is seen by commentators to extend the debate on frankness (over flattery) in friendship, and to develop a case both for friendship in marriage and for heterosexuality over homosexuality.

A few writers have commented specifically on separate works of Plutarch related to love and friendship. **Hadas** gives a brief introducton to his translation of selected essays of Plutarch under the title of *On Love, the Family and the Good Life*. There is a fairly extensive but selected bibliography given in **Luce**. **Licht**, **Foucault** and **Patterson** discuss Plutarch's 'Marital Advice' or 'Conjugal Precepts'. His essay, variously entitled 'On Love', 'Erotikos', or 'Amatorius' is the focus of **Martin**, **Brenk** (1988) and **Hershbell** (1988). Plutarch's symposium, 'The Dinner of the Seven Sages' is covered by many writers. **Babbitt**, **Licht** and **Defradas** debate whether this work is authentic Plutarch. **Flacelière** (1964) translates the first three chapters into French. **Gallardo** compares Plutarch's symposium with those of Plato and Xenophon. **Trench**, **Engberg-Pederson** and **Konstan** (1996b) discuss Plutarch's 'How to tell a flatterer from a friend'. So does **Greard** in his discusson of brotherly love, the number of friends, and the usefulness of enemies. **O'Neil** gives a summary of Plutarch's writings on friendship and focusses in particular on the Greek terms used in these works.

Fitzgerald (1996) is a collection of essays on friendship in the New Testament world from the 1992 annual meeting of the Society of Biblical Literature in San Francisco and includes discussion of Plutarch's essay on 'Friends and Flatterers' as part of a tradition of discourse during the era of early Christianity. Konstan's essay sees the connection between friendship, frankness and flattery as 'the product of a specific cultural moment'. The essay by Glad refers to Plutarch's use of frank criticism in the language of friendship. Engberg-Pederson gives a detailed analysis of Plutarch's essay and also examines the connection between the three concepts, seeing flattery as a contrast to friendship, and frank criticism as a means to an end, with friendship an end, something good in itself (75). **Konstan** (1997) also refers to

Plutarch's concern with the issue of unequal friends and flattery (108). Plutarch's emphasis on the importance of sincerity in friendship is covered by **Greard**. **Trench** briefly comments on Plutarch's essay, mainly contrasting the art of flattery to the 'essence' of true friendship which depends on speaking frankly (135).

Several writers discuss the influence of Socrates on Plutarch's work and compare Plutarch with Plato and Xenophon. **Hershbell** (1988) argues that Plutarch wrote in the tradition established by Plato and Xenophon and that he presents himself as Socrates' successor by assuming the role of the main speaker in 'Amatorius' (379-380). Hershbell feels that Plutarch's view of love in the 'Amatorius' differs from Plato's *Symposium*, but is basically that of the *Phaedrus* where Socrates claims that *eros* is a god or something divine (373). Hershbell acknowledges that Plutarch uses material from both the *Phaedrus* and the *Symposium*, but that he is 'quite un-Platonic in his references to women and their importance in awakening the soul to beauty' (372). **Wardman** sees Plutarch's 'Amatorius' as a variation on Plato's *Symposium*, which differs by idealising love between man and woman (61). **Martin** also looks at the influence of Plato on Plutarch's 'Amatorius', particularly from the *Symposium* and the *Phaedrus*, and provides a detailed comparison of these works. Martin acknowledges the debt to Plato but argues that the 'Amatorius' is Plutarch's 'own literary creation and no cheap imitation of the master' (87). Martin, like Hershbell, makes the point that by casting himself as his own spokesperson Plutarch 'presents himself as Socrates' successor' (87). **Gallardo** explores the literary styles and acknowledges Plato as the initiator of the philosophic tradition of symposia and the Socratic method. **Flacelière** (1954) contrasts the views of Epicurus, Plato and Plutarch on love and marriage where he sees Plato as defining love as a divine sentiment, Epicurus as advocating marriage without love, and Plutarch as condemning marriage without love. **Trench** also refers to a 'chasm' between Plutarch and the Epicureans' (93). **Desmarts de Saint-Sorlin** presents extracts from the works on the morals of Plutarch, Seneca, Socrates and Epictetus in French.

One of the major themes in the literature on Plutarch is the inclusion of women in his discussion of love and friendship. Plutarch has been credited by **Flacelière** (1962) with being responsible for the rehabilitation of heterosexuality (163). In an article which compares Plato, Epicurus and Plutarch, Flacelière (1954) identifies one of the central themes of Plutarch's 'Eroticos' as being that women, as well as boys, can inspire *eros*. **Russell** also refers to the topics of heterosexual versus homosexual love and arguments in favour of marriage as most important in Plutarch's 'Book of Love' (92). He claims that Plutarch was more in touch with common sentiments than were the Stoics in that he attaches a high moral value to sexual pleasure within marriage (91). **Foucault** devotes a section to Plutarch on love, friendship and marriage. Foucault claims that one of the most important ideas of 'Amatorius' is 'that the woman is just as capable as the man of inspiring amorous passion' (182 n) and that Plutarch 'transposes to the married couple the traits that had long been reserved for the *philia* of lovers of the same sex' (204). According to Foucault, the way in which Plutarch and others began to describe marriage reflected changes in Greek society. Plutarch's version of marriage emphasised a personal relationship between husband and wife, duties of reciprocity rather than mastery, and procreation combined with values of love, affection, understanding and mutual sympathy (148). Some commentators, however, believe that Plutarch's originality has been misinterpreted. **Patterson,** for example, argues that Foucault 'over-estimates Plutarch's originality by under-estimating the popular and traditional character' of his advice on marriage which could be traced back to the Odyssey (4713). Patterson feels that Plutarch's marital morality is not new but just a 'compendium of well-known advice'. But it is this focus on practical and personal advice about the relationship which distinguishes Plutarch from Plato, Xenophon and the Stoics (4722). **Brenk** (1988) claims that focussing on the heterosexual aspect of Plutarch's 'Erotikos' obscures the real novelty of his work which 'consists not so much in the aspect of reciprocal egalitarian love, as in the incorporation of this type of love into the Platonic goal of the vision of the beautiful and a new concept of what the Form of the beautiful is' (457). He agrees with Patterson that the sort of heterosexual married love which Plutarch describes was part of philosophical discourse long before Plutarch. Plutarch's originality for Brenk, lies in seeing marriage and sexuality within marriage as part of a Platonic ascent towards the Form of beauty.

     With reference to the value of women and the concept of marriage, Plutarch is often compared with Musonius Rufus. **Patterson** compares Plutarch to Musonius and to the Stoics, and discusses how Plutarch differs from Musonius who stresses the role of marriage for the polis (4715). In line with Patterson's theory that Plutarch's model of marriage can be traced back to the Odyssey, **Russell** cites Plutarch quoting a passage from the Odyssesy in his 'Book of Love' (92). Russell claims that Plutarch's attitude recalls that of Musonius Rufus, but that

Musonius Rufus is very different and is unlikely to have influenced Plutarch. Plutarch does contend that marriage is the basis of society; he lends more emphasis to sexual pleasure within marriage (91). Russell also claims that Plutarch uses Aristotle's classification of *philia* (93), that the influence of Plato is pervasive (95), that there are similarities to Cicero in Plutarch's essay on friends and flatterers (95) and that how to profit from your enemies is an old theme out of Xenophon (96).

Other influences both on Plutarch and by Plutarch are also considered. **Betz** refers to the fact that historians of Christianity have been struck by the similarities between Christian ethics and Plutarch's ethics. He explains this, not as Plutarch being influenced by Christianity, but 'by their dependence upon common traditions and by their sharing in common ethical concerns' (8). **Engberg-Pedersen** uses Plutarch's essay on friends and flatterers to illustrate the tie between Hellenistic moral philosophy and early Christianity (61). There is some discussion whether Plutarch was influenced by Pythagoreanism which was in vogue in his time. **Hershbell** (1984) argues that there is no great evidence of Pythagorean influence although some of Plutarch's friends were possibly affected by Pythagorean doctrines. **Russell** claims that Plutarch has 'more significantly perhaps than ... any single writer, educated Europe in the central, historical and moral traditions of classical antiquity' (17). **Emerson's** debt to Plutarch is acknowledged in his introduction to Goodwin's (1870) translation of *Plutarch's Morals,* in which he also refers to Montaigne's reliance on Plutarch's works on friendship (xii). **Berry** discusses Emerson's reliance, in particular, on Plutarch essay on love.

NOTES

1. A fuller form of this essay can be found in Preston King and Heather Devere (2000) *Friendship: Dominant Paradigm of Antiquity*, London: Frank Cass.
2. 'And never shall any man say that I, after leading Greeks into the land of the barbarians, betrayed the Greeks and chose the friendship of the barbarians ...', *Anabasis 1.3.5.*

BIBLIOGRAPHY

Adkins, A. (1963) Friendship and Self-Sufficiency in Homer and Aristotle. *Classical Quarterly*, 13 (1), pp.30-45.
Allcroft, A.H. and W.F. Masom (eds.) (1895) *Cicero de Amicitia*. London, University Tutorial Press Ltd.

Alline, H. (1912) Response to M.L. Robin 'Les Memorables de Xenophon et notre connaissance de la philosophie de Socrate'. *Revue des Etudes Grecques*, pp.25, 241-243.

Allman, Dwight David (1998) Ancient Friends, Modern Enemies. *South Atlantic Quarterly*, Winter 97(1), 113-135.

Alpern, K. (1983) Aristotle on the Friendships of Utility and Pleasure. *Journal of the History of Philosophy*, pp.21, 303-315.

Annas, Julia (1977) Plato and Aristotle on Friendship and Altruism. *Mind*, pp.86, 532-554.

Annas, Julia (1988) Self-Love in Aristotle. *The Southern Journal of Philosophy*, pp.27, Supplement, 1-18.

Anton, John P. and George L. Kustas (1972) *Essays in Ancient Greek Philosophy*. Albany, State University of New York Press.

Arieti, James A. (1990) *Interpreting Plato: The Dialogues as Drama*. Savage, Rowman and Littlefield.

Arnold, E.V. (1911) *Roman Stoicism*. London, Cambridge University Press.

Aubenque, Pierre (1998) On Friendship in Aristotle. *South Atlantic Quarterly*, Winter, 97 (1), pp.23-28.

Babbitt, Frank Cole (trans) (1927) *Plutarch's Moralia*. London, Heineman, New York, G.P. Putnam's Sons, Loeb Publications.

Babut, Daniel (1963) Les Stoiciens et l'amour. *Revue des Etudes Grecques*, 76, 55-63.

Badhwar, Neera Kapur (1993) *Friendship: A Philosophical Reader*. Ithaca, Cornell University Press.

Balsdon, J.P.V.D. (1983) *Roman Women: Their History and Habits*. New York, Barnes and Noble.

Bell, Susan Groag (ed.) (1973) *Women: From the Greeks to the French Revolution*. Stanford, Stanford University Press.

Benson, John (1990) Making Friends: Aristotle's Doctrine of Friend as Another Self in Loizou Andros and Harry Lesser (eds.) *Polis and Politics: Essays in Greek Moral and Political Philosophy*. Aldershot, Avebury.

Berry, Edmund G. (1961) *Emerson's Plutarch*. Cambridge, Massachusetts, Harvard University Press.

Betz, Hans Dieter (ed.) (1978) *Plutarch's Ethical Writings and Early Christian Literature*. Studia ad C.H.N.T.iii, Leiden, E.J. Brill.

Bickford, Susan (1996) Beyond Friendship: Aristotle on Conflict, Deliberation and Attention. *Journal of Politics*, 58 (2), May, pp.398-421.

Bloom, Allan (1993) *Love and Friendship*. New York, Simon and Schuster.

Blundell, Mary Whitlock (1989) *Helping Friends and Harming Enemies: A Study in Sophocles and Greek Ethics*. Cambridge, Cambridge University Press.

Bonnette, Amy L. (trans.) (1994) *Xenophon Memorabilia*. (with introduction by Christopher Bruell), Ithaca and London, Cornell University Press.

Brenk, F.W. (1977) *In Mist Apparelled: Religious Themes in Plutarch's Moralia and Lives*. Lugduni Batavorum, Leiden, E.J. Brill.

Brenk, Frederick S.J. (1988) Plutarch's *Erotikos* The Drag Down Pulled Up. *Illinois Classical Review*, 13, pp.457-471.

Brentlinger, John A. (ed.) and Suzy Q. Groden (trans.) (1970) *The Symposium of Plato*. Amherst, University of Massachusets Press.

Brown, Wendy (1988) "Supposing Truth were a Woman..." Plato's Subversion of Masculine Discourse. *Political Theory*, 16 (4), November, pp.594-616.

Bruell, Christopher (1984) Strauss on Xenophon's Socrates. *The Political Science Reviewer*, 14, pp.263-318.

Brunt, P.A. (1965) Amicitia in the late Roman Republic. *Proceedings of the Cambridge Philological Society*, 9, pp.1-20.

Buffière, Felix (1980) *Eros adolescent: la pédérastie dans la Grèce antique.* Paris, Société d'Edition Les Belles Lettres.
Campbell, Robin (trans.) (1985) *Seneca: Letters from a Stoic.* Harmondsworth, Penguin.
Carpenter, Edward (ed.) (1915) *Anthology of Friendship: Iolaus.* 3rd edn London, Allen and Unwin.
Chanter, Tina (1995) *Ethics of Eros: Irigaray's Rewriting of the Philosophers.* New York and London, Routledge.
Chroust, Anton-Hermann (1957) *Socrates: Man and Myth: The Two Socratic Apologies of Xenophon.* Routledge and Kegan Paul.
Cobb, William S. (1993) *The Symposium and the Phaedrus: Plato's Erotic Dialogues.* Albany, State University of New York Press, 1993.
Cooper, J.M. and J.F. Procope (eds.) (1975) *Seneca: Moral and Political Essays.* Cambridge, Cambridge University Press.
Cooper, John M. (1980) Aristotle on Friendship in Rorty, Amelia Oksenberg (ed.) *Essays on Aristotle's Ethics.* Berkeley, University of California Press.
Cooper, John M. (1976-1977) Aristotle on the Forms of Friendship. *Review of Metaphysics,* 30, pp.619-648.
Cooper, John M. (1977) Friendship and the Good in Aristotle. *Philosophical Review,* 86, pp.290-315.
Cooper, John M. (1993) Political Animals and Civic Friendship in Badhwar, Neera Kapur *Friendship: A Philosophical Reader.* Ithaca and London, Cornell University Press.
Cooper, John M. (1993) Rhetoric and the Passions. *Oxford Studies in Philosophy,* 11, pp.175-198.
Cornford, F.M. (1967) *The Unwritten Philosophy and Other Essays.* Cambridge, Cambrdige University Press.
Costa, C.D.N. (ed.) (1974) *Seneca.* London, Routledge and Kegan Paul.
Costa, C.D.N. (trans.) (1988) *Seneca: 17 Letters.* Warminster, Aris and Phillips Ltd.
Dawson, Miles Menander (1974) *The Ethics of Socrates.* New York, Haskell House Publishers.
Defradas (trans) (1954) *Plutarque: Le Banquet des Sept Sages.* Paris, Librairie C. Klincksieck.
den Boer, W. (1979) *Private Morality in Greece and Rome: Some Historical Aspects.* Leiden, Brill.
Derrida, Jacques (1994) *Politiques de l'amitié.* Paris; (1997) *Politics of Friendship.* translated by George Collins, London and New York, Verso.
Desmarets de Saint-Sorlin, J. (trans) (1655) *Les morales de Plutarque, Sénèque, Socrate, et Epictète.* Antointe de Sommerville.
Dover, K.J. (1966a) Aristophanes' Speech in Plato's *Symposium. The Journal of Hellenic Studies,* 87, pp.41-50.
Dover, K.J. (1966b) Eros and Nomos (Plato *Symposium* 182A-185C). *Bulletin of Institute of Classical Studies,* 11, pp.31-43.
Dover, K.J. (1973) Classical Greek Attitudes to Sexual Behaviour. *Arethusa,* 6 (1), pp.59-73.
Dover, K.J. (1978/1989) *Greek Homosexuality.* London, Duckworth.
Dziob, Anne Marie (1993) Aristotelian Friendship: Self-Love and Moral Rivalry. *Review of Metaphysics,* 46, June, pp.781-801.
Easterling, Pat (1989) Friendship and the Greeks in Roy Porter and Sylvana Tomaselli (eds.) *The Dialectics of Friendship.* London, Routledge.
Edwards, G.M. (1901) *The Memorabilia of Xenophon.* Cambridge, Cambridge University Press.
Eglinton, J.Z. (1964) *Greek Love.* New York, Oliver Layton.

Emerson, Ralph Waldo (1870) Introduction to *Plutarch's Morals.* revised by William W. Goodman. London, Sampson Low, Son and Marston.

Engberg-Pedersen, Troels (1996) Plutarch to Prince Philopappus on How to Tell a Flatterer from a Friend in Fitzgerald, John T. (ed.) *Friendship, Flattery and Frankness of Speech: Studies on Friendship in the New Testament World.* Leiden, E.J. Brill.

Epstein, D. (1987) *Personal Enmity in Roman Politics 218-43 BC.* London, Croom Helm.

Fantham, Elaine, Helene Peet Foley, Natalie Boymel Kampen, Sarah B. Pomeroy, H.A. Shapiro (1994) *Women in the Classical World: Image and Text.* New York, Oxford University Press.

Fau, Guy (1978) *L'émancipation feminine dans la Rome antique.* Paris, Société d'Edition Les Belles Lettres.

Feuerstein, Josef (1879) *Die Freundschaft Nach Xenophons Memorabilia und Platons Lysis.* Prog. des Gymnasiums, Krumau.

Fiore, Benjamin S.J. (1997) The Theory and Practice of Friendship in Cicero in Fitzgerald, John T. (ed.) *Greco-Roman Perspectives on Friendship.* Atlanta, Scholar Press.

Fitzgerald, John T. (ed.) (1996) *Friendship, Flattery and Frankness of Speech: Studies on Friendship in the New Testament World.* Leiden, E.J. Brill.

Fitzgerald, John T. (ed.) (1997) *Greco-Roman Perspectives on Friendship.* Atlanta, Scholar Press.

Flacelière, Robert (1961) A propos due *Banquet* de Xenophon. *Revue des Etudes Grecques,* 74, pp.93-118.

Flacelière, Robert (1954) Les Epicuriens et l'amour. *Revue des Etudes Grecques,* 67, pp.69-81.

Flacelière, Robert (1960) *L'amour en Grèce.* Paris, Hachette; (1962) *Love in Ancient Greece,* London, translated by James Cleugh Frederick Muller.

Flacelière, Robert (1964) *Sagesse de Plutarque.* Paris, Universitaires de France.

Foley, Helen P. (ed.) (1981) *Reflections of Women in Antiquity,* New York, Gordon and Breach Science Publishers.

Fortenbaugh, W.W. (1975) Aristotle's Analysis of Friendship: Function and Analogy, Resemblance, and Focal Meaning. *Phronesis,* 20, pp.51-62.

Foucault, Michel, *The History of Sexuality: Vol III 'The Care of the Self'* translated by Robert Hurley (1986) London, Penguin.

Fraisse, Jean-Claude (1974) *Philia: la notion d'amitié dans la philosophie antique.* Paris, Libraire Philosophique J. Vrin.

Gallardo, Maria Dolores (1972) Estado Actual de los Estudios Sobre los Simposios de Platon, Jenofonte y Plutarcho. *Cuadermos de Filologia Classica,* III, pp.127-191.

Gardner, Jane F. (1987)*Women in Roman Law and Society.* London and Sydney, Croom Helm.

Gardner, Jane F. (1993) *Being a Roman Citizen,* London, Routledge.

Gemoll, W. (1934) Der *Eros* in de Symposien Xenophons and Platons. *Philologische Wochenschrift,* 54, pp.30-32.

Glad, Clarence E. (1996) Frank Speech, Flattery and Friendship in Philodemus in Fitzgerald, John T. (ed.) *Friendship, Flattery and Frankness of Speech: Studies in Friendship in the New Testament Period,* Leiden, E.J. Brill.

Glidden, David (1980) The Language of Love: *Lysis* 212a8-213c9. *Pacific Philosophical Quarterly,* 61, pp.276-290.

Glidden, David (1981) The *Lysis* on Loving One's Own. *Classical Quarterly,* 31 (1) pp.39-59.

Goicoechea, David ed. (1995) *The Nature and Pursuit of Love: The Philosophy of Irving Singer.* New York, Prometheus.

Gonzalez, Francisco J. (1995) Plato's *Lysis*: An Enactment of Philosophical Kinship. *Ancient Philosophy,* 15 (1) pp.69-90.

Graham, Daniel W. (1992) Socrates and Plato. *Phronesis*, 37 (2), pp.141-165.

Grant, Michael (1971) *Cicero on the Good Life*. Harmondsworth, Penguin.

Greard, Octave (1866) *De la Morale de Plutarque*. Paris, Librairie de l'Hachette.

Grube, G.M.A. (1935) *Plato's Thought*. London, Hackett.

Gummere, Richard M. (trans.) (1953) *Seneca: Ad Lucilium Episulae Morales*. London, Heinemann, Cambridge Mass., Harvard University Press.

Hadas, Moses (trans.) (1957) *On Love, the Family and the Good Life: Selected Essays of Plutarch*. New York, New American Library.

Haden, James (1983) Friendship in Plato's *Lysis*. *Review of Metaphysics*, 37, December, pp.327-356.

Hadreas, Peter (1995) Eunoia: Aristotle on the beginning of friendship. *Ancient Philosophy*, 15, Fall, pp.393-402.

Halperin, David M. (1985) Platonic *Eros* and What Men Call Love. *Ancient Philosophy*, 5 (2), Fall, pp.161-204.

Halperin, David M. (1990) *One Hundred Years of Homosexuality and Other Essays on Greek Love*. New York and London, Routledge.

Halperin, David M., John J. Winkler and Froma I. Zeitlin (eds.) (1990) *Before Sexuality: The Construction of the Erotic Experience in the Ancient Greek World*. Princeton, Princeton University Press.

Helmbold, W.C. (trans.) (1939) *Plutarch's Moralia, Vol. V*. London, Heineman, Cambridge, Mass., Harvard University Press.

Herman, Gabriel (1987) *Ritualized Friendship and the Greek City*. Cambridge, Cambridge University Press.

Hershbell, Jackson P. (1988) Plutarch's Portrait of Socrates. *Illinois Classical Studies*, 13 (2), pp.365-381.

Hershbell, Jackson P. (1984) Plutarch's Pythagorean Friends. *The Classical Bulletin*, 60 (4), Fall, pp.73-79.

Higgins, W.E. (1977) *Xenophon the Athenian: The Problem of the Individual and the Society of the Polis*. Albany, New York, State University of New York Press.

Hirsh, Steven W. (1985) *The Friendship of the Barbarians: Xenophon and the Persian Empire*. Hanover and London, University Press of New England.

Hutter, Horst (1978) *Politics as Friendship: The origins of classical notions of politics in the theory and practice of friendship*, Wilfrid Laurier University Press, Waterloo, Ontario.

Hyland, Drew A. (1968) *Eros*, Epithumia and Philia in Plato. *Phronesis*, 13, pp.32-46.

Irigaray, Luce (1989) Sorcerer Love: A Reading of Plato's *Symposium*, Diotima's Speech. *Hypatia*, 3 (3), pp.32-61.

Irigaray, Luce (1993) *An Ethics of Sexual Difference*. Carolyn Burke and Gillian C. Gill (trans.), London, The Athlone Press.

Irwin, Terence (1995) *Plato's Ethics*. New York, Oxford University Press.

Jaffa, Harry V. (1952) *Thomism and Aristotelianism: A Study of the Commentary by Thomas Aquinas on the Nicomachean Ethics*. Westport, Greenwood Press.

Jones, L. Gregory (1987) The Theological Transformation of Aristotelian Friendship in the Thought of Thomas Aquinas. *New Scholasticism*, 61, pp.373-399.

Kahn, Charles H. (1981) Aristotle and Altruism. *Mind*, 90, pp.20-40.

Kelsen, Hans (1942-1946) Platonic Love. *The American Imago*, 3, pp.3-110.

Kenny, Anthony (1978) *The Aristotelian Ethics: A Study of the Relationship between the Eudemian and Nicomachean Ethics of Aristotle*. Oxford, Clarendon Press.

Konstan, David (1991) *Eros* in the Ephesus: The Nature of Love in Xenophon's Ephesian Tale. *Classicum*, 17 (2), October, pp.26-33.

Konstan, David (1994) *Sexual Symmetry: Love in the Ancient Novel and Related Genres*. Princeton, Princeton University Press.

Konstan, David (1994-95) Friendship and the State: The Context of Cicero's *De Amicitia*. *Hyperboreus*, 2, pp. 1-16.

Konstan, David (1995) Patrons and Friends. *Classical Philology*, 90, October, pp.328-342.

Konstan, David (1996a) Greek Friendship. *American Journal of Philology*, 117 (1) Spring, pp.71-94.

Konstan, David (1997) *Friendship in the Classical World*. Cambridge, Cambridge University Press.

Konstan, David (1996b) Friendship, Frankness and Flattery in Fitzgerald, John T. (ed.) *Friendship, Flattery and Frankness of Speech: Studies in Friendship in the New Testament Period*, Leiden, E.J. Brill.

Konstan, David and Martha Nussbaum (eds.) (1990) 'Sexuality in Greek and Roman Society' Special Issue of *Differences: A Journal of Feminist Cultural Studies*, 2 (1).

Kosman, L.A. (1976) Platonic Love in W.H. Werkmeister (ed.), *Facets of Plato's Philosophy*. Assen/Amsterdam, Van Gorcum.

Kraut, Richard (1973) Egoism, Love and Political Office in Plato. *The Philosophical Review*, 83, pp.330-344.

Kraut, Richard (1975) The Importance of Aristotle's Ethics. *Philosophy Research Archives*, 1, pp.300-322.

Kraut, Richard (1988) Comments on Julia Annas' 'Self-Love in Aristotle'. *The Southern Journal of Philosophy*, 27, Supplement, pp.19-23.

Lefkowitz, Mary R. and Maureen B. Fant (1982) *Women's Life in Greece and Rome*. London, Duckworth.

Levy, Donald (1979) The Definition of Love In Plato's *Symposium*. *Journal of the History of Ideas*, 40, pp.285-291.

Licht, Hans (1932) *Sexual Life in Ancient Greece*. London, Abbey Library.

Lipsius, Justus (trans.) (1739) *Select Epistles on Several Moral Subjects: L. Annaeus Seneca*. London, C. Rivington.

Litzinger, C.I., (trans) (1964) *St. Thomas Aquinas: Commentary on the Nicomachean Ethics*. Chicago, Henry Regnery Co.

Loizou, Andros and Harry Lesser (eds.) (1990) *Polis and Politics: Essays in Greek Moral and Political Philosophy*. Aldershot, Avebury.

Lodge, Thomas (trans.) (1614) *The Works of Lucius Annaeus Seneca*. London.

Luce, T. James (1982) *Ancient Writers: Greece and Rome: Vol.II*. New York, Charles Scribners Sons.

MacIntyre, Alisdair (1985) *After Virtue: A Study in Moral Theory*. 2nd edn. London, Duckworth.

MacKendrick, Paul with the collaboration of Karen Lee Singh (1989) *The Philosophical Books of Cicero*. London, Duckworth.

Martin, Herbert, Jr. (1984) Plutarch, Plato and *Eros*. *Classical Bulletin*, 60, pp.82-88.

Mendell, Clarence W. (1968) *Our Seneca*. Archon Books, Yale University Press.

Millgram, Elijah (1987) Aristotle on Making Other Selves. *Canadian Journal of Philosophy*, 17 (2), June, pp.361-376.

Morgan, Douglas N.(1964) *Love: Plato, the Bible and Freud*. Englewood Cliffs, Prentice-Hall.

Morrison, Donald R. (1988) *Bibliography of Editions, Translations, and Commentary on Xenophon's Socratic Writings 1600-Present*. Pittsburgh, Mathesis Publications.

Motto, Anna Lydia (1970) *Seneca Sourcebook: Guide to the Thought of Lucius Annaeus Seneca*. Amsterdam, Adolf M. Hakkert.

Motto, Anna Lydia (1985) *Seneca: Moral Epistles*. Chico, California, Scholars Press.

Motto, Anna Lydia and John R. Clark (1989) *Seneca: A Critical Bibliography: 1900-1980: Scholarship on his Life, Thought, Prose and Influence*. Amsterdam, Adolf M. Hakkert.

Motto, Anna Lydia and John R. Clark (1993) *Essays on Seneca*. Frankfurt am Main, New York, Peter Lang.

Nehamas, Alexander and Paul Woodruff (1989) *Plato's Symposium*. Indianapolis, Hackett.

Neumann, Harry (1965) Diotima's Concept of Love. *American Journal of Philology*, 86 (1), pp.33-59.

Nussbaum, Martha (1986) *The Fragility of Goodness: Luck and Ethics in Greek Tragedy and Philosophy*. Cambridge, Cambridge University Press.

Nye, Andrea (1989) The Hidden Host: Irigaray and Diotima at Plato's *Symposium*. *Hypatia*, 3 (3), Winter, pp.45-61.

Ollier, François (1961) *Xenophon: Banquet - Apologie de Socrate*. Société d'Editions Les Belles Lettres.

O'Neil, Edward N. (1997) Plutarch on Friendship in Fitzgerald, John T. (ed.) *Greco-Roman Perspectives on Friendship*. Atlanta, Scholar Press.

Pakaluk, Michael (1992) Friendship and the Comparison of Goods. *Phronesis*, 37 (1) pp.111-130.

Pakaluk, Michael (1991) *Other Selves: Philosophers on Friendship*. Indianapolis, Hackett.

Palmer, Ralph Graham (1953) *Seneca's de Remdiis Fortuitorum and the Elizabethans*. Chicago, Institute of Elizabethan Studies.

Patterson, Cynthia (1992) Plutarch's Advice on Marriage: Traditional Wisdom through a Philosophic Lens. *Aufstieg und Niedergang der Römischen Welt*, II 33 (6), Berlin, pp.4709-4723.

Peradotto, John and J.P. Sullivan (eds.) (1984) *Women in the Ancient World: The Arethusa Papers*. Albany, State University of New York Press.

Politis, Vasilis (1993) The Primacy of Self-Love in the *Nicomachean Ethics*. *Oxford Studies in Ancient Philosophy*, 11, Oxford, Clarendon Press, pp.153-174.

Pomeroy, Sarah B. (1975) *Goddesses, Wives, Slaves and Whores: Women in Classical Antiquity*. New York, Schocken Books.

Pomeroy, Sarah B. (ed.) (1991)*Women's History and Ancient History*. Durham, N.C., University of North Carolina Press.

Porter, Roy and Sylvana Tomaselli (1989) *The Dialectics of Friendship*. London, Routledge.

Powell, J.G. F., (trans.) (1990) *Cicero: Laelius, On Friendship and the Dream of Scipio*. Warminster, Aris and Phillips Ltd.

Powell, Jonathan (1995) Friendship and its Problems in Greek and Roman Thought, in Innes, Doreen, Harry Hine and Christopher Pelling (eds.) *Ethics and Rhetoric: Classical Essays for Donald Russell on his 75th Birthday*. Oxford, Clarendon Press.

Price, A.W. (1981) Loving Persons Platonically. *Phronesis*, 26 (1), pp.25-34.

Price, A.W. (1989) *Love and Friendship in Plato and Aristotle*. Oxford, Clarendon Press.

Rawson, Beryl (1978) *The Politics of Friendship: Pompey and Cicero*. Sydney, Sydney University Press.

Rees, D.A. (ed.) (1951) *Aristotle: The Nicomachean Ethics: A Commentary by the Late H.H. Joachim*. Oxford, Clarendon Press.

Reynolds, L.D. (1965) *The Medieval Tradition of Seneca's Letters*. Oxford, Oxford University Press.

Richard, H. (1896) The Minor Works of Xenophon: The *Symposium*. *The Classical Review*, 10, pp.292-295.

Rist, John M. (1964) *Eros and Psyche: Studies in Plato, Plotinus and Origin*. Phoenix, University of Toronto Press.

Robin, Léon (1964) *La théorie platonicienne de l'amour*.Nouvelle Edition, Paris, Presses Universitaires de France.

Rogers, Kelly, (1994) Aristotle on loving another for his own sake. *Phronesis*, 39 (3) pp.291-302.

Rorty, Amelie O. (ed.) (1980) *Essays on Aristotle's Ethics*. Berkeley, University of California Press.

Rouner, Leroy S. (ed.) (1994) *The Changing Face of Friendship*. Notre Dame, Indiana, University of Notre Dame Press.

Russell, D.A. (1973) *Plutarch*. London, Duckworth.

Saller, Richard (1989) Patronage and Friendship in early imperial Rome, in Wallace-Hadrill, Andrew (ed.) *Patronage in Ancient Society*. London and New York, Routledge.

Santas, Gerasimos (1979) Plato's Theory of *Eros* in the *Symposium*. *Nous*, 13, pp.67-75.

Santas, Gerasimos (1980) Plato on Love, Beauty and Good, in David J. Depew (ed.) *The Greeks and the Good Life*. Fullerton, California State University.

Santas, Gerasimos (1988) *Plato and Freud: Two Theories of Love*. Oxford, Blackwell.

Saxonhouse, Arlene W. (1976) The Philosopher and the Female in the Political Thought of Plato. *Political Theory*, 4 (2), May, pp.195-212.

Saxonhouse, Arlene W. (1984) *Eros* and the Female in Greek Political Thought: An Interpretation of Plato's *Symposium*. *Political Theory*, 12, pp.5-27.

Schoeman, Ferdinand (1985) Aristotle on the Good of Friendship. *Australian Journal of Philosophy*, 63 (3) September, pp.269-282.

Schollmeier, Paul (1994) *Other Selves: Aristotle on Personal and Political Friendship*. Albany, University of New York Press.

Sevenster, Jan N. (1961) *Paul and Seneca*. Leiden, E.J. Brill.

Sherman, Nancy (1987) Aristotle on Friendship and the Shared Life. *Philosophy and Phenomenological Research*, 47 (4) pp.589-613.

Singer, Irving (1966) *The Nature of Love: Plato to Luther*. New York, Random House.

Soble, Alan (1985) Love is not Beautiful: *Symposium* 200e-201c. *Apeiron*, 19 (1), pp.43-52.

Soble, Alan (1989) *Eros, Agape and Philia: Readings in the Philosophy of Love*. New York, Paragon House.

Spielvogel, Jorg (1993) *Amicitia und Res Publica*. Stuttgart, Franz Steiner Verlag.

Stannard, Jerry (1959) Socratic *Eros* and Platonic Dialectic. *Phronesis*, 4, pp.120-134.

Steinmetz, Fritz-Arthur (1967) Die Freundschaftslehre de Panaitios. Nach einer Analyse von Cicero, 'Laelius de amicitia'. *Palingensia* 3, Wiesbaden.

Stern-Gillet, Suzanne (1995) *Aristotle's Philosophy of Friendship*. Albany, State University of New York Press.

Strauss, Leo (1972) *Xenophon's Socrates*. Ithaca, Cornell University Press.

Thornton, Bruce S. (1997) *Eros: The Myth of Ancient Greek Sexuality*. Westview, Boulder.

Tracy, Theodore (1979) Perfect Friendship in Aristotle's *Nicomachean Ethics*. *Illinois Classical Studies*, 4, pp.65-75.

Tredennick, Hugh (trans) (1970) *Xenophon: Memoirs of Socrates and the Symposium*. Harmondsworth, Penguin.

Tredennick, Hugh and Robin Waterfield (trans) (1990) *Xenophon: Conversations with Socrates*. London, Penguin.

Trench, Richard Chenevix (1874) *Plutarch: His Life, His Parallel Lives, and His Morals: Five Lecturers*. London, Macmillan and Co.

Tuana, Nancy (ed.) (1994) *Feminist Interpretations of Plato*. University Park, Pennsylvania State University Press.

Vlastos, Gregory (1973) *Platonic Studies*. Princeton, Princeton University Press.

Waddell, Paul J. (1989) *Friendship and the Moral Life*. Notre Dame, University of Notre Dame Press.

Wagoner, Robert E. (1997) *The Meaning of Love: An Introduction to the Philosophy of Love*. Westport/London, Praeger.

Walker, A.D.M. (1979) Aristotle's account of Friendship in the Nicomachean Ethics. *Phronesis*, 24, pp.180-196.

Wardman, A. (1974) *Plutarch's Lives*. London.
Warner, Martin (1979) Love, Self and Plato's *Symposium*. *Philosophical Quarterly*, 29.
Wender, Dorothea (1973) Plato: Misogynist, Paedophile, and Feminist. *Arethusa*, 6(1), pp.75-90.
White, P. (1978) *Amicitia* and the Profession of Poetry in Early Imperial Rome. *Journal of Roman Studies*, 68, pp.74-92.
Winkler, John J. (1990) *The Constraints of Desire: The Anthropology of Sex and Gender in Ancient Greece*. New York, Routledge.
Wright, F.A. (1923) *Feminism in Greek Literature: From Homer to Aristotle*. New York/London, Kennikat Press.

Abstracts

The Role of Friendship in Aristotle's Political Theory
RICHARD MULGAN

Aristotle's theory of friendship is ambiguous in certain key points which has allowed it to be co-opted by both communitarians and liberal individualists. True friendship is possible only among close friends and family, thus ruling out the possibility of literally 'fraternal' citizenship. Aristotle is undecided whether derivative friendships, including business relationships and citizenship, involve goodwill. Political friendship is equated with unanimity or political consensus which is essential for political stability. But such consensus does not arise out of civic friendship which remains remote and instrumental.

Hume, Smith and Ferguson: Friendship in Commercial Society
LISA HILL and PETER McCARTHY

As the industrial revolution got under way in Britain, David Hume, Adam Smith and Adam Ferguson were all concerned with assessing the changing character of commercial society. An influential reading of those assessments, one focused on friendship, sees the three writers as essentially optimistic about the possibilities for new and better patterns of association in the 'new age'. The commercial age permits a more authentic quality of friendship because for the first time people are free to choose their friends. However, this reading overlooks significant differences between the three writers. Hume was most optimistic, welcoming a new sociability which he identified with the pleasures of politeness. Smith took a similar view, though he thought that most friendships were likely to be (and, indeed, should be) restrained. By contrast, Ferguson saw commerce as potentially destructive for social intimacy. Commerce brought with it the very real prospect of a society in which friendship was no longer possible. Friendships would be difficult to sustain in the face of rapacious competition between people and the demands of a market society governed by contract. Thus, the Scots present us with different, and in many ways troubling, pictures of the potential for friendship in the modern world.

Circles, Ladders and Stars: Nietzsche on Friendship
RUTH ABBEY

Considering Friedrich Nietzsche as a theorist of friendship seems odd if not misguided, given that he is usually associated with an ethos of ultra-individualism which glorifies independence and solitude. However, friendship is a real and powerful feature of the writings of Nietzsche's middle period. This article examines Nietzsche's views on friendship in these works, contending that he holds the capacity for friendship to be a central feature of higher individuals. Recognising this requires, in turn, a reconsideration of Nietzsche's views on solitude. The article concludes by comparing his very positive views on friendship in the middle period with those in his later writings.

Martin Buber and the Ontological Crisis of Modern Man
CHARLES RUSTIN

This article reintroduces the thought of Martin Buber to a modern audience. It is argued that Buber's philosophy of dialogue, which makes an ontological 'shift' away from the Cartesian cogito, provides philosophers and social theorists with an alternative means of interpreting and understanding global society and where the means to improve it might lie. Buber's motive for criticising Descartes is that when the individually conscious 'I' is understood as the foundation of truth and knowledge this results in societies in which subjective thought and differences of opinion become objectified into the unquestioned 'natural' norms of society. Human beings are then prepared to defend, with their lives if necessary, these 'objective' differences which originated in somebody's mind. It is this negative aspect of difference which Buber examined in order to illustrate the potentially unifying force of relation which precedes the objectifying moment.

Derrida and Friendship
FRED DALLMAYR

While celebrated in antiquity as an important political bond, friendship in later times has tended to be sidelined and even placed under siege. As inaugurated by Descartes, modern Western philosophy erected the thinking ego into a bulwark of self-certainty against the 'external world' (comprising nature and other selves). Subsequently, liberal theory deployed individual self-interest as the chief engine of politics and market economics, with the result that friendship – to the extent that it persisted – was increasingly internalised and privatised. This paper explores Jacques Derrida's contributions to the rethinking of friendship, including political friendship, in our time. The first part recapitulates Derrida's main arguments as stated especially in 'The Politics of Friendship' and later in the book *Politics of Friendship*. The paper next turns to an immediate rejoinder formulated by Thomas McCarthy (from a largely Habermasian angle). The concluding section assesses the strengths and possible weaknesses to Derrida's position as captured in the phrase 'Oh my friends there is no friend'. While appreciating Derrida's deconstructive elan as an antidote to consumerism and social conformism, the paper questions the focus on rupturing and the accent on 'without' in such repeated formulas as 'friendship without friendship, community without community', wondering whether the notion of an anchoritic 'non-community', may not have disempowering connotations for democracy.

The Virtue of Solitude and the Vicissitudes of Friendship
HORST HUTTER

Friendship is universal but expresses itself variably in different cultural settings. Friendship in advanced industrial societies is different in view of the mobility, solitude and uncertainty they impose. This essay has two foci - the modern setting on the one hand and classical theory on the other. Modern society may be viewed as one in which the schizoid condition is normal. This is because human beings can not locate an ultimate end – as in Christian metaphysics - and are thus internally

divided between the drive to serve some public good on the one hand
and their natural egoisms on the other. A defective friendship is often
established through a process of negative 'othering' as among 'new age'
religious sects, and the various hate groups, where principles of enmity
(-friendship) and difference (-sameness) supply a basis for identity. But
modernity has not destroyed friendship altogether. New forms – such
as 'friendship in mind' and 'stellar friendship' – have emerged as
adaptations to the mobility, solitude and uncertainty characteristic of
modern life. Hence the Epicurean paradigm of friendship may seem
more appropriate to our circumstances than that supplied by Plato and
Aristotle.

Reviving Greco-Roman Friendship: A Bibliographical Review
HEATHER DEVERE

This essay surveys recent collections and commentaries on friendship
and love, with especial reference to Classical Greece and Rome. The
terminology itself is complex as in 'friendship' and 'love'; *philia*, *eros*
and *xenia*; *amor*, *amicitia* and *erotica*; as well as the more Christian
notion of agape. Many traditions of love and friendship are debated
in the literature: carnal v. spiritual, homosexual v. heterosexual,
chastity v. prostitution as well as whether friendship can exist only
between men, or whether friendships between women or between
women and men are also possible. The essay concludes with a
distillation of recent works on Xenophon, Plato, Aristotle, Cicero,
Seneca and Plutarch.

Notes on Contributors

Preston King is Professor of Political Philosophy at Lancaster University. He is the author of such books as *Fear of Power*, *The Ideology of Order* and *Federalism and Federation*. His latest book is *Thinking Past a Problem: Essays on the History of Ideas* (Frank Cass, 2000).

Richard Mulgan lectures in the Public Policy Program, Australian National University. He was formerly professor of Classics at the University of Otago and professor of political studies at the Universities of Otago and Auckland. He is the author of *Aristotle's Political Theory* (Oxford UP, 1977) and articles on Greek political thought. He has written extensively on both Australian and New Zealand politics.

Lisa Hill is a Fellow in political science at the Research School of Social Sciences, Australian National University. She has published in such journals as *Applied Philosophy*, *History of Political Thought*, *History of Economic Ideas* and the *Archives Européennes de Sociologie*. Her primary interest is in eighteenth-century thought, but her current research interests are broad and range from classical political economy to the history of feminist thought and Australian politics.

Peter McCarthy is a Visitor in political science at the Research School of Social Sciences, Australian National University. His primary interests are in the history of ideas and in the theory and practice of political deliberation.

Ruth Abbey is Senior Lecturer in Philosophy, University of Notre Dame, in Fremantle, Western Australia. She is the author of 'Nietzsche's

Middle Period' (Oxford University Press, 2000). She is currently writing a book on the thought of Charles Taylor.

Charles Rustin is a PhD candidate in the Department of International Relations, Hebrew University of Jerusalem, where he has received a number of awards and research grants. He is currently researching the political and social thought of Martin Buber.

Fred Dallmayr has been Packey J. Dee Professor of Political Theory at the University of Notre Dame, South Bend, Indiana since 1978. He took earlier degrees in law and political science from Munich and from Duke. His many publications include *Twilight of Subjectivity* (1981), *Margins of Political Discourse* (1989), *Life-World, Modernity and Critique* (1991), *G.W.F. Hegel: Modernity and Politics* (1993), *Beyond Orientalism: Essays on Cross-Cultural Encounter* (1996) and *Alternative Visions: Paths in the Global Village* (1998).

Horst Hutter is Professor of Political Theory and director of the graduate programme in political science at Concordia University, Montreal. He regularly teaches courses on Plato and Nietzsche, as well as Hellenistic and Enlightenment political theory. He has lectured in Austria, Germany and the United States. His book on *Politics as Friendship* (1978) has gained a wide readership. He has written on other topics including the ideas of Schiller, cynicism and the politics of anger. He is currently at work on a book concerning political passions and the passion for politics.

Heather Devere PhD is Senior Lecturer in Politics and Ethics at the Auckland University of Technology. She has written on women's issues, women's attitudes, civil rights and the politics of the media. She is currently editing with Preston King a series of books on the philosophy of friendship. Her contribution to this issue of *CRISPP* constitutes an abbreviated review of the literature.

Index